P9-DYJ-810

Also by Kenneth Tynan

He That Plays the King
Persona Grata
Alec Guinness
Bull Fever
Curtains
Tynan Right and Left
A View of the English Stage 1944–63
The Sound of Two Hands Clapping

PLAYS:

The Quest for Corbett
Oh! Calcutta
Carte Blanche

SHOW PEOPLE

Profiles in Entertainment

Kenneth Tynan

SIMON AND SCHUSTER · NEW YORK

Copyright © 1979 by Kenneth Tynan
All rights reserved
including the right of reproduction
in whole or in part in any form
Published by Simon and Schuster
A Division of Gulf & Western Corporation
Simon & Schuster Building
Rockefeller Center
1230 Avenue of the Americas
New York, New York 10020
Designed by Edith Fowler
Manufactured in the United States of America

2 3 4 5 6 7 8 9 10

Library of Congress Cataloging in Publication Data

Tynan, Kenneth, date.
  Show people.

    1. *Entertainers—United States—Addresses, essays,*
lectures.   2.   Theater—Great Britain—Addresses, essays,
lectures.   I. Title.
PN2285.T9   791'092'2   79-19093
ISBN 0-671-25012-4

The text of this book appeared originally in *The New Yorker.*

The author is grateful for permission to reprint the following excerpts:
From Christopher Logue's poem (page 119), reprinted by permission
of Alfred E. Knopf, Inc., from *New Numbers,* © 1969 by Christopher
Logue.
From T. S. Eliot's "Love Song of J. Alfred Prufrock" (page 83),
reprinted by permission of Harcourt, Brace, Jovanovich, Inc., from
Collected Poems 1909–1962, © 1962 by T. S. Eliot, and by permission
of Faber and Faber, from *Collected Poems 1909–1962* by T. S. Eliot.

Contents

Foreword

THIS BOOK consists of word portraits of five people who have two qualities in common—(1) they all work in show business, and (2) I admire them enormously.

I have called these portraits "profiles." Until a few decades ago, they would have been described as "essays," but in recent years "essay" has become a dirty word in certain literary circles. Many critics maintain that the essay is an inferior form; and many publishers believe that modern readers care only for long-distance, marathon writing, and that there is no room left for such middle-distance, eight hundred metre stuff as essays. Out of the window—if these experts are right—goes Montaigne. To the bonfire with William Hazlitt, closely followed by Max Beerbohm, Sainte-Beuve and John Aubrey. A brusque kiss-off to Francis Bacon, Charles Lamb, La Bruyère and the best of Mencken, not to mention Suetonius's *Lives of the Caesars*; and into the garbage goes Samuel Johnson's *Lives of the Poets*, perhaps the finest book of profile-essays ever written. The list could be indefinitely extended. Any theory that regards works like these as second-class literature is transparently dotty. It is as if art critics were to judge pieces of sculpture by their bulk.

I am not, of course, claiming a place for myself among the masters I have named above. (Although, when Lamb is at his most whimsical, I sometimes feel I could go a couple of rounds with him and not make a total fool of myself.) I have spent much of my life as a literary sprinter, writing thousand-word reviews of plays and movies. But I have also aspired to be a middle-distance man, and the pieces that follow are my latest efforts in this genre.

Their subjects are show people, inhabitants of the overlapping worlds of theatre, cinema, and television which I have professionally observed for the past three decades. Together, they make up a royal flush of talent—talent to which, over the years, I have happily responded and which I have felt the need to define in print. Not with the comprehensive detail of a biography, nor yet with the epigrammatic brevity of a thumbnail sketch, but in the space of twenty thousand words or so, enough to convey the essential facts of a man's life and to explore the nature of his gifts.

My chosen quintet includes a great actor (Sir Ralph Richardson), a great television virtuoso (Johnny Carson), a great screen beauty (Louise Brooks), a great comic creator (Mel Brooks), and a uniquely inventive playwright (Tom Stoppard) who has more than once been within hailing distance of greatness and may, any season now, earn a permanent niche in the dramatic pantheon. Each of them has a style that is as inimitable as a fingerprint. All but one (the exception being Stoppard) are performers—a fact that reflects my abiding obsession with the skills that enable a man or woman to seize and hold the rapt attention of a multitude. Last and far from least, they all rank high on the list of people whom I would invite to an ideal dinner party.

KENNETH TYNAN

At three minutes past eight
you must dream
—RALPH RICHARDSON

SIR RALPH RICHARDSON celebrated his seventy-fourth
birthday on December 19, 1976, the day after Harold
Pinter's *No Man's Land*, in which he co-starred with his old
friend Sir John Gielgud, ended its Broadway run at the
Longacre. Sir Ralph played Hirst, a wealthy Englishman with
an awe-inspiring thirst, incessantly slaked, for vodka and
Scotch. Hirst is also a famous writer, although we do not
discover this until page 67 of the published text (which ends
on page 95)—a little late in the day, some may think, for
such an important disclosure. Some, indeed, would get
downright shirty if another playwright were thus to withhold
essential information that could easily have been revealed
in the first ten minutes; but when Mr. Pinter does it, audiences marvel at what they have been taught to recognize as
his skill in creating an atmosphere of poetic suspense. At all
events, Hirst, protected by a pair of sinister servants called
Foster and Briggs, lives in a palatial Hampstead house,
where he is bearded by Spooner, a threadbare poetaster
(played by Sir John) whom he may or may not have

cuckolded—Mr. Pinter leaves us in poetic doubt—on the
eve of the Second World War. Spooner, who seeks employment as Hirst's secretary, is under pressure throughout the
play to quit the household. I don't propose to offer an
interpretation of *No Man's Land*, but it may not be irrelevant
to point out that all of its four characters are named after
English cricketers who flourished around the turn of the
century. Mr. Pinter is known to be a fanatical lover of
cricket—a game in which a batsman (e.g., Spooner) invades
the territory of the opposing team (e.g., Hirst, Foster, and
Briggs), which then attempts, by a variety of ploys that include bluff, deceit, and physical intimidation, to dismiss him
from the field. The dialogue, garlanded with bizarre non
sequiturs, is often hilarious. Whether the play is more than
a cerebral game is a decision that will have to wait until we
see it performed by second-rate actors. Fortunately for Mr.
Pinter, the English theatre is well equipped with senior
players who can bestow on whatever material comes their
way a patina of seignorial magic.

Sir Ralph is one such. Devotees of the Richardson cult—
who had last seen their idol on Broadway in 1970, when he
appeared (also with Sir John) as a benevolent lunatic in
David Storey's *Home*—observed with relief that immersion
in Pinterdom had left his professional trademarks unchanged.
There was the unique physical presence, at once rakish and
stately, as of a pirate turned prelate. There was the balsawood
lightness of movement, which enabled him to fall flat on his
face three times in the course of a single act—a rare feat for
septuagenarians. There was the peculiar method of locomo-
tion, whereby he would spring to his feet and, resembling a
more aloof and ceremonious Jacques Tati, propel himself
forward with the palms of his hands turned out, as if wading
through waist-deep water. There was the pop-eyed, poleaxed
look, with one eyebrow balefully cocked, whenever he was
faced with a remark that was baffling or potentially hostile.
Above all, there was the voice, which I once described as
"something between bland and grandiose: blandiose, per-

haps." Or, as I wrote in another context, when he played
Cyrano de Bergerac in 1946:

> His voice is most delicate; breath-light of texture; more
> buoyant even than that of M. Charles Trenet. . . . It is a
> yeasty, agile voice. Where Olivier would pounce upon
> a line and rip its heart out, Richardson skips and lilts
> and bounces along it, shaving off pathos in great flakes.

A personal note: The noise that Sir Ralph makes has
sometimes struck me as the vocal equivalent of onionskin
writing paper—suave, crackling, and resonant. This curious
association is no doubt strengthened by my memories of his
definitive performance as Peer Gynt, in 1944—specifically,
of the scene in which Peer tries to find his true identity by
symbolically peeling an onion, only to discover that beneath
the last layer of skin there is no core of selfhood but, simply
and literally, nothing. Sir Ralph has often been at his best
when playing men in whose lives, gamely though they keep
up appearances, there is a spiritual emptiness, a certain terror
of the void. One of his greatest regrets is having turned down
Samuel Beckett's *Waiting for Godot* in the early nineteen-
fifties, when he and Alec Guinness were invited to play the
two Godot-forsaken tramps. They were dissuaded in part by
Gielgud, who decried the play—in a phrase of which he is
now thoroughly ashamed—as "a load of old rubbish." Sir
Ralph, then appearing at the Haymarket Theatre in London,
asked Beckett to come and discuss the script with him. "I'd
drawn up a sort of laundry list of things I didn't quite
understand," Sir Ralph recalls. "And Beckett came into my
dressing room—wearing a knapsack, which was very mysterious—and I started to read through my list. You see, I
like to know what I'm being asked to do. March up the hill
and charge that blockhouse! Fine—but I wasn't sure which
was the hill and where the blockhouse was. I needed to have
a few things clear in my mind. But Beckett just looked at
me and said, 'I'm awfully sorry, but I can't answer any of
your questions.' He wouldn't explain. Didn't lend me a hand.

And then another job came up, and I turned down the greatest play of my lifetime."

Richardson became an indisputably great actor in the latter half of 1944. Since then, despite some wildly misguided choices of roles, he has continued to ripen. Today, both as a man and as a performer, he is more expansive in his uniqueness and his eccentricity than ever before. He is the eldest of a formidable trio of English actors—the others being Gielgud and Laurence Olivier, his juniors by, respectively, two and five years—who were born early in the century, and whose careers, which have frequently crisscrossed, form a map that covers most of the high points of English theatre in the past five decades. (Richardson and Olivier were knighted in 1947; Gielgud had to wait for his accolade until 1953.) Gielgud and Olivier, from their earliest days in the profession, were that godsend to critics, a pair of perfect opposites. You could list their qualities in parallel columns:

GIELGUD	OLIVIER
Air	Earth
Poet	Peasant
Mind	Heart
Spiritual	Animal
Feminine	Masculine
John Philip Kemble	Edmund Kean
Introvert	Extrovert
Jewel	Metal
Claret	Burgundy

Concerning the great Shakespearean parts that both actors have played, the critical consensus is that Gielgud has defeated Olivier as Hamlet and Romeo, while Olivier has knocked out Gielgud as Othello, Antony, and Macbeth. King Lear has outpointed both of them. But where does this all leave Sir Ralph? Very much the odd man out. Many of his greatest Shakespearean successes have been in parts like Falstaff, Caliban, Bottom, and Enobarbus, which the other

members of the triumvirate have never attempted. In 1960, he
contributed a series of autobiographical pieces to the London
Sunday Times, in one of which he wrote, "Hamlet, Lear,
Macbeth and Othello are the four glorious peaks of dramatic
literature." Of Macbeth, a role he played in 1952, he said,
"I couldn't do it for nuts—not for a second did I believe in
the air-drawn dagger, and if I couldn't, no wonder no one
else did." In 1938, he failed as Othello, though he cannot
have been much helped by his Iago: Olivier, who elected to
play the part along Freudian lines, as a man consumed by
a smoldering homosexual passion for the Moor, but who
neglected to inform Sir Ralph that he intended, in the
course of the performance, to kiss him full on the lips. James
Agate, the leading London critic of the time, headed his
review "Othello Without the Moor." In it he sombrely
concluded:

> The truth is that Nature, which has showered upon this
> actor the kindly gifts of the comedian, has unkindly
> refused him any tragic facilities whatever. His voice has
> not a tragic note in its whole gamut, all the accents
> being those of sweetest reasonableness. He cannot blaze.

As for Hamlet and Lear, Sir Ralph has avoided them both
—wrongly, I think, as far as the latter role is concerned, but
this is a point to which I'll return. "Clearly," he wrote in 1960,
"I don't belong to the first division. It could be that my place
is in doomed second." Alternatively, it could be just that he
lacks the traditional (but now surely outdated) attributes
of the tragic hero—the rumbling voice, the aquiline nose, the
high cheekbones, the profile of ruined beauty. Critics have
written of his "round, sober cheese-face," his "broad moony
countenance," which has also been likened to a "sanctified
potato." Interviewed on British TV in 1975, he said, "I
don't like my face at all. It's always been a great drawback
to me." He is utterly sincere about this, the proof being that
although he has been working in the cinema since 1933, he

has never seen any of the rushes. "It discourages me," he says of his physical appearance. "I lose confidence in myself." Yet, despite this alleged handicap, and despite his failure to conquer the tragic Big Four, he has remained, both in and out of the classics, a star with an assured place in the Big Three—a wine to be judged on the same level as Burgundy and claret, even if nobody can quite manage to locate the vineyard.

To explain his continued presence in the top trio, a special category had to be invented for him. Ralph Richardson, it was said, represented not the Tragic Hero or the Poetic Hero but the Common Man. I once asked him how he differed as a performer from Olivier. He ruminated for a moment and then replied, "I've not his size or range. I'm a more rotund kind of actor. Laurence is more the spiky sort. I haven't got his splendid fury." Fury, of course, takes many forms that are not explicit, and hearty bluffness can veil many kinds of desolation and misanthropy. To this matter, too, I shall return. During the thirties and early forties, it became an article of theatrical faith that Richardson was Everyman, the chap you cast when you wanted an embodiment of common-place decency, of sterling (if slightly tongue-tied) honesty— in short, a sort of human dobbin. Not everyone was deceived. Barbara Jefford, a handsome classical actress with whom he has worked at the Old Vic, once said to me, "People called him the epitome of the ordinary man, I suppose because of his round face. They were absolutely wrong. I can imagine him as a kind of Thomas Hardy hero—a plebeian type transmogrified and exalted. But he could never be your average worker." In 1963, she went on, she appeared with Sir Ralph in Pirandello's *Six Characters in Search of an Author*. He played the father, a fictitious creature perma-nently condemned to a twilit half existence, since the play-within-a-play of which he is the protagonist is never com-pleted. "And, of course, he was superb," Miss Jefford said, "*because he was playing a ghost*. That's the point about Ralph. There's always something spectral about him. He really is a man from Mars." In 1957, he scored a great hit in *Flowering Cherry*, Robert Bolt's first stage success, as a dowdy suburban husband with delusions of grandeur. His performance gave the lie to the theory that he was Everyman reborn in Surbiton. "To any role that gives him half a chance," I wrote at the time, "he brings outsize attributes, outsize euphoria, outsize dismay. Those critics who hold that he excels in portraying the Average Man cannot, I feel, have met many Average Men. . . . He gives us fantasy, not normality."

If Sir Ralph was not Everyman, what was he? Two quotations may be helpful. One is from George Jean Nathan: "Drama is a two-souled art: half divine, half clownish." The other is from Sir Ralph himself: "The ability to convey a sense of mystery is one of the most powerful assets possessed by the theatre." If Sir Ralph was the odd man out, the operative word was "odd." Mystery, clownishness, oddity: all of them forms of protective carapace—smokescreens, layers of the onion.

First Interlude: 5 P.M. on June 14, 1976. Interview between Sir Ralph and me at his London house, which is extremely grand—designed by Nash and overlooking Regent's Park. The meeting has been easy to fix: strangely, for a man so deeply private in other respects, he does not bother to have an unlisted telephone number. I have known him slightly for twenty-odd years: Will he remember that I described him in *Macbeth* as "a sad facsimile of the Cowardly Lion in *The Wizard of Oz*" and as "the glass eye in the forehead of English acting"? I ascend by lift (still a great rarity in London houses) to wait in a resplendent L-shaped living room with floor-to-ceiling windows. My qualms are allayed when he bursts in beaming and asks if I'd care to join him in one of his special cocktails. I accept with thanks. He pads across to a well-stocked drinks table, selects two half-pint tumblers, and pours into each of them three fat fingers of Gordon's gin, followed by a huge slug of French vermouth.

I reach out for my drink. He shakes his head and adds a
lavish shot of Italian vermouth. I repeat business; he repeats
headshake. Into each glass he now pours three *thumbs* of
vodka. "That," he says gravely, "is what makes the difference." I can well believe him. Three things are known about
Sir Ralph's relationship with alcohol. One: He enjoys it.
Two: On working days he restricts himself, until the curtain
falls, to a couple of glasses of wine, taken with luncheon.
Three: He is never visibly drunk. I recall a story told me by
a former director of a famous classical repertory theatre,
who wanted Sir Ralph to join the company and went to his
home to discuss what parts he might play. "There was this
long mahogany table," my informant said, "Ralph sat at one
end and put a full bottle of gin in front of me. 'That,' he
said, 'is for you.' Then he got another full bottle and placed
it at his end of the table. 'And that,' he said, 'is for me.'
Then he sat down. 'Now, my dear fellow,' he said, 'what do
we want to talk about?' "

I stealthily consult some notes I have made about his
career, but before I have framed my first question he says,
"I've no idea what we're going to say to each other. After
all, where did we come from? Did you ever have a vision of
the place we came from before we were born? I did, when I
was about three years old. I used to dream about it a good
deal. I even drew pictures of it." He leans forward con-
fidentially. "*It looked rather like Mexico*," he says with quiet
emphasis. Wind utterly removed from sails, I am silenced:
Who else would start a conversation like this? I sip his lethal
cocktail, which he leaps up to replenish as soon as the level
falls more than half an inch below the rim of the glass. From
life before birth it is a short step to life after death. "I've
been very close to death," he muses. "It's like dropping into
an abyss—very drowsy, rather nice." Is he referring to wartime experiences in the Fleet Air Arm or to the motorbike
on which, pipe in mouth, he habitually zooms around
London? In a conversation recently recorded in the London
Observer, Gielgud said to Sir Ralph, "The last time you

took me on the pillion, I practically had a fit. I was a stretcher case." Sir Ralph nodded and esoterically replied, "I have been killed several times myself." Meanwhile, he pursues his metaphysical speculations: "God is very economical, don't you think? Wastes nothing. Yet also the opposite. All those galaxies, stars rolling on forever . . ."

By a mighty effort, I turn the conversation to contemporary realities. What does he think, after all these years, of his old partner Olivier? He springs from his seat, arms outstretched above his head. "I *hate* Larry. Until I see him. Then he has more magnetism than anyone I've ever met. Except Alexander Korda. I had a film contract with Korda from 1935 until he died, in 1956. I would go to see him with a furious speech about what I wanted, and what I'd do if I didn't get it. And all the time he'd be staring at my feet. When I'd finished, he'd say, 'Where did you get those marvellous shoes? I'd give anything to have shoes like those.' And I would be defeated." He subsides into a chair. "I admire anyone who has a talent that makes me tingle. Like Chopin, or Conrad, or Pinter, or Beckett. Though not the later Beckett. I am sadly literal-minded, and in Beckett's recent work I find obscurity instead of mystery. And, of course, I worship Ethel Merman."

We talk about Peter Hall, who succeeded Olivier as artistic director of Britain's National Theatre, and for whom Sir Ralph has lately worked in Ibsen's *John Gabriel Borkman* as well as in *No Man's Land*. A few months earlier, Hall confided to his associates that Sir Ralph was "the greatest poetic actor alive, with perhaps two or three good years left in him," adding that it was their duty to make sure that he spent these precious days at the National. Accordingly, Hall acquired the rights to *The Kingfisher*, a new play written for Sir Ralph by the popular boulevard dramatist William Douglas Home and originally intended for presentation in the commercial theatre. Hall's ingenious plan was that after a token run of a few weeks at the National the play should be moved to the West End. The director (Hall) and any stars in his cast would then be remunerated at West End levels, which are considerably higher than those at the National, since they include percentages of the box-office gross. A profitable operation for all concerned—though there were purists who doubted whether the true function of a national theatre was to stage commercial productions for quick moneymaking transfers to the West End. Sir Ralph makes no claims for the play as a work of art: *"The Kingfisher* is two bits of cobweb stuck together with stamp edging and sticking plaster. It's about two elderly people—Celia Johnson plays the woman—who very nearly had an affair when they were much younger but didn't quite. He's now an old novelist, and her husband has just died. They try to begin again where they left off all those years ago. Things like that happen all the time. When I was, oh, about twelve, I met a girl named Francesca. I never kissed her, never even touched her, doubt if I saw her more than a couple of times, but as long as I live I shan't forget her." Topping up our drinks, he lowers his voice. "Don't you think Peter Hall has something *Germanic* about him? I do hope he doesn't get Germanic with the Willie Douglas Home play, because if he does we shall all go down with the Titanic." Pause. Then a broad, beatific smile: "Or the Teutonic." (Since this conversation took place, Hall has had a change of heart. Influenced, perhaps, by the increasingly vocal doubts of the purists, the National has relinquished the play to the commercial theatre, where it will be staged by another director, with Sir Ralph still in the lead, but without the aid of public subsidy.)

Before we part, he reminisces about his pet ferret. He really used to have a pet ferret. He washed it every week in Lux soap flakes. (There were rabbits, too, and hamsters. "Whether it's a ferret or a motorbike or a firework," said Barbara Jefford, "he concentrates entirely on his extraordinary enthusiasms. It's a boy we're talking about, a great boy.") "Goodbye, my dear chap," he says, waving me into the lift. I leave feeling (a) that I have known this man all my life, and (b) that I have never met anyone who more adroitly buttonholed me while keeping me firmly at arm's length.

Sir Ralph once said, "I've never given a good performance, that has satisfied me, in any play." Is this false modesty or genuine diffidence? A young actor I know appeared with Sir Ralph in a recent production. One evening, as they stood in the wings awaiting their entrance, Sir Ralph turned to my friend and murmured, "I had a little talent once. A very little talent. If you should ever come across a tiny talent labelled R. R., please let me know." Then the cue came, and he surged imperiously into the spotlight.

Ralph Richardson was born in 1902 in the intensely respectable West Country town of Cheltenham. His mother was a devout Catholic and his father a Quaker—according to Sir Ralph, "a shortish man with a beard and cold blue eyes," who wore bright-colored waistcoats and taught art at the local Ladies' College. Ralph had two elder brothers, of whom—as of Cheltenham and, indeed, of his father—he remembers very little, since when he was four his mother ran away from home, taking him with her. When he is asked why she bolted, he maintains a silence that may betoken either tact or ignorance. On a minute allowance of two pounds and ten shillings a week, provided by his father, they lived at Shoreham-by-Sea, in Sussex, in a pair of disused railway carriages standing side by side on the beach and joined together by a tin roof. This meant that they had, in Sir Ralph's words, "a front door and a back door, as well as about twenty side doors." Their neighbors were few. "I had one friend for a time," Sir Ralph has written, "until I was accused of murder." It seems that when he was idly twirling an iron hoop on a stick it flew off and accidentally struck his friend, a small girl, on the head. Unfortunately, her mother was an explosive pioneer feminist on a very short fuse, who came storming out of her nearby bungalow and howled, "You brute! You have killed my daughter!" He had in fact merely grazed her scalp. Since his mother had hopes of grooming him for the priesthood, he was sent to several Catholic schools; one of them was a seminary, from which, to her great disappointment, he ran away. Academic subjects bored him: "I was not passionate enough and had not the character to be rebellious. I think I was just a big oaf."

He recalls from his school days only one moment of fulfill-ment, when a teacher called on him to get up and recite a passage from Macaulay's *Lays of Ancient Rome*. He ac-cepted the challenge and astounded himself. "It frightened the life out of the class, and it frightened the life out of me. They were horrified, they were electrified. It was really very good. I never read again. No one ever asked me to." Around 1910, he and his mother moved to South London, and thence to Brighton, living in a succession of cheap flats, hotels, and boarding houses. "I had no education at all, really," he later told a TV interviewer. "I was sort of professionally ill when I was a little boy." He was forever catching things—mumps, scarlet fever, diphtheria—and his mother, a lonely and possessive woman, as well as an expert hypochondriac in her own right, saw to it that he stayed at home as much as possible. There was money on the Richardson side of the family, which included prosperous leather manufacturers in Newcastle-upon-Tyne, but Ralph's father had forfeited his share of the fortune by abjuring commerce and taking to the arts. Even so, the boy remem-bered his paternal grandfather, controller of the dynastic loot, with fondness:

> He came to take me out in London one day when he was about eighty. Wonderful white beard and very ironic, like a pirate in a good mood. It was my day, he said, and we'd do exactly what I liked. I took him to the Crystal Palace and we spent hours on the switchbacks; he never turned a whisker. I was told afterwards I might have killed him.

What follows could easily be a novel by H. G. Wells modulating into a novel by J. B. Priestley. In 1919, young Richardson is employed as an office boy in a Brighton insurance company. Being a sprightly lad with a taste for heights and none for his job, he amuses himself one day by shuffling his way around the office building on a narrow outside ledge, vertiginously overlooking Brighton High Street. Crowds gather on the sidewalk, watching him in horror. (He later admitted that he was partly motivated by exhibitionism; after all, "the Alpine climber's audience is sparse.") He has timed his exploit to coincide with a period when the boss will be out of the building. His timing is off. The boss reenters his office to find Richardson passing slowly by outside his window, and freezes in the act of removing his hat. Richardson smiles and waves in a friendly manner. Receiving no response, he puts his head in over the top of the window and affably explains, "I was chasing a pigeon." His employer, too nonplussed to take disciplinary action, nods vaguely and makes a mental note: "Richardson is not reliable."

Soon afterward, Richardson's Newcastle grandmother died—a wealthy woman he had hardly met. When he was six, she summoned him to visit her. He took with him a pet mouse named Kim. The servant who met him at the station shook her head and said, "You'll never be allowed to take that creature up to the big house." "Why not?" said Ralph. "I've been invited to see my grandmother, and I never travel without Kim." "She won't let it in the house," said the servant. "In that case," said Ralph, "when's the next train back to Brighton?" He stood his ground, and the matriarch was forced to capitulate; but she was so impressed by his stubbornness that she remembered him in her will. In fact, she left him five hundred pounds—a sum large enough to change the course of his life. "Kim cost me sixpence," he reflected later. "It was the happiest buy I ever made."

He gave up insurance and enrolled in the Brighton School of Art. But not for long. A few months afterward, Sir Frank

Benson and his renowned Shakespearean company appeared
at the Theatre Royal, and Richardson went to see them in
Hamlet. This was "the decisive moment that moved my
compass," he wrote later. "I suddenly realized what acting
was and I thought: By Jove, that's the job for me." He
abandoned painting and applied for work with a semiprofessional troupe run in Brighton by a stubby, hooknosed actor-
manager named Frank R. Growcott. He chose as his audition
piece a speech by Falstaff. Growcott was appalled. "That is
quite awful," he said. "It is shapeless, senseless, badly
spoken. . . . You could never, never be any good as Falstaff."
(This diatribe burned itself into Richardson's mind. When
Olivier, a quarter of a century later, asked him to play
Falstaff, his first reaction was to say that he couldn't possibly
do it.) Nonetheless, Growcott agreed to hire him for six
months. During the first half of the engagement he would
pay Growcott ten shillings a week, after which Growcott
would pay him the same sum. In the following year, 1921,
he achieved full professional status. He joined a touring
repertory company led by a now forgotten Irish actor called
Charles Doran. The Doran productions were rehearsed in
London, so Richardson—who until then had never seen a
play on the West End stage—was able to study the work of
people like Charles Hawtrey ("I think the best actor I've
ever seen") and Mrs. Patrick Campbell ("who knocked me
flat"). For three years, he toured with Doran, building a
solid Shakespearean technique on the basis of parts like
Orlando, Macduff, and Bottom. A fellow member of the
troupe was Muriel Hewitt, whom he married in 1924, and
later summed up as "the perfect example of the natural
actress." They went on to work together at the Birmingham
Repertory Theatre, which was then the most adventurous
regional ensemble in Britain, and in 1926 Richardson made
his West End debut, in *Yellow Sands*, a Birmingham success
by Eden and Adelaide Phillpotts that moved to London and
ran for over six hundred performances, with Cedric Hard-

wicke in the leading role. Richardson's wife was also in the cast. In his own words:

> Her career on the stage was brilliant but brief, and her courage was terribly tested, for after a few years of work she fell under some rare nervous attack, perhaps akin to polio, and some years later she died.

"Ralph's first wife contracted some kind of sleeping sickness in Croydon," John Gielgud told me recently. "Her death was long and painful." It finally took place in 1942. "They were devoted to each other," Gielgud added.

Richardson's first real blossoming began in 1930 at the Old Vic, where, over a period of two years, he played a full range of classical roles, among them Prince Hal in *Henry IV*, part I, Caliban, Bolingbroke, Iago, Toby Belch, the Bastard in *King John*, Petruchio, Kent in *King Lear*, Enobarbus, and Henry V. Gielgud remembers "his marvellous performances of shaggy-dog faithfulness—the kind of part Shakespeare wrote so well," and says, "He was unforgettable as the Bastard and Enobarbus and Kent. And he always gave them a touch of fantasy. But he couldn't bear fights. When I played Hotspur to his Hal, and he had to kill me, he used to count the strokes out loud. 'Come on, cockie,' he'd say. 'One, and two, and three, and four . . .' I never really felt his heart was in it."

By the midthirties, he was an established star in modern plays (*For Services Rendered* and *Sheppey*, both by Somerset Maugham, and J. B. Priestley's *Eden End*) as well as the classics. In 1935, Broadway saw him for the first time, playing the Chorus and Mercutio in *Romeo and Juliet*, with Katharine Cornell as the Capulet heiress. A year later, back in London, he plunged into the title role of *The Amazing Dr. Clitterhouse*, a long-running thriller, in which he was supported by Meriel Forbes, who subsequently became—as she still is—his wife. Thus far, he was a thoroughly respected actor, versatile and dependable, yet somehow earthbound. Agate had written of "his stolid, inexpressive mien, altogether admirable . . . in all delineations of the downright," and the phrase epitomized what up to that point most playgoers felt about him. His stage persona, however, did not reflect the combustible *bizarrerie* of the man within.

Second Interlude: November 5, 1937 or 1938. (None of the surviving participants is quite sure of the year.) It is Guy Fawkes Day, on which the British let off fireworks to celebrate the discovery (and frustration) of a Catholic plot to blow up the Houses of Parliament. It is also Vivien Leigh's birthday. She and Olivier—as yet unmarried, because Olivier's divorce from his first wife, Jill Esmond, is not final—have moved into a tiny house in Chelsea. Miss Leigh has spent months and a great deal of money turning it into (Olivier's phrase) "a perfect little bandbox," full of costly trinkets, with a minuscule garden behind. Instead of giving a large house-warming party, they decide to invite only two old friends— Ralph Richardson and Meriel Forbes, the latter known by the nickname of Mu. What follows is Sir Ralph's account of the festivity, as he recalled it for me last year: "I took great trouble and care. I arrived at the house with Mu and a huge box of fireworks that I had bought with loving joy. I took the biggest rocket out into the garden—it was one of the kind you use to attract attention if your ship is sinking— and there I set it off. It came straight back into the dining room and burned up the curtains and set the pelmet on fire." According to Olivier, it also wrecked a lot of priceless antique crockery and left him and Vivien, who were cowering behind the sofa, blackened about the face like Al Jolson. "I knew that Vivien had taken great trouble with her decorations, and that her pelmet was unpleasantly burned. But it was my *benevolence* that had caused it all. 'Let's get out of here,' I said to Mu. 'These people don't understand us.' I grabbed the doorknob, and through no fault of mine it came off in my hand. I have to admit that I was very hurt, next day, when nobody rang me up to say, 'How kind of you, Ralph, to have thought of bringing those fireworks.' "

Some years later, Sir Ralph mentioned to Olivier that he had given birth to a splendid idea for the National Theatre, should it ever come into being. Every night (he said), as the curtain went up, a synchronized rocket should rise from the roof of the theatre, to inform the populace that an event of national significance was about to take place. It would be known as Ralph's Rocket. This suggestion was adopted, and in March, 1976, when the National Theatre finally moved into its new home, on the south bank of the Thames, the first rocket was duly launched. Sir Ralph himself lit the fuse.

It was not until 1944, after five wartime years spent as a pilot in the Fleet Air Arm, that Ralph Richardson's great period began. He outgrew his humility, burst the bounds of sobriety that had theretofore constrained him, and started to allow his fantasy free flight. "He had always wanted to be a matinee idol," Gielgud says, "and felt inadequate because he couldn't be." Or, as Barbara Jefford puts it, "he was always a wonderfully flexible film performer—better in many ways than Gielgud or Olivier—but he never had the obvious good looks you expect of The Great Actor." Now that he had entered his forties, this lack of physical glamour began to seem less important. He joined the revived Old Vic company, which was to be temporarily housed at the New Theatre, in the West End, since its original (and much humbler) home, south of the Thames, had been gutted by German bombs. Richardson shared the artistic director-ship with Olivier and a promising newcomer named John Burrell, and launched the inaugural season, on August 31, 1944, by playing the title role in *Peer Gynt*. Tyrone Guthrie directed, with assistance "in grouping and movement" from Robert Helpmann, then at the height of his powers as dancer and choreographer. Sybil Thorndike, Margaret Leighton, and Olivier (in the small but spine-chilling part of the Button-Molder) were in the supporting cast; and Richardson,

as the peasant who circumnavigates the globe in fruitless
search of self-fulfillment, gave the most poetic performance
of his life—volatile, obsessed, constantly surprising. (He has
said that Peer Gynt, who is "a little mad," is his favorite
part.) In the same season he played Bluntschli, the pragmatic
soldier in Shaw's *Arms and the Man*; Richmond to Olivier's
overwhelming Richard III; and Uncle Vanya in the tender,
unsparing play of that name. In the autumn of 1945, he
opened as Falstaff in both parts of Shakespeare's *Henry IV*.
These were the productions that—coupled with those left
over from the previous season, and augmented by the flabber-
gasting double bill in which Olivier played Sophocles'
Oedipus and (after the intermission) Mr. Puff in Sheridan's
The Critic—established the highwater mark of English acting in the twentieth century.

"Falstaff," Sir Ralph wrote in 1960, "proceeds through
the plays at his own chosen pace, like a gorgeous ceremonial
Indian elephant." As an undergraduate at Oxford, I said
of his performance, "Here was a Falstaff whose principal
attribute was not his fatness but his knighthood. He was Sir
John first and Falstaff second." I continued:

> The spirit behind all the rotund nobility was spry and
> elastic. . . . There was also, when the situation called for
> it, great wisdom and melancholy. ("Peace, good Doll!
> do not speak like a death's head: do not bid me
> remember mine end" was done with most moving
> authority.) Each word emerged with immensely careful
> articulation, the lips forming it lovingly and then spitting
> it forth. In moments of passion, the wild white halo of
> hair stood angrily up and the eyes rolled majestically;
> and in rage one noticed a slow, meditative relish taking
> command . . . it was not a sweaty fat man, but a dry
> and dignified one. . . . He had good manners and also
> that respect for human dignity which prevented him
> from openly showing his boredom at the inanities of
> Shallow and Silence. . . . He was not often jovial, laughed
> seldom, belched never. . . . After the key-cold rebuke

[from Prince Hal, once his fellow-boozer, now his monarch], the old man turned, his face red and working in furious *tics* to hide his tears. . . . "I shall be sent for soon at night."

But we know, of course, that he will not. Of the preceding scenes, lyrically comic, set in a twilit Gloucestershire orchard, where Falstaff basks in the sycophantic adulation of Justice Shallow (Olivier), a shrivelled drinking crony of his youth, I see no reason to revise what I wrote thirty years ago: "If I had only half an hour more to spend in theatres, and could choose at large, no question but I would have these." In the 1946–47 season, Sir Ralph's exuberent, opportunistic performances as Cyrano de Bergerac and Face, the scheming servant in Jonson's *The Alchemist*, set the seal on his new reputation. Always excepting Olivier, no actor in England was riding higher.

Third Interlude: The summer of 1946. Ralph and Meriel Richardson are motoring down to spend the weekend at Notley Abbey, in Buckinghamshire. The Oliviers have recently acquired the fifteenth-century abbot's lodge, and converted it, at ridiculous expense, into a stately home. Stopping his car on the brow of a hill that overlooks the abbey and its domain, Richardson turns to Mu and says (they both recall the exact words), "I hope to God I don't put my foot in it this time." Since the Chelsea holocaust, purely social contacts between the two couples have been limited—mainly because the war has kept them apart but also because of a lingering sense (on Mrs. Olivier's part) that there is something inherently hazardous, almost poltergeistic, about Richardson's presence.

The day passes sweetly. The guests are shown over the estate. Across a candlelit dinner table, good stories are told, and plans made for the future of the Old Vic. Richardson conducts himself with extreme caution, a man walking on eggshells. Olivier talks of the abbey's history, and of some remarkably preserved frescoes painted by the monks on beams in the attic. Wouldn't the Richardsons (he suggests after dinner) like to come up and see them? Mu declines the invitation; her husband, the model guest, accepts. The men having left, the wives chat over their coffee. Mrs. Olivier feels obscurely uneasy, but after five, ten, fifteen minutes have passed without incident, she is ready to scoff at her qualms. At this moment, there is a prolonged splintering noise from above, followed by a colossal crash that makes the whole house shake. The women dash upstairs, where, in the main guest room, lovingly decorated under Mrs. Olivier's personal supervision, they find Richardson flat on his back and covered in plaster, on a bed that has collapsed under his weight. Above it there is a gaping hole in the ceiling, through which he has evidently fallen. It emerges that the attic has no floor and can be traversed only on narrow rafters. Olivier had brought a flashlight, with which he directed Richardson's attention to the paintings on the beams above their heads. Two versions exist of what happened next. According to Sir Ralph, "Larry said to me, 'Why don't you take a step back to see the pictures better?' " Olivier denies this, saying, "Ralph just whirled round in pure wonderment and toppled off." At all events, Mrs. Olivier was seen to be foaming with rage, like a Cassandra whose prophecies of doom have gone unheeded.

"I felt pretty dogsbody, I can tell you," Sir Ralph remarked to me later. At the time, he thought himself slightly more sinned against than sinning, but now he admits that his hostess had some cause to be upset. "There was a rational basis to Vivien's fury, which we must salute," he said to me the other day. "If you prod a tigress twice in her lair, you must not expect her to purr."

Knighted (along with Olivier) in 1947, his film career thriving, Sir Ralph was at his perihelion when, in a fit of collective paranoia, the governors of the Old Vic did an extraordinary thing. Fearing that the company had lost its identity as a people's theatre offering high art at low prices, and was in danger of becoming a gilded playground for West End stars, they fired the entire directorship at a stroke, without warning, in the middle of the 1948–49 season. "We felt rather badly treated," Sir Ralph told me years afterward, with the stoicism of hindsight, "but a fired butler doesn't complain of his master."

Burrell, Olivier, and Richardson were jobless overnight. It did not, of course, take them long to find other employment; but the three men, despite differences of temperament, had formed a spectacularly successful and cohesive team, like a jazz trio in which contrasting styles coalesce into a whole that is greater than the sum of its parts. The decision to axe them changed the course of theatrical history in England, and during the years that followed, Sir Ralph, bereft of the stimulation that group leadership can provide in the theatre (for the leaders no less than the led), sometimes looked a little lost. Something he said of his colleagues in the Fleet Air Arm may also apply to his co-directors at the Vic: "They brought the best out of you by being so absolutely certain you'd got the best in you." He continued, of course, to have his triumphs—as Peggy Ashcroft's glacially possessive Papa in *The Heiress* (adapted from Henry James's *Washington Square* and directed by Gielgud) and as Vershinin, the philosopher-philanderer in Chekhov's *The Three Sisters*. But the creative interplay, the artistic checks and balances, the argumentative crosscurrents of the Old Vic days had gone forever. Thenceforward, Sir Ralph was on his own.

His plague year was 1952, in which he went to Stratford-upon-Avon to play Prospero, Macbeth, and Volpone, and failed in all three. He said himself, "I don't know which was the worst." The night I saw his Volpone, many of the lines eluded him, and replacements were smuggled in from other plays. At one point, he stunned his fellow actors by addressing them as "Ye elves of hills, brooks, standing lakes, and groves," and went on (since there was clearly no going back) to favor us with the rest of the famous speech from *The Tempest* which begins with that phrase. In 1953, having seen him in *The White Carnation*, a puny play by R. C. Sherriff, I wrote:

> He has taken to ambling across our stages in a spectral, shell-shocked manner, choosing odd moments to jump and frisk, like a man through whom an electric current is being intermittently passed.

The year 1956 brought us a most erratic *Timon of Athens*, containing "gestures so eccentric that their true significance could be revealed only by extensive trepanning." But even at his most aberrant he remained supremely watchable. Once the curtain had risen, you could never be sure (nor, it seemed at times, could he) what he would do next. A moment of pure dottiness might be followed by a flash of revelation. More and more, he was bringing the aura of his own private world onto the stage with him, like a glass bell with which to protect himself from the audience—for whom, in any case, he had never felt any overpowering fondness. "I'm rather inclined," he told a man from *The Guardian* last year, "to think of them as a cage of bloody tigers that will bite you, and will put you out of the stage door if they can. . . . You must never let them command." (Even the theatregoers of Brighton, to whose applause he had so often bowed during his apprenticeship, he described in 1975 as "very dangerous.") A master of all the stratagems of self-protection, he has always been extremely wily if he suspects that an attempt is being made, in Hamlet's phrase, to pluck out the heart of his mystery. Not long ago, he and Gielgud were photographed by Jane Bown, of the London *Observer*. She had hardly arrived when Sir Ralph began to profess amnesia about his identity. "The trouble is I can never remember who I am whenever I'm photographed. Who *am* I? I find I'm no one in particular."

"However close you get to him, he's still distant," Barbara Jefford says. "In life and onstage, he has a kind of remote intimacy. When you're acting with him there's no eye contact. He never looks at you. And he never touches people onstage. I played his stepdaughter in *Six Characters in Search of an Author*, and there's a big scene where he's supposed to grope me. He never even touched me. And yet I'm told the audience got a very sensual impression from the whole scene." The play was staged by the American director William Ball. Miss Jefford recalls, "The most typical thing that Ralph did happened during rehearsals. One morning, Bill called the company together and said, 'Today, I want us all to throw away our scripts and improvise our way through the play.' Ralph didn't say a word. He was perfectly polite. He just quietly rose and left the room. Oh, he was *about*, he didn't leave the building, but he didn't come back to that room. He couldn't bear the thought of *exposing* himself like that."

In 1964, as part of the festivities in honor of the quatercentenary of Shakespeare's birth, the British Council sent Sir Ralph on a tour of Mexico (his prenatal homeland), South America, and Europe, playing Shylock in *The Merchant of Venice* and Bottom in *A Midsummer Night's Dream*. Miss Jefford went along as Portia and Helena. Lady Richardson, although she had never before appeared in Shakespeare, decided at the last moment to volunteer her services as Titania. I saw *The Merchant* before it left England. It had a lot of very old-fashioned sets, with equally old-fashioned blackouts between scenes, and was memorable chiefly for Sir Ralph's physical appearance. He wore a bright yellow skullcap, set off by lurid green makeup, and he brandished what I took to be a shepherd's crook. "He looks like the Demon King in a pantomime," a junior member of the cast had told me, with awe in his voice, before the performance. I paid a brief visit to Sir Ralph's dressing room afterward. When I asked about the shepherd's crook, he explained although he based his interpretation on the assump-

tion that Shylock was "a gent," it was vital not to forget that
"the Jews were a race of nomadic shepherds." He added,
"Shylock knows all about breeding sheep. Look at his speech
about Jacob and Laban and the ewes and the rams—typical
piece of Shakespearean illumination." The notion of a
pastoral Shylock was something I was not quite ready for,
and, as I remember, our conversation ended there. During
the months that followed, however, I often thought of this
strange, glaucous, eerily imposing apparition, and what the
citizens of Lima or Buenos Aires must have made of it as it
came looming at them over the Andes. Miss Jefford has
vivid memories of Sir Ralph off duty during the three-month
tour. "In Latin America, he became intensely English, very
much the squire, with a yellow waistcoat and a panama hat
at a jaunty angle." In another vignette, he is standing beside
her in the wings, watching his wife—an excellent actress in
modern roles—tackling Titania. "She tries very hard," he
muses. "But"—and here he mimes the gestures of a violinist
—"she hasn't got the *bowing*."

He and Miss Jefford met in 1956 when they were at the
Old Vic together, though not in the same plays. "He was
only in *Timon*, so I didn't know him at all, but one night he
came to see me as Imogen in *Cymbeline*. Next day, I got one
of his beautiful little notes, written in exquisite script, so
delicately arranged on the page, with wide, wide margins all
covered with little sketches. He said that in the bedroom,
when Iachimo creeps out of the trunk to examine me, he
thought my *sleep* was especially convincing. Rather an odd
tribute, considering that I didn't move a muscle throughout
the scene. But I appreciated it." A great Richardson fan, Miss
Jefford concedes that he was below his best as Shylock. She
says shrewdly, "He's not good at portraying *mundane* sins and
desires. There isn't enough poetry in Shylock for Ralph." She
agrees with me that he ought to have a crack at King Lear.
There's no doubt that he would be heartbreaking in the final
exchanges with Cordelia:

We too alone will sing like birds i' the cage:
When thou dost ask me blessing, I'll kneel down,
And ask of thee forgiveness.

In these passages, Lear has fought his way through to a
simplicity and an emotional sanity that lie on the far side of
complexity and madness. (It is the early Lear, the capricious
and egocentric despot of the opening scene, who is truly
mad.) I have heard it objected that Sir Ralph lacks the
vocal firepower for the "Blow, winds, and crack your cheeks"
aria on the storm-blasted health; but the point, nearly
always forgotten, about this speech is that Lear is not attack-
ing the storm or trying to shout it down. Its fury confirms
his misanthropy: *he is on its side.* Played thus (as I have yet
to see it played), the speech would be well within Sir Ralph's
compass.

At 5 P.M. on January 11, 1976, I visit Sir John Gielgud in
his suite at the Drake Hotel in New York. My host is spruce,
poker-backed, voluble, eyes wickedly gleaming—a lighthouse
spraying words instead of candlepower. "It's true that Ralph
is wary about the audience," Sir John says. "He watches it
like a hawk. Quite often he'll say to me, 'Did you notice that
man in the fifth row groping that girl during the second
act?'" We talk about *No Man's Land*: "I always think that
Hirst, the character Ralph plays, is very much like Hamm,
the hero of Beckett's *Endgame*—a sort of tyrant who's
dominated by his domestic staff. Did you know, by the way,
that Larry wanted to play the part? I think Ralph is so
marvellous in the second act, when he's doing his bland-
clubman stuff. In some ways, he's the great successor to A. E.
Matthews." (Not, perhaps, the most overwhelming of
tributes: Matthews, a brilliantly accomplished light comedian
who went on acting into his eighties, was never regarded as
a player of the first rank.) Since the two knights co-starred in
Home seven years ago, they have been endlessly interviewed

and photographed together, and are frequently mistaken for one another on the street. "We're like the Broker's Men in *Cinderella*," Gielgud says, referring to a pair of slapstick clowns in traditional English pantomime. For interview purposes, he and Sir Ralph have evolved what amounts to a double act, in which certain routines and catch phrases (including the one about the Broker's Men) ritually recur. There's usually a formal exordium, such as the following, taken from the London *Observer* in October, 1975, during the West End run of *No Man's Land*:

> SIR RALPH: You're looking very well, by the way.
> SIR JOHN: Thank you.
> SIR RALPH: I haven't seen much of you lately.
> SIR JOHN: We meet in costume.
> SIR RALPH: We meet as other people.

These encounters, normally held in restaurants at lunchtime, seldom pass without providing opportunities for Sir Ralph, a fervent and mercurial gourmet, to leap into action. Here are three examples:

> I love bread so much; I want it to be taken out of my temptation. I have made a vow. I am going to give up my beautiful rolls. (*The Guardian*, November, 1976.)

> It has been my experience, in the past, that most of the wine served in American restaurants is cat's urine, disguised in French labels. (Luncheon with present writer, though without Gielgud, November, 1976.)

> SIR RALPH (*suddenly jumps, points to his plate dramatically. Waiters surround him*): What is THAT?
> SIR JOHN: I think it's a bit of liver, Ralph.
> SIR RALPH: Never touch it. Take the liver away. . . . Bear the offending liver away. (*The Observer*, October, 1975.)

This confirms what Gielgud now tells me—that Sir Ralph, though a superb host, is not a good guest. "I eat out of tins, but Ralph always insists on the best." From the same *Observer* interview, Gielgud recalls Sir Ralph's response when Peter Brook was mentioned as a director of world renown:

> SIR RALPH: What was that *terrible* production Brook did? . . . That *ghastly* thing. You were in it.

He was referring to Seneca's *Oedipus*, directed by Brook for the National Theatre, in which Gielgud played the protagonist. It was far from ghastly, at least in my opinion; I was working for the National at the time and selected the play for its repertoire. I don't deny, however, that there were unusual elements in Brook's staging, notably in his handling of the chorus. Let Sir Ralph continue:

> SIR RALPH: When I went to see the production, somehow I hadn't got a programme. So I said to Mu, 'Leave it to me.' And I went down the aisle to a chap, but he was lashed to a pillar. I didn't know what was going on. It turned out that he was in the show. I think he was one of the chorus. But the show hadn't started yet. Mu said, 'Did you get a programme?' And I had to say it wasn't possible because all the programme-sellers were lashed to the dress circle. Very strange.
>
> SIR JOHN: But what did the poor actor who was lashed to the pillar say to you?
>
> SIR RALPH: Well, of course, when I asked him for a programme all I got were these strangled sounds. He was gagged, you see. The whole experience upset me very much. I'm a very *square* man.

Gielgud first appeared with Sir Ralph in 1930, and has enormous respect for his old confrere. "He loves the craftsmanship of his art. He prepares his work and exhibits it with the utmost finesse. It's like Edith Evans—she used to open a window to her heart and then slam it shut, so that you'd come back the next night to see more. My own tendency, on the other hand, is always to show too much. Ralph says he never thinks anything he does is a success. He doesn't even want to repeat his Falstaff. I wish he would; it's his greatest performance. And he was wonderful as John Gabriel Borkman at the National last year. I shall never forget the noise he made when Borkman died. As if a bird had flown out of his heart."

We sip white wine while Gielgud recalls Sir Ralph as he first knew him: "He had a very unhappy early life as an actor. He used to walk with his behind stuck out, and thought he was terribly unattractive to women. He was very poor, and then there was his first wife's dreadful illness. But now he's acquired such control of movement, such majesty. Of course, he does have a violent side to his nature—a powerful sadistic streak, sudden outbursts of temper. But you have to remember that he went through a really wretched time before he was able to marry Mu." Gielgud smiles. "He used to expect her to be the perfect hostess during dinner, and then, after coffee was served, to kick up her legs like a chorus girl. It must have been difficult, at times, to reconcile those two demands."

Fourth Interlude: 1:45 P.M. on November 11, 1976. Luncheon with Sir Ralph at the Algonquin Hotel. He arrives late, bustling through the crowded restaurant, mustache bristling, eyes moist with apology. We talk first about the honorary D. Litt. he received from Oxford University in 1969. It was bestowed by Harold Macmillan, the Chancellor of the University and former Prime Minister, who delivered a Latin oration. "What he said, in essence, was that the gods have been graceful and lucky for you, and that we of this university wish to add to their smiling," Sir Ralph says. When we have ordered, I ask Sir Ralph whom he would invite to an ideal dinner party, given free choice from the living and the dead. His list, like a good deal more about him, is highly idiosyncratic. "Samuel Butler, demolisher of Victorian fathers. Robert Louis Stevenson. Joseph Conrad, provided that he admired Shakespeare. Scott of the Antarctic. And another explorer, Shackleton, to whom I'm distantly related. Einstein, definitely. And, above all, David Lloyd George, that rascally fellow-actor, that bandit, that savior of our country, without whom Kaiser Bill might even now be walking through Buckingham Palace waxing his mustache." Sir Ralph eats for a while in silence, apparently—and to my great relief—with pleasure. "I've just been reading some of Freud's lectures. Amazing how these tiny little childhood things can have repercussions like the atomic bomb. I wouldn't mind having him at our dinner table. He had such a great sense of humor." Another pause for eating. "I've always been intrigued by his picture of life—the sex down there, the caretaker up here. But I wouldn't put sex ace high, No. 1, the thing that winds up the whole clock. I think murder is more basic. Before you get the woman, you must kill the man who possesses her. Hunger is the first impulse of all. But then I must *possess* something. And then I must *enjoy* something. And that may involve destroying somebody else. For reasons of policy and politeness, of course, we put the brakes on."

It is getting late, and the room has emptied. The waiters are laying tables for dinner. For a moment, Sir Ralph watches them. Then he says, "I wouldn't mind running through this restaurant and smashing all those glasses. I see them glittering there." A pause. "One is putting the brakes on all the time." While we wait for the check, his mind reverts to *No Man's Land*: "Hirst is capable of murder, you know. I believe he was responsible for the drowning of a girl in a lake, although Mr. Pinter might not necessarily agree. He is certainly capable of killing Spooner. We all have original sin. Hirst has it. *I* have it." Sir Ralph's eyes are blazing. As I escort the former altar boy (for such he was in his papist youth) to his limousine, he says, "I would much rather be able to terrify than to charm. I like malevolence. What an enjoyable lunch."

In September, 1975, Sir Ralph went on London Weekend Television and gave a sixty-minute interview by which (his finest stage performances apart) I would not mind remembering him. He was freewheeling and free-associating, seeming artless in his candor, yet laying artful diversionary smokescreens whenever anything central to his privacy appeared to be threatened. We were watching a master mesmerist. No great lover of publicity for its own sake, he had undertaken this chore at the behest of the National Theatre, by whom he was currently employed. His interlocutor was Russell Harty, a dapper North Countryman, who runs the most popular chat show on the British commercial channel. The setting was the usual studio mockup—in this case, a semicircular arrangement of window draperies with nothing behind it, and a low window seat and a pair of tulip-shaped chairs (one of them occupied by Harty) in front of it. A packed house applauded as Harty urged it to welcome "one of the most distinguished actors in the British theatre."

Sir Ralph enters around one side of the draperies, wearing a tweed suit, a pink satin tie, and bright-yellow socks. Instead of taking his expected place in the empty chair, he walks straight past it (and Harty) toward the audience, before whom he halts, bounteously beaming. He seems in a genial frame of mind. Cameras whirl round to keep him in shot, none too successfully.

> Sir Ralph (*to Harty, over his shoulder*): You've got a very nice place here, haven't you? It's a great deal bigger than my place, where you came to see me the other day.
>
> Harty (*left high and dry, but keeping his cool*): Yes, but it's not as posh as yours.
>
> Sir Ralph: No, but you've got a lot more friends than I have.

In his voice we note a false bonhomie, as of a Dr. Watson
—played, of course, by Nigel Bruce—behind whose slightly
fatuous facade a canny, Holmeslike intelligence is at work.

> SIR RALPH: Are they friends of yours? Or are they
> enemies?
> HARTY: Well, we don't know.
> SIR RALPH: Shall I address them? Ladies and gentle-
> men of the jury, I assure you that this man Harty is
> innocent.

Who said he was guilty? Already Sir Ralph has taken
control.

> SIR RALPH: You've got a lot more cameras in your
> place than I've got in mine. Cameras always make me
> rather nervous. They sort of prowl in on you. Of course,
> you know them. You probably feed them. What do they
> eat? Celluloid and chips?

Thus far, he has been strolling around inspecting the
technology. He now wanders past Harty, still glued to his
tulip, toward the window seat. On this he sits, and he peeps
gently through the draperies at what we know perfectly well
is the wall of the studio.

> SIR RALPH: I say, what a wonderful view you've got
> here! I mean, you could see anything from here, couldn't
> you—the Tower of London, Buckingham Palace, the
> Post Office Tower? I'll bet you could.

Consenting at last to occupy a chair, Sir Ralph immediately
begins to interview Harty, asking him about his past career
and whether his parents have secure and pensionable jobs.
Some time passes before Harty manages to sneak in a question about the Pinter play.

> SIR RALPH: There isn't any plot. But that never
> bothers an actor. And the characters are never really

rounded off. They don't quite know who they are. But
that's rather natural in a way. We don't know exactly
who we are, do we? We hardly know anybody else,
really completely. We none of us know when we're
going to die. . . . We're a mystery to ourselves, and to
other people.

He goes on to say that acting is never boring, because the
audiences are always different.

SIR RALPH: In music, the punctuation is absolutely
strict, the bars and the rests are absolutely defined. But
our punctuation cannot be quite strict, because we have
to relate it to the audience. In other words, we are con-
tinually changing the score. . . . For me, what gives our
work its special fascination is the challenge that has to
do with time. If you're a writer or a painter, you write
or paint whenever you want to. But we have to do this
task at a precise moment. At three minutes past eight,
the curtain goes up, and you've got to pretend to believe,
because no one else will believe you unless you believe it
yourself. A great deal of our work is simply making ourselves dream. That is the task. At three minutes past
eight you must dream.
HARTY: Do you dream when you go to bed?
SIR RALPH: Yes, I dream a lot. I lead a fairly sheltered
life. Things are fairly peaceful, and nobody tries to
murder me much. . . . Fortunately, I am able to remember my nightmares. They help me in my work. When
I'm asleep, I'm earning my living if I have a nightmare.
I get murdered a good deal. I get stabbed quite a bit.

Harty suggests that Sir Ralph doesn't much like his own
body. Conceding the point, Sir Ralph proposes that they
might swap. Perhaps feeling cornered, he fires a sudden
question at Harty: "Do you hate your face?" Commendably
unfazed, Harty replies that he hates not only his face but his
name and his body from the waist down. "Oh, really?" says

Sir Ralph. "I can't see anything the matter with it." Harty now tries yet again to seize the initiative.

> HARTY: I wondered whether you'd gone into acting because you weren't satisfied with your face or your body.
> SIR RALPH (*not to be drawn*): There are lots of reasons why people become actors. Some to hide themselves, and some to show themselves. As for my face, I've seen better-looking hot cross buns.

Before long, Sir Ralph, back in the driver's seat, is asking Harty what kind of people he finds the easiest to talk to. Having given a long and honest answer, Harty reverses the question.

> SIR RALPH: I like talking to engineers best. They build bridges, they're very precise, they're very disciplined, yet I find they have roving minds. They can talk about anything. My other favorite people are explorers and potholers. To *choose* to be brave is a great sign of character, I think. They have great accuracy, and also great fantasy.

Harty shows a clip from Sir Ralph's latest film, *Rollerball*, and afterward points out to the viewers that throughout the excerpt Sir Ralph busied himself with lighting his pipe and carefully averted his eyes from the screen. Emitting clouds of smoke, Sir Ralph resumes the questioning. Does Russell Harty like his own name? Harty says that he doesn't. Sir Ralph hastens to reassure him.

> SIR RALPH: I think Russell Harty is a jolly decent name. . . . I'm very fond of Russell because half my family are Russells. My mother was a Russell, so I'm very used to the name. And I don't mind Richardson. I think it suits me, because it's rather plain.

Here he drifts off into free association, before the eyes of approximately twelve million viewers.

> SIR RALPH: How weird it is, the way people's names seem to suit them—how they get a name and grow up to be like it. . . . Shakespeare, for instance—it's an arresting, an aggressive word. You can see the man. . . . And Velazquez—how the name suits the painter! It's a delicious sound; you can feel him laying on the paint, you could almost eat the paint itself. And Rembrandt— he's an old ruminative man, drawing old things with long memories. . . . But I tell you, I like the name Richardson, and I like the name Russell. . . .
>
> HARTY: Are you viewing the prospect of old age with regret or happiness?
>
> SIR RALPH: I'm amazed that I'm as old as I am. I always had the idea that when I was old I'd get frightfully clever. I'd get awfully learned, I'd get jolly sage. People would come to me for advice. But nobody ever comes to me for anything, and I don't know a thing.

Later, as if it were a matter of trifling consequence, he remarks that he has "never been particularly afraid of dying." Finally, at Harty's gentle instigation, he goes to a lectern and brings their conversation to an end by reading Keats's "To Autumn," that being the season of the year.

As I watched, I remembered him, thirty years ago, as the dying Cyrano, sitting in a convent garden, with autumn leaves twirling and floating around him. Sir Ralph looked, even then, very odd, and absentminded, and solitary, and absurd, and noble, and desolate. When he spoke, he sounded at once defiant and merciful. There has always been in his voice a mixture of challenge and benison.

Like Gielgud, I wanted to see him again as Falstaff, a role of which W. H. Auden once wrote:

> Falstaff never really does anything, but . . . the impression he makes on the audience is not of idleness

but of infinite energy. He is never tired, never bored, and until he is rejected he radiates happiness as Hal radiates power, and this happiness without apparent cause, this untiring devotion to making others laugh becomes a comic image for a love which is absolutely self-giving.

Very delicately, Auden goes on to suggest nothing less than that Falstaff is a comic symbol of Jesus Christ. When the Christian God presents himself on earth, "the consequence is inevitable," as Auden points out. "The highest religious and temporal authorities condemn Him as a blasphemer and a Lord of Misrule, as a Bad Companion for mankind." Which, of course, is what happened to Falstaff. Quite apart from its fun and its lunatic grandeur, there was a charity about Sir Ralph's performance, a magnanimity and a grief, that made you wonder whether Auden's audacious hint might not be the simple truth, after all.

In fact, to take a step further, if a playwright were to revive the anthropomorphic conception of the deity and write a play about God himself, and if he were then to ask my help in picking an actor for the central role, I know exactly in which direction I would point him. I would find it entirely credible that the creator of the universe as we know it was someone very like Sir Ralph. This does not mean either that I accept the Christian hypothesis or that I approve of the current state of the world; but if we imagine its maker as a whimsical, enigmatic magician, capable of fearful blunders, sometimes inexplicably ferocious, at other times dazzling in his innocence and benignity, we are going to need an actor who can imply metaphysical attributes while remaining—to quote C. S. Lewis on God—"a positive, concrete, and highly articulated character." Someone, in short, who is at once unapproachable and instantly accessible. Sir Ralph's number, as I have said, is in the book.

[1977]

Withdrawing with style from the chaos

—TOM STOPPARD

IN *Jumpers*, a play by Tom Stoppard, whose other works include *Rosencrantz and Guildenstern Are Dead, Travesties,* and *Dirty Linen,* a man carrying a tortoise in one hand and a bow and arrow in the other, his face covered with shaving cream, opens the door of his apartment. Standing outside is a police inspector bearing a bouquet of flowers. There is a perfectly rational explanation for this.

In *After Magritte,* a much shorter play by the same author, we learn that a one-legged blind man with a white beard, who may in fact have been a handicapped football player with shaving cream on his face, has been seen hopping, or perhaps playing hopscotch, along an English street, wearing striped pajamas, convict garb, or possibly a West Bromwich Albion football jersey, waving with one arm a white stick, a crutch, or a furled parasol while carrying under the other what may have been a football, a wineskin, an alligator handbag, or a tortoise. (One of the characters, discounting the hypothesis that the man was blind, scornfully inquires whether it was a seeing-eye tortoise.) There is also a perfectly rational, though much longer, explanation for this.

In "The Language of Theatre," an address delivered by the same author in January, 1977, at the University of California at Santa Barbara, the lecturer began by stating that he was not going to talk about the language of theatre. ("That was just a device to attract a better class of audience," he said, eying the spectators. "I see it failed.") Instead— and among other things—he told a story about a man he knew who bought a peacock on impulse and, shortly afterward, while shaving in his pajamas, observed the bird escaping from his country garden. Dropping his razor, he set off in pursuit and managed to catch the feathered fugitive just as it reached a main road adjoining his property. At that moment, a car flashed by, middle-aged husband at the wheel, wife at his side. For perhaps five seconds—*vrrooommm*— they caught sight of this perplexing apparition. Wife: "What was that, dear?" Husband: "Fellow in his pajamas, with shaving cream all over his face and a peacock under his arm." There was, as we know, a perfectly rational explanation. (Stoppard went on to say that several of his plays had grown out of images such as this. He added that when he tried the peacock anecdote out on the members of a literary society at Eton College, it was received in bewildered silence. He soon realized why: "They all *had* peacocks.")

In none of the same author's plays will you find any reference to (or echo of, or scene derived from) the following singular, and partly equivocal, story. During the nineteen-thirties, there lived in Zlin—a town in Czechoslovakia that is now known as Gottwaldov—a middle-class physician named Eugene Straussler, who worked for a famous shoe company. Either he or his wife (nobody seems quite sure which) had at least one parent of Jewish descent. In any case, Dr. Straussler sired two sons, of whom the younger, Thomas, was born on July 3, 1937. Two years later, on the eve of the Nazi invasion of their homeland, the Strausslers left for Singapore, where they settled until 1942. The boys and their mother then moved to India. Dr. Straussler stayed behind to face the Japanese occupation. He died in a Japanese air raid, or in a prisoner-of-war camp, or on a Japanese prison ship torpedoed by the British (nobody seems quite sure which). In 1946, his widow married a major in the British Army, who brought the family back with him to England. The two Straussler scions assumed their stepfather's surname, which was Stoppard. Thomas, who claims to have spoken only Czech until the age of three, or possibly five and a half (he does not seem quite sure which), grew up to become, by the early 1970s, one of the two or three most prosperous and ubiquitously adulated playwrights at present bearing a British passport. (The other contenders are Harold Pinter, who probably has the edge in adulation, and Peter Shaffer, the author of *Equus*, whose strong point is prosperity.) There is no perfectly rational explanation for any of this. It is simply true.

Preliminary notes from my journal, dated July 24, 1976:

Essential to remember that Stoppard is an émigré. A director who has staged several of his plays told me the other day, "You have to be foreign to write English with that kind of hypnotized brilliance." An obvious comparison is with Vladimir Nabokov, whom Stoppard extravagantly admires. Stoppard said to me not long ago that his favorite parenthesis in world literature was this, from *Lolita*: "My very photogenic mother died in a freak accident (picnic, lightning) when I was three." He is at present adapting Nabokov's novel *Despair* for the screen; Rainer Werner Fassbinder, who commissioned the script, will direct. Stoppard loves all forms of wordplay, especially puns, and frequently describes himself as "a bounced Czech." Like many immigrants, he has immersed himself beyond the call of baptism in the habits and rituals of his adopted country. Nowadays, he is *plus anglais que les anglais*—a phrase that would please him, as a student of linguistic caprice, since it implies that his

Englishness can best be defined in French. His style in dress is the costly-casual dandyism of London in the nineteen-sixties. According to his friend Derek Marlowe, who wrote the best-selling novel *A Dandy in Aspic*, "Tom goes to some very posh places for his clothes, but he finds it hard to orchestrate all his gear into a sartorial unity. The effect is like an expensive medley." (Told of this comment, Stoppard protests to me that Marlowe is exaggerating. "Derek," he says, "is a fantasist enclosed by more mirror than glass.") Because Stoppard has a loose, lanky build, a loose thatch of curly dark hair, liver tinted lips, dark, flashing eyes, and long, flashing teeth, you might mistake him for an older brother of Mick Jagger, more intellectually inclined than his frenetic sibling.

Stoppard often puts me in mind of a number in *Beyond the Fringe*, the classic English revue of the sixties, in which Alan Bennett, as an unctuous clergyman, preached a sermon on the text "Behold, Esau my brother is an hairy man, and I am a *smooth* man." The line accurately reflects the split in English drama which took place during (and has persisted since) this period. On one side were the hairy men—heated, embattled, socially committed playwrights, like John Osborne, John Arden, and Arnold Wesker, who had come out fighting in the late fifties. On the other side were the smooth men—cool, apolitical stylists, like Harold Pinter, the late Joe Orton, Christopher Hampton (*The Philanthropist*), Alan Ayckbourn (*The Norman Conquests*), Simon Gray (*Otherwise Engaged*), and Stoppard. Earlier this year, Stoppard told an interviewer from the London weekly *Time Out*, "I used to feel out on a limb, because when I started to write you were a shit if you weren't writing about Vietnam or housing. Now I have no compunction about that. . . . *The Importance of Being Earnest* is important, but it says nothing about anything." He once said that his favorite line in modern English drama came from *The Philanthropist*: "I'm a man of no convictions—at least, I *think* I am." In *Lord Malquist and Mr. Moon* (1966),

Stoppard's only novel to date, Mr. Moon seems to speak for his author when he says, "I distrust attitudes because they claim to have appropriated the whole truth and pose as absolutes. And I distrust the opposite attitude for the same reason." Lord Malquist, who conducts his life on the principle that the eighteenth century has not yet ended, asserts that all battles are discredited. "I stand aloof," he declares, "contributing nothing except my example." In an article for the London *Sunday Times* in 1968, Stoppard said, "Some writers write because they burn with a cause which they further by writing about it. I burn with no causes. I cannot say that I write with any social objective. One writes because one loves writing, really." On another occasion, he defined the quality that distinguished him from many of his contemporaries as "an absolute lack of certainty about almost anything."

Seeking artistic precedents for this moral detachment, this commitment to neutrality, I come up with four quotations. The first is from Oscar Wilde:

> A Truth in art is that whose contradictory is also true.

The second is from Evelyn Waugh's diary:

> I . . . don't want to influence opinions or events, or expose humbug or anything of that kind. I don't want to be of service to anyone or anything. I simply want to do my work as an artist.

Then these, from John Keats's letters:

> It struck me what quality went to form a Man of Achievement, especially in Literature, and which Shakespeare possessed so enormously—I mean *Negative Capability*, that is, when a man is capable of being in uncertainties, mysteries, doubts, without any irritable reaching after fact and reason. . . .

> The only means of strengthening one's intellect is to
> make up one's mind about nothing—to let the mind be
> a thoroughfare for all thoughts, not a select party.

In Stoppard's case, "negative capability" has been a
profitable thoroughfare. When I asked him, not long ago,
how much he thought he had earned from *Rosencrantz and
Guildenstern Are Dead*, his answer was honestly vague:
"About—a hundred and fifty thousand pounds?" To the
same question, his agent, Kenneth Ewing, gave me the
following reply: "*Rosencrantz* opened in London in 1967.
Huge overnight success—it stayed in the National Theatre
repertory for about four years. The Broadway production
ran for a year. Metro bought the screen rights for two
hundred and fifty thousand dollars and paid Tom a hundred
thousand to write the script, though the movie was never
made. The play had a short run in Paris, with Delphine
Seyrig as Gertrude, but it was quite a hit in Italy, where
Rosencrantz was played by a girl. It did enormous business
in Germany and Scandinavia and—oddly enough—Japan.
On top of that, the book sold more than six hundred thousand copies in the English language alone. Up to now, out of
Rosencrantz I would guess that Tom had grossed well over
three hundred thousand pounds."

And now, on this sunny Saturday afternoon, to Gunners-
bury Park, in West London, where a cricket match is to be
played. Cricket, to which I am addicted, is a pastime of great
complexity and elegance. Shapeless and desultory to the out-
sider, it has an underlying structure that only the initiate
perceives. At the international level, a match may last five
days, end in a draw, and still be exciting. Cricket may seem
to dawdle, to meander, to ramble off into amorphous perversity; but for all its vagaries and lapses into seeming inco-
herence there is, as in a Stoppard play, a perfectly rational
explanation. Not surprisingly, Stoppard is a passionate fan
of the game—an enslavement he shares with many British
writers of the cool school. Generalization: Cricket attracts

artists who are either conservative or nonpolitical; e.g., P.G. Wodehouse, Terence Rattigan, Samuel Beckett, Kingsley Amis, Harold Pinter, and Stoppard, all of them buffs who could probably tell you how many wickets Tich Freeman, the wily Kent spin bowler, took in his record-breaking season of 1928. Leftists, on the whole, favor soccer, the sport of the urban proletariat. It's hard to imagine Wesker, Arden, Trevor Griffiths, or the young Osborne (the middle-aged Osborne has swung toward right-wing anarchism and may well, for all I know, have taken up the quarterstaff) standing in line outside Lord's Cricket Ground. As a cricket-loving radical, I am an anomaly, regarded by both sides with cordial mistrust.

Today's game is an annual fixture: Mr. Harold Pinter's XI versus the *Guardian* newspaper's. The field, rented for the occasion, is impressively large, with a well-equipped pavilion, inside which at 2:30 P.M., the advertised starting time, both teams are avidly watching another match—England versus the West Indies—on television. Eight spectators, including two children and me, have turned up. The *Guardian* XI looks formidably healthy, featuring several muscular type-setters and the paper's industrial correspondent. The Pinter squad seems altogether less businesslike. To begin with, only nine of the players are present, the principal batsman having discovered on his arrival that he had left his contact lenses at home. Since he lives in an outlying northern suburb, the game may easily be over by the time he returns. More-over, Skipper Pinter, inscrutable as always, has decided at the last moment to absent himself, thereby leaving his lads leaderless. Among the nine remaining are a somewhat bald fortyish publisher, a retired Chelsea football player, Pinter's teenage son Daniel (already a published poet, who has lately won a scholarship to Magdalen College, Oxford), and —by far the most resplendent, in gauntlets of scarlet leather and kneepads as blindingly white as Pitz Palu—Tom Stoppard, the team's wicketkeeper, who swears to me that he has not played cricket for over a year.

He asks me to take the place of the myopic batsman. I refuse, on the ground that I have no white flannels. Characteristically, Dandy Tom has 'brought a spare pair. I counter by pleading lack of practice, not having put bat to ball for roughly twenty years, and am grudgingly excused. Why, I wonder, has Pinter let down the side? The answer, gleaned from his teammates, is that his estranged wife, the brilliant but temperamental actress Vivien Merchant (who made no secret of her vexation when, a year earlier, Pinter left home to live with Lady Antonia Fraser, the biographer of Cromwell and Mary Queen of Scots), has announced her intention of watching the game, ostensibly to see her son in action. Anxious to avoid a scene, the captain has retired to a nearby Thames-side pub, where—doubtless biting his nails, for he is a deeply competitive man—he will await the result. (As it happened, he need not have worried: Mrs. Pinter failed to show up until the game was over.) Many amateur cricket teams have specially designed ties; I learn from Stoppard that the Pinter outfit does not. "But if it had," he adds, alluding to the pauses for which Pinter's plays are famous, "the club insignia would probably be three dots." The *Guardian* XI, having torn itself away from TV and won the toss, has elected to bat first; it is time for the Pinter XI (reduced to IX) to take the field. Stoppard goes out, managing as he does so to drop a smoldering cigarette butt between kneepad and trousers. "There may be a story here," he calls back to me. " 'Playwright Bursts Into Flames at Wicket.' "

Having no fast bowlers, who are the match-winning thunderbolts of cricket, the Pinter team is forced to rely on slow spinners of the ball, oblique and devious in their approach. To hazard an analogy: Pinter onstage is a masterly spinner, but his surrogates on the field, lacking his precision, are mercilessly bashed about by their opponents. The tough and purposeful *Guardian* team scores eighty-three runs, and the figure would be much higher if it were not for the elastic leaps and hair-trigger reflexes of Stoppard behind the stumps, where (in the role that approximates the catcher's in baseball) he dismisses no fewer than four of the enemy side. This leaves room for hope—though not for all that much, as we realize when the Pinter IX starts to bat. Its acting captain, the somewhat bald publisher, holds his own, scoring with occasional suave deflections, the picture of public-school unconcern; but the *Guardian* bowlers have muscle and pace, and wicket after wicket falls to their intimidating speed. The game is all but lost when Stoppard ambles in to bat, with the score at sixty and only two men to follow him. Within ten minutes, in classic style, he has driven three balls to the boundary ropes for four runs apiece. Six more graceful swipes bring his personal total to twenty, thereby making him the top scorer and winning the game for his side. He is welcomed back to the pavilion with cheers.

We repair to the riverside pub, where Skipper Pinter, accompanied by Lady Antonia, has just heard the news. Bursting with pride, he embraces Stoppard and buys expensive drinks for the whole team. (Lady A. sips chilled cider.) He has been informed of certain crass errors made in the course of play, and sharply chides those responsible. It is like listening to Wellington if an attack of gout had kept him away from Waterloo. (Pinter's record commands respect: turning out every Saturday afternoon, he has a batting average that has seldom dipped below seventy, which is very high indeed.) In T-shirt and slacks, this sun-drenched evening, he looks dapper and superbly organized behind his thick horn-rimmed spectacles. Pinter has two basic facial expressions, which alternate with alarming rapidity. One of them, his serious mask, suggests a surgeon or a dentist on the brink of making a brilliant diagnosis. The head tilts to one side, the eyes narrow shrewdly, the brain seems to whirr like a computer. His stare drills into your mind. His face, topped by shiny black hair, is sombre, intent, profoundly concerned. When he smiles, however, it is suddenly and totally transformed. "Smile" is really the wrong word: what comes over his face is unmistakably a *leer*. It reveals gleaming, voracious teeth, with a good deal of air between them, and their owner resembles a stand-up comic who has just uttered a none too subtle sexual innuendo. At the same time, the eyes pop and lasciviously swivel. There seems to be no halfway house between these two extremes, and this, as Pinter is doubtless aware, can be very disconcerting.

Pinter's absence from the field, which might have spelled disaster, has in fact made no difference at all, thanks to Stoppard's dashing performance. Where a lesser man might have been nettled, Pinter is genuinely delighted. Team spirit has triumphed: the leer is positively euphoric. Stoppard makes his farewells and departs (to keep a date with his wife), leaving the skipper surrounded by disciples. One might, I suppose, discern a kind of metaphorical significance in the fact that while the top-ranking English playwright's back was turned the runner-up nipped in and seized the victor's crown. But, as Noël Coward said in *The Scoundrel*, I hate stooping to symbolism.

Back home after the match, I decided that for Stoppard art is a game within a game—the larger game being life itself, an absurd mosaic of incidents and accidents in which (as Beckett, whom he venerates, says in the aptly entitled *Endgame*) "something is taking its course." We cannot know what the something is, or whither it is leading us; and it is therefore impermissible for art, a mere derivative of life, to claim anything as presumptuous as a moral purpose or a social function. Since 1963, when the first professional performance of a script by Stoppard was given, he has written one novel, four full-length plays, one miniplay (*Dirty Linen*) that was cheekily passed off as a full-length entertainment, five one-acters for the stage, and ten pieces for radio or television. Thus far, only one of his performed works (*Jumpers*, to my mind his masterpiece, which was first produced in 1972) could be safely accused of having a moral or political message; but the critics are always sniffing for

ulterior motives—so diligently that Stoppard felt it necessary
to announce in 1974, "I think that in future I must stop
compromising my plays with this whiff of social application.
They must be entirely untouched by any suspicion of useful-
ness. I should have the courage of my lack of convictions."
In another interview, he said he saw no reason that art
should not concern itself with contemporary social and
political history, but added that he found it "deeply em-
barrassing . . . when, because art takes notice of something
important, it's claimed that the art is important. It's not."
Hating to be pinned down, politely declining to be associated
with the opinions expressed by his characters, he has often
remarked, "I write plays because dialogue is the most
respectable way of contradicting myself." (Many of his
apparent impromptus are worked out beforehand. Himself
a onetime journalist, he makes a habit of anticipating questions and prefabricating effective replies. Indeed, such was
his assurance of eventual success that he was doing this long
before anyone ever interviewed him. When he read the
printed result of his first conversation with the press, he
said he found it "very déjà vu." Clive James, the Australian
critic and satirist, now working in London, has rightly
described him as "a dream interviewee, talking in eerily
quotable sentences whose English has the faintly extrater-
ritorial perfection of a Conrad or a Nabokov.")

Philosophically, you can see the early Stoppard at his
purest in Lord Malquist and Mr. Moon, which sold only four
hundred and eighty-one copies in 1966, when it was published. Malquist says:

> Nothing is the history of the world viewed from a
> suitable distance. Revolution is a trivial shift in the
> emphasis of suffering; the capacity for self-indulgence
> changes hands. But the world does not alter its shape or
> its course. The seasons are inexorable, the elements
> constant. Against such vast immutability the human
> struggle takes place on the same scale as the insect
> movements in the grass, and carnage in the streets is no

more than the spider-sucked husk of a fly on a dusty
window-sill.

Later, he adds, "Since we cannot hope for order, let us
withdraw with style from the chaos."

When Moon, his biographer and a professed anarchist,
attacks Malquist's antihumanism on the ground that whatever he may say, the world is made up of "all *people,* isn't
it?" Malquist scoffs:

> What an extraordinary idea. People are not the
> world, they are merely a recent and transitory product
> of it. The world is ten million years old. If you think of
> that period condensed into one year beginning on the
> first of January, then people do not make their appear-
> ance in it until the thirty-first of December; or to be more
> precise, in the last forty seconds of that day.

Such trivial latecomers sound barely worth saving.

Though Stoppard would doubtless deny it, these pro-
nouncements of Malquist's have a ring of authority which
suggests the author speaking. They reflect a world view of
extreme pessimism, and therefore of conservatism. The
pessimist is necessarily conservative. Maintaining, as he does,
that mankind is inherently and immutably flawed, he must
always be indifferent or hostile to proposals for improving
human life by means of social or political change. The
radical, by contrast, is fundamentally an optimist, embracing
change because he holds that human nature is perfectible.
The Malquist attitude, whatever its virtues, is hardly con-
ducive to idealism. I recall a conversation with Derek Marlowe about Stoppard's private beliefs. "I don't think,"
Marlowe said, "that there's anything he would go to the
guillotine for." I found the choice of instrument revealing.
We associate the guillotine with the decapitation of aristo-
crats. Marlowe instinctively identified Stoppard with the
nobility rather than the mob—with reaction rather than
revolution.

•   •

There are signs, however, that history has lately been forcing Stoppard into the arena of commitment. Shortly after I wrote the above entry in my journal, he sent me a typescript of his most recent work. Commissioned by André Previn, who conducts the London Symphony Orchestra, it is called *Every Good Boy Deserves Favour*—a mnemonic phrase familiar to students of music, since the initial letters of the words represent, in ascending order, the notes signified by the black lines of the treble clef. Involving six actors (their dialogue interspersed with musical contributions from Mr. Previn's big band), it had its world première in July, 1977, at the Royal Festival Hall, in London. It started out in Stoppard's mind as a play about a Florida grapefruit millionaire, but his works have a way of changing their themes as soon as he sits down at his typewriter. The present setting is a Russian mental home for political dissidents, where the main job of the staff is to persuade the inmates that they are in fact insane. What follows is a characteristic exchange between a recalcitrant prisoner named Alexander and the therapist who is assigned to him:

> PSYCHIATRIST: The idea that all the people locked up in mental hospitals are sane while the people walking about outside are all mad is merely a literary cliché, put about by the people who should be locked up. I assure you there's not much in it. Taken as a whole, the sane are out there and the sick are in here. For example, *you* are here because you have delusions that sane people are put in mental hospitals.
> ALEXANDER: But I *am* in a mental hospital.
> PSYCHIATRIST: That's what I said.

Alexander, of course, refuses to curry Favour by being a Good Boy. Beneath its layers of Stoppardian irony, the play (oratorio? melodrama?) is a point-blank attack on the way in which Soviet law is perverted to stifle dissent. In the script I read, Alexander declares, at a moment of crisis, "There are truths to be shown, and our only strength is personal example." Stoppard, however, had crossed this line out, perhaps being reluctant to put his name to a platitude, no matter how true or relevant it might be. Simplicity of thought—in this piece, as elsewhere in his work—quite often underlies complexity of style. *E.G.B.D.F.* rests on the assumption that the difference between good and evil is obvious to any reasonable human being. What else does Stoppard believe in? For one thing, I would guess, the intrinsic merits of individualism; for another, a universe in which everything is relative, yet in which moral absolutes exist; for a third, the probability that this paradox can be resolved only if we accept the postulate of a presiding deity. In 1973, during a public discussion of his plays at the Church of St. Mary Le Bow, in London, he told his interlocutor, the Reverend Joseph McCulloch:

> The whole of science can be said, by a theologian, to be operating within a larger framework. In other words, the higher we penetrate into space and the deeper we penetrate into the atom, all it shows to a theologian is that God has been gravely underestimated.

Nietzsche once said that convictions were prisons—a remark that the younger Stoppard would surely have applauded. Later, I shall try to chart the route that has led Stoppard, the quondam apostle of detachment, to the convictions he now proclaims, and to his loathing for the strictly unmetaphorical prisons in which so many people he respects are at present confined.

Stoppard's childhood was full of enforced globe-trotting. Much of it was spent on the run from totalitarianism, of both the European and the Oriental variety. By the time he was five years old, he had moved from his Czechoslovakian birthplace to Singapore and thence—with his mother and elder brother—to India. His father, as we have seen, stayed in Singapore, where he died in circumstances that remain obscure. (Not long ago, I asked Stoppard why this question, like that of the family's Jewish background, could not be cleared up by his mother, who, together with his stepfather, nowadays lives in the Lake District. "Rightly or wrongly, we've always felt that she might want to keep the past under a protective covering so we've never delved into it," he said. "My father died in enemy hands, and that's that.") Stoppard attended a multiracial, English-speaking school in Darjeeling. There his mother managed a shoe store and met Major Kenneth Stoppard, of the British Army in India, whom she married in 1946. By the end of the year, Major Stoppard had brought his new family back to England. Demobilized, he prospered as a salesman of machine tools, and Tom went through the initial hoops of a traditional middle-class education. From a preparatory boarding school in Nottinghamshire he moved on to "a sort of minor public school" in Yorkshire. He summed up his extracurricular activities for me in a recent letter:

> I wrote a play about Charles I when I was twelve. It was surprisingly conventional: he died in the end. I edited no magazines but I did debate. I remember being completely indifferent as to which side of any proposition I should debate on.

In 1954, aged seventeen, he left school to live with his family in the West Country port of Bristol, where they had settled a few years earlier. He bypassed higher education and plunged into local journalism, first at the *Western Daily Press* and later at the Bristol *Evening World*, in a variety of posts, including those of news reporter, humorous columnist, feature writer, and reviewer of plays and films. For a while, although he was unable to drive, he held down the job of motoring correspondent on the *Daily Press*. ("I used to review the upholstery," he says.) He rejoiced in the life of a newspaperman, relished "the glamour of flashing a press card at flower shows," and had no higher ambition than to make a gaudy mark in Fleet Street. He did not contemplate becoming a playwright until the late nineteen-fifties, when a new breed of English authors, led by John Osborne, began to assert themselves at the Royal Court Theatre, in London. Simultaneously, a new breed of actors emerged, to interpret their work. One of the latter, the then unknown Peter O'Toole, joined the Bristol Old Vic—probably the best of Britain's regional repertory companies—and in the course of the 1957–58 season he played a series of leading parts, among them the title role in *Hamlet* and Jimmy Porter in Osborne's *Look Back in Anger*. (This was the unique and original O'Toole, before he submitted his profile to surgical revision, which left him with a nose retroussé and anonymous enough to satisfy the producer of *Lawrence of Arabia*.) Years later, at a seminar in California, a student asked Stoppard, "Did you get into the theatre by accident?" "Of course," he said innocently. "One day, I tripped and fell against a typewriter, and the result was *Rosencrantz and Guildenstern*." In reality, it was O'Toole's blazing performances—and the plays they adorned in Bristol—that turned Stoppard on to theatre. By the end of the season, he was incubating a new vocation.

Meanwhile, he stuck to journalism, writing two columns (both pseudonymous) in every issue of the *Daily Press*. "They became a bit tiring to read, because they were a little too anxious to be funny," he says nowadays. "At the time, I was desperate to be printed in *Punch*. I was overextended." During this period, Bristol was a seedbed of theatrical talent. Geoffrey Reeves, who directed the first performance of *After Magritte* and collaborated with Peter Brook on several of the latter's productions, was then a research student in Bristol University's Drama Department. He recalls Stoppard as "a cynical wit in a mackintosh, one of the very few sophisticated journalists in town—though I would never have thought of him as a potential playwright." Peter Nichols (the author of *A Day in the Death of Joe Egg*) and Charles Wood (who wrote the screenplays of *The Knack, How I Won the War*, and *The Charge of the Light Brigade*) were both growing

up in Bristol when Stoppard was there. Wood remembers
Stoppard as "a sort of Mick Jaggerish character, who wrote
some rather unfunny newspaper columns," and adds, "He
wasn't a part of our world." Nichols's recollections are
similarly tinged with waspishness: "Tom was a great figure in
Bristol, to be mentioned with bated breath. His comings
and goings were reported as if he were Orson Welles." When
Nichols told me this, he had just returned from Minneapolis,
where one of Stoppard's works was being performed. With
a glint of malice in his voice, he continued, "Tom is very
big in Minneapolis. Unlike a lot of modern British drama,
his stuff travels well. No rough edges on Tom. None of those
awkward local references. There never were." During the
nineteen-sixties, Stoppard's *Rosencrantz and Guildenstern*,
Wood's *H* (a chronicle of the Indian Mutiny of 1857), and
Nichols's *The National Health* were all to be presented at
the National Theatre, thereby provoking rumors of a Bris-
tolian conspiracy to dominate British drama. *H*, stunningly
written but structurally a mess, was a box-office failure; the
Nichols play, in which a hospital ward symbolized the invalid
state of the nation, had a great success with British audiences;
but Stoppard's was the runaway smash, at home and abroad,
with critics and public alike.

His career as a playwright began in 1960, when he wrote a
one-act piece called *The Gamblers*, which he described to me
in a recent letter as "*Waiting for Godot* in the death cell—
prisoner and jailer—I'm sure you can imagine the rest." (It
was staged in 1962 by Bristol University undergraduates, and
has never been revived.) Later in 1960, he spent three months
writing his first full-length play, *A Walk on the Water*. It
was so weightily influenced by Arthur Miller and by Robert
Bolt's *Flowering Cherry* that he has come to refer to it as
"Flowering Death of a Salesman." He said in 1974 that,
although it worked pretty well onstage, "it's actually phony
because it's a play written about other people's characters—
they're only real because I've seen them in other people's
plays." A few years afterward, indulging in his hobby of self-

contradiction, he told a group of drama students, "What I like to do is take a stereotype and betray it, rather than create an original character. I never try to invent characters. All my best characters are clichés." This is Stoppard at his most typical, laying a smoke screen designed to confuse and ambush his critics. Run the above statements together and you get something like this: "It's wrong to borrow other writers' characters, but it's all right as long as they're clichés." A *Walk on the Water* is about George Riley, a congenital self-deceiver who declares roughly once a week that he is going to achieve independence by leaving home and making his fortune as an inventor. Never having won more bread than can be measured in crumbs, he is entirely dependent— for food, shelter, and pocket money—on his wife and their teenage daughter, both of whom are wearily aware that, however bravely he trumpets his fantasies of self-sufficiency in the local pub, he is sure to be back for dinner. For all his dottiness (among his inventions are a pipe that will stay perpetually lit provided it is smoked upside down and a revolutionary bottle opener for which, unfortunately, no matching bottle top exists), Riley has what Stoppard describes as "a tattered dignity." This attribute will recur in many Stoppard heroes, who have nothing to pit against the hostility of society and the indifference of the cosmos except their obstinate conviction that individuality is sacrosanct. C. W. E. Bigsby says in a perceptive booklet he wrote on Stoppard for the British Council:

> While it is clear that none of his characters control their own destiny . . . it is equally obvious that their unsinkable quality, their irrepressible vitality and eccentric persistence, constitute what Stoppard feels to be an authentic response to existence.

The first performance of A *Walk on the Water* (and the first professional production of any Stoppard play) was given on British commercial television in 1963. Considerably

rewritten, and retitled *Enter a Free Man,* it was staged in
the West End five years later, when *Rosencrantz and Guildenstern* had established Stoppard's reputation. Both versions
of the text are indebted not only to Miller and Bolt but to
N. F. Simpson (the whimsical author of *One Way Pendu-
lum,* a gravely surreal farce that contains a character whose
ambition is to train a team of speak-your-weight machines to
sing the "Hallelujah Chorus"), and both pay respectful
homage to P. G. Wodehouse and to British music-hall
comedy, especially in the exchanges between Riley and a
saloon-bar companion named Brown. In one of these, Riley
insists that Thomas Edison was the inventor of the lighthouse. Brown, anxious to avoid a row, hints at the probable
source of his friend's misapprehension by gently singing the
opening lines of the well-known folk song: "My father was
the keeper of the Eddystone light and he met a mermaid
one fine night." This causes "a terrible silence," after which:

> RILEY: Your father was what?
> BROWN: Not my father.
> RILEY: Whose father? . . . Whose father was a mer-
> maid?
> BROWN: He wasn't a mermaid. He *met* a mermaid.
> RILEY: Who did?
> BROWN: This man's father.
> RILEY: Which man's father?
> BROWN (*testily*): I don't know.
> RILEY: I don't believe you, Jones.
> BROWN: Brown.
> RILEY: This is just sailors' talk, the mythology of the
> seas. There are no such things as mermaids. I'm sur-
> prised at a grown man like you believing all that super-
> stitious rubbish. What your father saw was a sea lion.
> BROWN: My father didn't see a sea lion!
> RILEY (*topping him*): So it *was* your father!

Both scripts are flawed by a running gag that the passage of
time has tripped up. The invention that is supposed to

demonstrate Riley's invincible stupidity beyond all doubt—
viz., an envelope with gum inside and out, so that it can be
used twice—has since been widely adopted as an efficient
method of sending out bills. (Hazards of this kind are
endemic to humorists who mistrust the march of science.
Cf. the English wit J. B. Morton, who convulsed his readers
in the nineteen-thirties by predicting the advent of an electric
toothbrush.) Wherever the 1968 text differs from the original,
the changes are for the better, as witness the addition of
Riley's crowning fancy—a device that supplies indoor rain
for indoor plants. From Stoppard's deletions, however, we
learn something crucial about the nature and the limitations
of his talent.

"Tom cares more about the details of writing than
anyone else I know," Derek Marlowe told me. "He's startled
by the smallest minutiae of life. He'll rush out of a room to
make a note of a phrase he's just heard or a line that's just
occurred to him. But the grand events, the highs and lows of
human behavior, he sees with a sort of aloof, omniscient
amusement. The world doesn't impinge on his work, and
you'd think after reading his plays that no emotional experience had ever impinged on his world. For one thing, he
can't create convincing women. His female characters are
somewhere between playmates and amanuenses. He simply
doesn't understand them. He has a dual personality, like the
author of *Alice in Wonderland*. His public self is Charles
Dodgson—he loves dons, philosophers, theorists of all kinds,
and he's fascinated by the language they use. But his private
self is Lewis Carroll—reclusive, intimidated by women, unnerved by emotion."

Geoffrey Reeves agrees with this analysis: "However
abstract Beckett may seem, he always gives you a gut reaction.
But Tom hasn't yet made a real emotional statement."

This is not to say that he hasn't tried. In the telecast of
A Walk on the Water, as in the stage version, Riley's
daughter is horrified to discover that her lover, whom she
thought to be unmarried, has a wife. Before the play reached

the theatre, however, Stoppard excised the following outburst, addressed by the girl to her mother:

> He said he loved me. Loved me enough to have me on
> the side, didn't he? For his day off. . . . I asked him if
> he'd meant it, about loving me, really, and he said, he
> liked me a lot. It's murder. . . . If I was king, I'd hang
> people for that. Everybody saying they love each other
> when they only like each other a lot—they'll all be *hung*
> and there'll be no one left except hangmen, and all of
> them will say how they love each other when they only
> like each other a lot, until there's only one left, and he'll
> say—That's everybody, king, except me, your only true
> and loving hangman. And I'll say, you don't love me,
> you only like me a lot, and I'll *hang* him, and I'll be
> king, and I'll like myself a lot.

There was more in that vein, which playgoers were luckily
spared. Not long ago, I asked Stoppard what he thought of
Marlowe's charge that his plays failed to convey genuine
emotion. He reflected for a while and then replied, "That
criticism is always being presented to me as if it were a
membrane that I must somehow break through in order to
grow up. Well, I don't see any special virtue in making my
private emotions the quarry for the statue I'm carving. I
can do that kind of writing, but it tends to go off, like fruit.
I don't like it very much even when it works. I think that
sort of truth-telling writing is as big a lie as the deliberate
fantasies I construct. It's based on the fallacy of naturalism.
There's a direct line of descent from the naturalistic theatre
which leads you straight down to the dregs of bad theatre,
bad thinking, and bad feeling. At the other end of the scale,
I dislike Abstract Expressionism even more than I dislike
naturalism. But you asked me about expressing emotion. Let
me put the best possible light on my inhibitions and say
that I'm waiting until I can do it well." And what of Marlowe's comment that he didn't understand women? "If Derek

had said that I don't understand *people*, it would have made
more sense."

(A word on Stoppard and women. It is felt by some of
his friends that his sexual ambitions, compared with his
professional ambitions, have always been modest. He has
been twice married. He met his first wife, a nurse called
Jose Ingle, in London in 1962; Derek Marlowe remembers
her as being "svelte and sun-tanned." Their marriage produced two sons, who bear the Dickensian names of Oliver
and Barnaby. But the dramatic change in Stoppard's way of
life that followed the triumph of *Rosencrantz and Guildenstern* in 1967 was more than Jose could cope with, and that
familar show-business phenomenon—the ditching of the pre-
success partner—took its sad accustomed course. According
to one observer, "Jose was a feminist before her time, and she
got bloody-minded about being overshadowed by Tom." At
all events she finally suffered a nervous breakdown. Now fully
recovered, she lives in a flat on the northern outskirts of
London and is studying at a technical college for a teaching
diploma. Divorce proceedings began when Stoppard left
home, in 1970. Shortly afterward, he set up house with
Miriam Moore-Robinson, a dark-haired pouter pigeon of a
girl, buxom and exuberantly pretty, whom he had known,
on and off, for about four years, and whose marriage to a
veterinary surgeon was already at the breaking point. Miriam
was the same age as Stoppard, and her ancestry included a
Jewish grandparent who was born in Czechoslovakia. A
qualified doctor, she worked for a pharmaceutical company
that specialized in birth-control research, and has gone on to
become its managing director. She has also made vivacious
appearances on popular-science programs on British TV,
answering questions on biology, zoology, and sex. Since 1972,
when she and Stoppard were married, she has given him two
more sons, William and Edmund. In matters of emotion,
Stoppard is one of nature's Horatios; you could never call
him passion's slave, or imagine him blown off course by a

romantic obsession. He thrives in the atmosphere of a family nest. "I can't work away from domestic stability," he once told me.)

To revert to chronology: In 1960, the text of A *Walk on the Water* landed on the desk of Kenneth Ewing, the managing director of a newly formed script agency, which now represents such writers as Michael Frayn, Charles Wood, Adrian Mitchell, and Anthony (*Sleuth*) Shaffer. Ewing sent Stoppard an encomiastic letter; the two men lunched in London; and Ewing has ever since been Stoppard's agent. "When I first met him, he had just given up his regular work as a journalist in Bristol, and he was broke," Ewing says. "But I noticed that even then he always travelled by taxi, never by bus. It was as if he knew that his time would come." In 1962, Stoppard heard that a new magazine called *Scene* was about to be launched in London; he applied for a job on the staff and was offered, to his amazement, the post of drama critic, which he instantly accepted. He then left Bristol for good and took an apartment in Notting Hill Gate, a dingy West London suburb. Derek Marlowe lived in the same dilapidated house. "Tom wrote short stories, and smoked to excess, and always worked at night," Marlowe recalls. "Every evening, he would lay out a row of matches and say, 'Tonight I shall write twelve matches'—meaning as much as he could churn out on twelve cigarettes." *Scene* made its debut early in 1963. Virulently trendy in tone and signally lacking in funds, it set out to cover the whole of show business. In seven months (after which the money ran out and *Scene* was no longer heard from), Stoppard reviewed a hundred and thirty-two shows. Years later, in a sentence that combines verbal and moral fastidiousness in a peculiarly Stoppardian way, he explained why he thought himself a bad critic: "I never had the moral character to pan a friend—or, rather, I had the moral character never to pan a friend."

Since the magazine was ludicrously understaffed, he filled its pages with dozens of pseudonymous pieces, most of which he signed "William Boot." The name derives from

Evelyn Waugh's novel *Scoop,* in which William Boot is the
nature columnist of a national newspaper who, owing to a
spectacular misunderstanding, finds himself shipped off to
cover a civil war in Africa. (As things turn out, he handles
the assignment rather well.) Boot took root in Stoppard's
imagination, and soon began to crop up in his plays, often
allied to or contrasted with a complementary character
called Moon. As a double act, they bring to mind Lenin's
famous division of the world into "Who" and "Whom"—
those who do and those to whom it is done. In Stoppard's
words, "Moon is a person to whom things happen. Boot is
rather more aggressive." Early in 1964, BBC radio presented
two short Stoppard plays entitled *The Dissolution of
Dominic Boot* and *M Is for Moon Among Other Things.*
The leading characters in *The Real Inspector Hound* (1968)
are named Birdboot and Moon. Apropos of the eponymous
heroes of *Rosencrantz and Guildenstern,* the English critic
Robert Cushman has rightly said:

> Rosencrantz, being eager, well-meaning, and con-
> sistently oppressed or embarrassed by every situation in
> which he finds himself, is clearly a Moon; Guildenstern,
> equally oppressed though less embarrassed and taking
> refuge in displays of intellectual superiority, is as ob-
> viously a Boot.

Cushman once asked Stoppard why so many of his characters were called Moon or Boot. Stoppard crisply replied that
he couldn't help it if that was what their names turned out
to be. "I'm a Moon, myself," he went on. "Confusingly, I
used the name Boot, from Evelyn Waugh, as a pseudonym
in journalism, but that was because Waugh's Boot is really a
Moon, too." Having thus befogged his interviewer, he added
a wry etymological touch. "This is beginning to sound
lunatic," he said.

In 1964, a cobbler sticking to his last, Stoppard wrote a
ninety-minute TV play called *This Way Out with Samuel*

Boot, which he equipped with a *pair* of Boots, who represent diametrically opposed attitudes toward material possessions. Samuel Boot, a fortyish man of evangelical fervor, preaches the total rejection of property. Jonathan, his younger brother, is a compulsive hoarder of objects, unable to resist mail-order catalogues, who fills his home with items bought on credit which are constantly being repossessed, since he never keeps up the payments. ("It's like Christmas in a thieves' kitchen," Samuel cries, surveying a room stacked with vacuum cleaners, goggles, filing cabinets, miners' helmets, boomerangs, knitting machines, miniature Japanese trees, and other oddments.) At one point, a salesman comes to deliver a hearing aid for a week's free trial. Having fitted the device into Jonathan's ear, he shouts into the box, "There! That's better, isn't it?" "You don't have to shout," says Jonathan sharply. "I'm not deaf." He demands to know who told the salesman that he suffered from this infirmity.

SALESMAN: It was an assumption.
JONATHAN: If I told you I'd got a wooden leg, would you assume I was one-legged?
SALESMAN: Yes.
JONATHAN: Well, I have. And you may have noticed I'm wearing skis. You seem to be making a lot of nasty assumptions here. You think I'm a deaf cripple.

This *reductio ad absurdum* is pure Stoppard. An unreasonable man uses rational arguments to convince a reasonable man that he (the latter) is irrational. The salesman flees in panic, but Jonathan still has the hearing aid. Though both brothers are Boots by name, Samuel turns out to be a Moon by nature. He ends up defeated by his own innocence. When he claims to have found an exit from the commercial rat race, Jonathan brutally demolishes his dream:

There's no out. You're in it, so you might as well fit. It's the way it is. Economics. All this stuff I've got . . .

people have been paid to make it, drive it to the ware-
house, advertise it, sell it to me, write to me about it,
and take it away again. They get paid, and some of
them buy a carpet with the money. [He has just had a
carpet repossessed.] That's the way of it and you're in it.
There's no way out with Samuel Boot.

Jonathan has a vast collection of trading stamps. Samuel
steals them and holds a public meeting at which he proposes
to give them away. He is mobbed and killed by a crowd of
rapacious housewives. "He died of people," says one of his
disciples, a young deserter from the army. "They trod on
him." To this, Jonathan replies, "That's what it is about
people. Turn round and they'll tread on you. Or steal your
property." The deserter delivers Samuel's epitaph:

> He was a silly old man, and being dead doesn't change
> that. But for a minute . . . his daft old crusade, like he
> said, it had a kind of dignity.

Whereupon he picks up, as a souvenir of Jonathan's
acquisitive way of life, a newly delivered vacuum cleaner.
Rising to the defense of property, Jonathan shoots him dead
with a mail-order harpoon gun.

Samuel Boot is patchily brilliant, an uneasy blend of
absurdist comedy and radical melodrama. I have dwelt on it
because (a) it is the last Stoppard play with a message (i.e.,
property is theft) that could be described as leftist, and (b) it
is one of the few Stoppard scripts that have never been
performed in any medium. Kenneth Ewing offered it to a
London commercial-TV company and took Stoppard with
him to hear the verdict. It was negative. "Stick to theatre,"
he advised his dejected client on the way back. "Your work
can't be contained on television." Then Ewing's thoughts
moved to Shakespeare, and for no reason that he can now
recall, he brought up a notion he had long cherished about
Hamlet. Quoting the speech in which Claudius sends Hamlet
to England with a sealed message (borne by Rosencrantz and

Guildenstern) enjoining the ruler of that country to cut off
Hamlet's head, Ewing said that in his opinion the King of
England at the time of their arrival might well have been
King Lear. And, if so, did they find him raving mad at
Dover? Stoppard's spirits rose, and by the time Ewing dropped
him off at his home he had come up with a tentative title:
Rosencrantz and Guildenstern at the Court of King Lear. A
seed had clearly been planted. It pleases Ewing to reflect that
agents are not necessarily uncreative.

In the spring of 1964, the Ford Foundation awarded grants
to four British playwrights (or would-be playwrights)
enabling them to spend six months in West Berlin. The
senior member of the chosen quartet was James Saunders,
then thirty-nine years old and very much in vogue as the
author of *Next Time I'll Sing to You*, a lyrical-whimsical
play that seemed to some critics anemic and to others a
near-masterpiece. The remaining grants went to Derek Marlowe, Piers Paul Read (son of Sir Herbert, the illustrious poet
and critic), and Stoppard, an avowed admirer of Saunders,
by whose penchant for fantasy and wordplay his own work
had been visibly affected. The four authors were installed,
courtesy of Ford, in a mansion on the shore of the Wannsee.
"We were there as cultural window dressing," Saunders says,
"to show the generosity of American support for European
art." They were all eager to see Brecht's Berliner Ensemble,
in East Berlin, and three of them immediately did so.
Stoppard alone hung back, and did not make the trip until
his stay in Berlin was nearly over. He had never set foot in
Communist territory, and the prospect of crossing the border
repelled him. Although his passport was British, it stated
that he was born in Czechoslovakia, and this had planted in
him a superstitious fear that, once in East Berlin, he might
never be allowed to return.

In the house by the Wannsee, he wrote a one-act comedy
in verse, *Rosencrantz and Guildenstern Meet King Lear*. His
work, like that of his colleagues, was performed by English
amateur actors in one-night stands at a theatre on the

Kurfürstendamm, with no decor apart from a large photograph of the author. Saunders, having seen Stoppard's *jeu
d'esprit*, urged him to expand it into a full-length play. In
his spare time, Stoppard was recruited by a young Dutch
director to appear in a low-budget film based on a short
story by Borges. He played a cowboy, and Marlowe has
vivid memories of a sequence that showed Stoppard
belligerently twirling a pair of six-shooters in front of the
Brandenburg Gate. While Stoppard was in Germany, a
Hamburg theatre presented the first stage production of *A
Walk on the Water*, and he flew from Berlin for the
premiere. The performance passed off in silence but without
incident; and when the curtain fell Stoppard's German agent
rashly urged him to go onstage and take a bow. He did so,
with a cigarette between his lips—perhaps in emulation of
Oscar Wilde, who had once used the same method of showing his indifference to audience reaction. He was greeted, for
the first time in his life, by a storm of booing. It was directed,
as he readily admits, at the text, not the tobacco.

Summing up his impressions of Stoppard, in Berlin and
afterward, James Saunders says, "Diffident on the surface,
utterly unworried underneath. He's extremely cautious about
being thought too serious. I've heard him quote Auden's
famous remark to the effect that no poet's work ever saved
anyone from a concentration camp. Well, that may be true,
but it's terrible to *admit* that it's true. After all, the writer's
job is constantly to redefine the role of the individual: What
can he do? What *should* he do? And also to redefine the
role of society: How can it be changed? How *should* it be
changed? As a playwright, I live between these two respon-
sibilities. But Tom—Tom just plays safe. He enjoys being
nice, and he likes to be liked. He resists commitment of any
kind, he hides the ultimate expression of his deepest concerns. He's basically a displaced person. Therefore, he
doesn't want to stick his neck out. He feels grateful to
Britain, because he sees himself as a guest here, and that
makes it hard for him to criticize Britain. Probably the most

damaging thing you could say about him is that he's made
no enemies." Since Berlin, Stoppard's star has risen while
Saunders's has tended to decline. I asked Saunders how this
had affected their relationship. He smiled, and quoted a
well-known British dramatist who had once told him,
"Whenever I read a rave review of a young playwright in
the Sunday papers, it spoils my whole day." He continued,
"When Tom first became famous, he gave a series of expensive lunches at the Café Royal to keep in touch with his old
pals. I thought that was pretty ostentatious behavior. Meeting him nowadays I do feel a sort of cutoff." He made a
gesture like a portcullis descending. "I don't think that he's
overrated, as much as that many other writers are underrated.
He has distracted attention from people who have an equal
right to it."

(A word on Stoppard and friendship. Most of those who
know him well regard him as an exemplary friend. "He
actually drops in unannounced, which hardly anyone does in
London," says a close female chum, "and he usually brings
an unexpected but absolutely appropriate present. And he
mails huge batches of postcards, which are not only funny
but informative and helpful. He really works on his friendships." When Derek Marlowe wrote a novel entitled *Nightshade*, Stoppard, who knew that Marlowe venerated Ray-
mond Chandler, sought out an antique pulp magazine containing a Chandler story called "Nightshade," and arranged
for it to reach Marlowe on publication day.)

After Stoppard returned from Berlin, he shared a flat in
Westminster with Marlowe and Piers Paul Read. "At this
period, his idol was Mick Jagger," Marlowe says. "He looked
like him, he dressed like him, and he was thrilled when he
found out that Jagger loved cricket as much as he did."
Stoppard transmuted *Rosencrantz and Guildenstern* from
verse into prose, and turned out a couple of short plays for
television; but for the greater part of 1965 "he lived on the
Arabs," as Kenneth Ewing puts it. "For some unfathomable

reason, the BBC hired him to write the diary of an imaginary
Arab student in London, which was then translated into
Arabic and broadcast on the Overseas Service. He alternated
with another author, and every other week he was paid forty
pounds for five episodes. As far as I know, he had never met
an Arab in his life. But the job kept him going for about
nine months." Eager to scan the results of this bizarre
assignment, I approached the BBC for permission to consult
its files. I was told that no copies of the scripts were in
existence—a body blow to theatrical history but conceivably
good news to Stoppard.

Early in 1965, the Royal Shakespeare Company took a
twelve-month option on a play that was by then called
Rosencrantz and Guildenstern Are Dead. The company failed
to fit the play into its repertoire, and after the option expired
the script went to several other managements, all of which
rejected it. In the summer of 1966, the president of the
Oxford Theatre Group walked into Kenneth Ewing's office
and asked for permission to present an amateur production
of the play on the Fringe of the forthcoming Edinburgh
Festival. (The Fringe is Edinburgh's Off and Off-Off Broadway.) At first reluctant, Ewing eventually consented. He did
not regret his decision. The opening night got a handful of
bad notices, but over the weekend the momentous, life-
changing review appeared. Ronald Bryden, writing in the
Observer, described the play as an "erudite comedy, punning,
far-fetched, leaping from depth to dizziness," and continued, "It's the most brilliant debut by a young playwright
since John Arden's." At the time, I was working for Laurence
Olivier as literary manager of the National Theatre, whose
company was housed at the Old Vic. Minutes after reading
Bryden's piece, I cabled Stoppard, requesting a script. Olivier
liked it as much as I did, and within a week we had bought
it. Directed by Derek Goldby, it opened at the Vic in April,
1967. Very seldom has a play by a new dramatist been hailed
with such rapturous unanimity. Harold Hobson, of the

Sunday Times, called it "the most important event in the British professional theatre of the last nine years"; that is, since the opening of Harold Pinter's *The Birthday Party.* Stoppard, who had subtly smoothed and improved the text throughout rehearsals, found himself overnight with his feet on the upper rungs of Britain's theatrical ladder, where several hobnailed talents were already stamping for primacy.

When *Rosencrantz and Guildenstern* had its London triumph, Vaclav Havel was thirty years of age, just nine months older than Stoppard. He wore smart but conservative clothes, being a dandy in the classic rather than the romantic mode. Of less than average height, he had the incipient portliness of the gourmet. His hair was trimmed short, and this gave him a somewhat bullet-shaped silhouette. He both walked and talked with purposeful briskness and elegance. He drove around Prague (where he was born on October 5, 1936) in a dashing little Renault, bought with the royalties from his plays—for in 1967 Havel was the leading Czechoslovakian playwright, and the only one to have achieved an international reputation since Karel Capek wrote *R. U. R.* and (with his brother Josef) *The Insect Play,* between the wars. Havel's family connections were far grander than Stoppard's. Vera Blackwell, a Czech émigrée who lives in London and translates Havel's work into English, has said that "if Czechoslovakia had remained primarily a capitalist society Vaclav Havel would be today just about the richest young man in the country." One of his uncles was a millionaire who owned, apart from vast amounts of real estate and a number of hotels, the Barrandov studios, in Prague, which are the headquarters of the Czech film industry. All this was lost in the Communist takeover of 1948, and during the dark period of Stalinist rigor that followed, Havel's upper-class background prevented him from receiving any full-time education above grade-school level. Instead, he took a menial job in a chemical laboratory, spending most of his off-duty hours at evening classes, where he studied science. In 1954, he began two years of military service, after which he made repeated attempts to enter Prague University. All his applications were turned down. His next move was to offer himself for any theatrical work that was going. He found what he was looking for in the mid-sixties, when he was appointed *Dramaturg* (i.e., literary manager, a post that in Europe quite often means not only play selector and script editor but house playwright as well) at the Balustrade Theatre, which was Prague's principal showcase for avant-garde drama.

We nowadays tend to assume that the great thaw in Czech socialism began and ended with the libertarian reforms carried out by Alexander Dubcek's regime in the so-called Prague Spring of 1968. By that time, artistic freedom had in fact been blooming for several ebullient years: a period that saw the emergence of filmmakers like Milos Forman, Ivan Passer, Jan Nemec, and Jan Kadar; of theatrical directors like Otomar Krejca and Jan Grossman (who ran the Balustrade); and of a whole school of young dramatists, at whose head Vaclav Havel swiftly established himself. In one sense, he was a traditional Czech writer. Using a technique that derived from Kafka, Capek, and countless Central European authors before them, he expressed his view of the world in nonrealistic parables. His plays were distorting mirrors in which one recognized the truth. Stoppard belongs in precisely the same tradition, of which there is no Anglo-Saxon equivalent. Moreover, Havel shares Stoppard's passion for fantastic word juggling. Some critics have glibly assigned both writers to the grab bag marked Theatre of the Absurd. But here the analogy falters, for Havel's Absurdism is very different from Stoppard's. Vera Blackwell says:

> Havel does not protest against the absurdity of man's life *vis-à-vis* a meaningless universe, but against the absurdity of the modern Frankenstein's monster:

bureaucracy. . . . The ultimate aim of Havel's plays . . .
is the improvement of man's lot through the improvement of man's institutions. These, in their turn, can
become more "human" only insofar as the individual
men and women who invent and people these institutions are prepared to be fully human—i.e., fully responsible for their actions, fully aware of their responsibility.

If Dubcek's policies represented what Western journalists
called "Socialism with a human face," Havel's work gave
Absurdism a human face, together with a socially critical
purpose.

Like Stoppard, he had his first play performed in 1963.
Entitled *The Garden Party*, it was staged by Grossman at
the Balustrade. The hero, Hugo Pludek, is a student whose
consuming interest is playing chess against himself. "Such
a player," says his mother sagely, "will always stay in the
game." His parents, a solid bourgeois couple, base their
values on a storehouse of demented proverbs that they never
tire of repeating; e.g., "Not even a hag carries hemp heed
to the attic alone," "He who fusses about a mosquito net
can never hope to dance with a goat," "Not even the Hussars
of Cologne would go to the woods without a clamp," and—
perhaps the most incontrovertible of all—"Stone walls do
not an iron bar." They worry about Hugo, since he shows no
inclination to apply for work in the ruling bureaucracy.
Under their pressure, he attends a garden party thrown by
the Liquidation Office, where he poses as a bureaucrat so
successfully that before long he is put in charge of liquidating
the Liquidation Office. From a high-ranking member of the
Inauguration Service—the opposite end of the scale from the
Liquidation Office—he learns the Party line on intellectual
dissent: "We mustn't be afraid of contrary opinions. Everybody who's honestly interested in our common cause ought
to have from one to three contrary opinions." Eventually,
the authorities decide to liquidate the Inauguration Service,
and the question arises: Who should inaugurate the process

of liquidation—an inaugurator or a liquidator? Surely, not
the former, since how can anyone inaugurate his own liquidation? But, equally, it can't be the latter, because liquidators
have not been trained to inaugurate. Either liquidators must
be trained to inaugurate or vice versa. But this poses a new
question: Who is to do the training? At the end of the play,
driven mad by living in a society in which all truths are
relative and subject to overnight cancellation, Hugo feels his
identity crumbling. He knows what is happening to him, but,
good bureaucrat that he now is, he cannot resist it. In the
course of a hysterical tirade, he declares:

> Truth is just as complicated and multiform as every-
> thing else in the world—the magnet, the telephone,
> Impressionism, the magnet—and we are all a little bit
> what we were yesterday and a little bit what we are
> today; and also a little bit we're not these things. Any-
> way . . . some of us are more and some of us are more
> not; some only are, some are only, and some only are
> not; so that none of us entirely is, and at the same time
> each one of us is not entirely.

This was Absurdism with deep roots in contemporary
anxieties. The play was an immediate hit in Prague, and went
on to be performed in Austria, Switzerland, Sweden, Finland,
Hungary, Yugoslavia, and West Germany. Meanwhile, Havel
composed a series of "typographical poems" to amuse his
compatriots. One of them, labelled "Philosophy," went

```
! ! ! ! ! ! ! ! ! ! ! ! ! ! ! ! ! ! ! ! ! ! ! ! ! !
! ! ! ! ! ! ! ! ! ! ! ! ! ! ! ! ! ! ! ! ! ! ! ! ! !
! ! ! ! ! ! ! ! ! ! ! ! ! ! ! ! ! ! ! ! ! ! ! ! ! !
! ! ! ! ! ! ! ! ! ! ! ! ! ! ! ! ! ! ! ! ! ! ! ! ! !
! ! ! ! ! ! ! ! ! ! ! ! ! ! ! ! ! ! ! ! ! ! ! ! ! !
! ! ! ! ! ! ! ! ! ! ! ! ! ! ! ! ! ! ? ! ! ! ! ! ! !
! ! ! ! ! ! ! ! ! ! ! ! ! ! ! ! ! ! ! ! ! ! ! ! ! !
```

Another, wryly political, was printed thus:

```
                        FORWARD
           FORWARD                  FORWARD
           FORWARD                  FORWARD
           FORWARD                  FORWARD
           FORWARD                  FORWARD
           FORWARD                  FORWARD
           FORWARD                  FORWARD
           FORWARD                  FORWARD
           FORWARD                  FORWARD
           FORWARD                  FORWARD
                        FORWARD
```

And the following is Havel's succinct comment on the role of humor under Stalinism:

```
100%  100%  100%  100%  100%  100%  100%
100%  100%  100%  100%  100%  100%  100%
100%  100%  100%  100%  100%  100%  100%
100%  100%  100%  100%  100%  100%  100%
100%  100%  100%  100%  100%  100%  100%
100%  100%  100%  100%  100%  100%  100%
100%  100%  100%  100%  100%  100%  100%
100%  100%  100%  100%  100%  100%  100%
100%  100%  100%  100%  100%  100%  100%
100%  100%  100%  100%  100%   99%  100%
100%  100%  100%  100%  100%  100%  100%
100%  100%  100%  100%  100%  100%  100%
```

It is captioned "Constructive Satire."

Authentic satire operates on the principle of the thermos flask: it contains heat without radiating it. Havel's second play, *The Memorandum* (1965), was a splendid example: burning convictions were implicit in a structure of ice-cold logic and glittering linguistic virtuosity. His target was the use of language to subvert individualism and enforce conformity. Josef Gross, the managing director of a huge but undefined state enterprise, grows unsettled when he discovers that, on orders from above, the existing vernacular is being replaced by a synthetic language called Ptydepe, uncontaminated by the ambiguities, imprecisions, and emotional vagaries of ordinary speech. Its aim is to abolish similarities between words by using the least probable combinations of letters, so that no word can conceivably be mistaken for any other. We learn from the Ptydepe instructor who has been assigned to Gross's organization, "The natural languages originated . . . spontaneously, uncontrollably, and their structure is thus, in a certain sense, dilettantish." For purposes of official communication, they are utterly unreliable. In Ptydepe, "the more common the meaning, the shorter the word." The longest entry in the new dictionary has three hundred and nineteen letters and means "wombat." The shortest is "f" and at present has no meaning, since science has not yet determined which word or expression is in commonest use. The instructor lists several variations of the interjection "Boo" as it might be employed in a large company when one worker seeks to "sham-ambush" another. If the victim is in full view, unprepared for the impending ambush and threatened by a hidden colleague, "Boo" is rendered by "Gedynrelom." If, however, the victim is *aware* of the danger, the correct cry is "Osonfterte"—for which "Eg gynd y trojadus" must be substituted if *both* parties are in full view and the encounter is meant only as a joke. If the sham-ambush is seriously intended, the appropriate expression is "Eg jeht kuz." Jan Ballas, Gross's ambitious deputy, points out to his baffled boss that normal language is fraught with undesirable emotional overtones: "Now, tell me sincerely, has the word 'mutarex' any such overtones for you? It hasn't, has it! You see! It is a paradox, but it is precisely the surface inhumanity of an artificial language that guarantees its truly human function!" Gross's problems are compounded by the fact that he has received an official memorandum in Ptydepe, but in order to get a Ptydepe text translated one must make an application in Ptydepe, which Gross does not speak. "In other words," he laments, "the only way to know what is in one's memo is to know it already." Ever willing to compromise (and this is Havel's

underlying message), he does not complain when he loses
his job to Ballas; and it is through no effort of his own that
he regains it at the end. The authorities have observed that, as
one of their spokesmen resentfully puts it, wherever Ptydepe
has passed into common use, "it has automatically begun to
assume some of the characteristics of a natural language:
various emotional overtones, imprecisions, ambiguities."
Therefore, Ptydepe is to be replaced by a new language,
Chorukor, based on the principle not of abolishing but of
intensifying the similarities between words. Gross, reinstated
to spearhead the introduction of Chorukor, remains what
he has never ceased to be: a time-serving organization man.

This small masterpiece of sustained irony was staged
throughout Europe and at the Public Theatre, in New York,
where it won the 1968 *Village Voice* award for the best
foreign play of the Off Broadway season. In April of that
year, Havel's next work, *The Increased Difficulty of Concentration*, opened in Prague. If the logical games and verbal
pyrotechnics of *The Memorandum* suggested analogies with
Stoppard, there were aspects of the new piece which antic-
ipated a play that Stoppard had not yet written; namely,
Jumpers. Havel's central character is Dr. Huml, a social
scientist engaged (like Professor Moore in *Jumpers*) in
dictating a bumbling lecture on moral values which goes
against the intellectual grain of his society. He is interrupted
from time to time by a couple of technicians bearing an
extremely disturbed and unreliable computer with which
they propose to study his behavior patterns. Here are some
telescoped samples of Huml at work, with Blanka, his
secretary:

> HUML: Where did we stop?
> BLANKA (*reads*): "Various people have at various times
> and in various circumstances various needs—"
> HUML: Ah yes! (*Begins to pace thoughtfully to and
> fro while dictating to Blanka, who takes it down in*

shorthand)—and thus attach to various things various values—full stop. Therefore, it would be mistaken to set up a fixed scale of values—valid for all people in all circumstances and at all times—full stop. This does not mean, however, that in all of history there exist no values common to the whole of mankind—full stop. If those values did not exist, mankind would not form a unified whole—full stop. . . . Would you mind reading me the last sentence? . . . There exist situations—for example, in some advanced Western countries—in which all the basic human needs have been satisfied, and still people are not happy. They experience feelings of depression, boredom, frustration, etc.—full stop. In these situations man begins to desire that which in fact he perhaps does not need at all—he simply persuades himself he has certain needs which he does not have—or he vaguely desires something which he cannot specify and thus cannot strive for—full stop. Hence, as soon as man has satisfied one need—i.e., achieved happiness—another so far unsatisfied need is born in him, so that every happiness is always, simultaneously, a negation of happiness.

Can science help man to solve his problems? Not entirely, says Huml, because science can illuminate only that which is finite, whereas man "contains the dimensions of infinity." He continues:

I'm afraid the key to a real comprehension of the individual does not lie in a greater or lesser understanding of the complexity of man as an object of scientific knowledge. . . . The unique relationship that arises between two individuals is thus far the only thing that can —at least to some extent—mutually unveil their secrets. Values like love, friendship, compassion, sympathy, even mutual conflict—which is as unique and irreplaceable as mutual understanding—are the only tools we have at our disposal. By other means we may perhaps be able to explain man, but never to understand him. . . . The fundamental key does not lie in his brain, but in his heart.

Meanwhile, the computer has broken down, and emits a shrill bombardment of imbecile questions, endlessly repeated:

Which is your favorite tunnel? Are you fond of musical instruments? How many times a year do you air the square? Where did you bury the dog? Why didn't you pass it on? When did you lose the claim? Wherein lies the nucleus? Do you know where you're going, and do you know who's going with you? Do you urinate in public, or just now and then?

On August 21, 1968, the Soviet Union, alarmed by the experiment in free socialism that was flowering in Czechoslovakia, invaded the country and imposed on it a neo-Stalinist regime. One of the first acts of the new government was to forbid all performances of Havel's plays.

By the summer of 1968, Stoppard had had his third London premiere within fourteen months. *Enter a Free Man*, which I've already discussed, had opened to mixed notices at the St. Martin's Theatre in March, and *The Real Inspector Hound*, to which I'll return later, had been more happily received (the *Observer* compared it to a Fabergé Easter egg) when it arrived at the Criterion Theatre, in June, just two months before the Russian tanks rolled into Prague. *Rosencrantz and Guildenstern* remained a great drawing card in the repertory—a hand already stacked with aces—of the National Theatre. A couple of weeks before its first night, in 1967, I had written a piece on the performing arts in Prague. In it I said that the new Czech theatre was "focussing its attention not only on man vs. authority but on man vs. mortality," and that "the hero is forced to come to terms not merely with the transient compulsions of society but with the permanent fact of death." Under liberal governments, I added, authors tend to concern themselves with "the ultimate problem of dying as well as the immediate problems of living." With the benefit of hindsight, I realize that every word of this might have been written about *Rosencrantz and Guildenstern*: it fitted perfectly into my group portrait of Czech drama. (Perhaps the most memorable speech in the play occurs when the former and dumber principal character asks, "Whatever became of the moment when one first knew about death?"—that shattering instant, surely inscribed on everyone's memory, which for some reason no one can remember.) Of course, one can also spot Western influences. The sight of two bewildered men playing pointless games in a theatrical void while the real action unfolds offstage inevitably recalls Beckett. Stoppard has said, "When *Godot* was first done, it liberated something for anybody writing plays. It redefined the minima of theatrical validity. It was as simple as that. He got away. He won by twenty-eight lengths, and he'd done it with so little—and I mean that as an enormous compliment." When Guildenstern says, "Wheels have been set in motion, and they have their own pace, to which we are . . . condemned," we think once more of Beckett's doom-laden slogan, "Something is taking its course." The debt to Eliot's "Love Song of J. Alfred Prufrock" is equally transparent:

> No! I am not Prince Hamlet, nor was meant to be;
> Am an attendant lord, one that will do
> To swell a progress, start a scene or two . . .
> Full of high sentence, but a bit obtuse;
> At times, indeed, almost ridiculous—
> Almost, at times, the Fool.

"Prufrock and Beckett," Stoppard has said, "are the two syringes of my diet, my arterial system." But has anyone noticed another mainline injection? Consider: Rosencrantz and Guildenstern are unaccountably summoned to a mysterious castle where, between long periods of waiting, they receive cryptic instructions that eventually lead to their deaths. They die uncertain whether they are the victims of chance or of fate. It seems to me undeniable that the world they inhabit owes its atmosphere and architecture to the master builder of such enigmatic fables—Franz Kafka, whose birthplace was Prague, and who wrote of just such a castle.

Stoppard is nothing if not eclectic. His play even bears traces of Wittgenstein, according to whose *Philosophical Investigations* (1953) it is conceivable that:

> . . . two people belonging to a tribe unacquainted with chess should sit at a chessboard and go through the moves of a game of chess. . . . And if we were to see it, we would say they were playing chess. But now imagine a game of chess translated, according to certain rules, into a series of actions which we do not ordinarily associate with a *game*—say, into yells and stamping of feet. And now suppose these two people to yell and stamp instead of playing the form of chess that we are used to. . . . Should we still be inclined to say they were playing a game? What *right* would one have to say so?

Stoppard's twin heroes are clearly involved in "a series of actions which we do not ordinarily associate with a game." They are caught up in a strict and ferocious plot—both onstage and off, people are being killed—but the total experience, however unplayful it looks, may still be a kind of game, as formal in its rules as chess.

Again, Oscar Wilde (a good fairy, in the elfin sense of the word, who has more than once waved an influential wand over the *accouchement* of a Stoppard work) supplies an apt quotation, from *De Profundis*:

> I know of nothing in all Drama more incomparable from the point of view of Art, or more suggestive in its subtlety of observation, than Shakespeare's drawing of Rosencrantz and Guildenstern. They are Hamlet's

college friends. They have been his companions. . . .
At the moment when they come across him in the
play he is staggering under the weight of a burden
intolerable to one of his temperament. . . . Of all this,
Guildenstern and Rosencrantz realise nothing.

Which they prove in the funniest speech of Stoppard's play,
when, having been told to "glean what afflicts" Hamlet, the
two spies quiz each other about his state of mind and come
up with the following conclusion:

> ROSENCRANTZ: To sum up: your father, whom you
> love, dies, you are his heir, you come back to find that
> hardly was the corpse cold before his young brother
> popped on to his throne and into his sheets, thereby
> offending both legal and natural practice. Now why
> exactly are you behaving in this extraordinary manner?

Wilde goes on:

> They are close to his secret and know nothing of it.
> Nor would there be any use in telling them. They are
> little cups that can hold so much and no more. . . . They
> are types fixed for all time. To censure them would show
> a lack of appreciation. They are merely out of their
> sphere: that is all.

Despite its multiple sources, *Rosencrantz and Guildenstern*
is a genuine original, one of a kind. As far as I know, it is the
first play to use another play as its decor. The English critic
C. E. Montague described *Hamlet* as "a monstrous Gothic
castle of a poem, full of baffled half-lights and glooms."
This is precisely the setting of *Rosencrantz and Guildenstern*:
it takes place in the wings of Shakespeare's imagination. The
actor-manager who meets the two travellers on the road to
Elsinore says that in life every exit is "an entrance somewhere
else." In Stoppard's play, every exit is an entrance somewhere
else in *Hamlet*. Sometimes he writes like a poet:

> We cross our bridges when we come to them and
> burn them behind us, with nothing to show for our
> progress except a memory of the smell of smoke, and a
> presumption that once our eyes watered.

And at other times with fortune-cookie glibness:

> Eternity is a terrible thought. I mean, where's it going
> to end?

But we are finally moved by the snuffing out of the brief
candles he has lit. Tinged perhaps with sentimentality, an
emotional commitment has nonetheless been made. To quote
Clive James:

> The mainspring of "Rosencrantz and Guilderstern Are
> Dead" is the perception—surely a compassionate one—
> that the fact of their deaths mattering so little to
> Hamlet was something that ought to have mattered to
> Shakespeare.

The Real Inspector Hound, which joined *Rosencrantz and
Guildenstern* on the London playbills in June, 1968, need
not detain us long. It is a facetious puzzle that, like several
of Stoppard's minor pieces, presents an apparently crazy
series of events for which in the closing moments a rational
explanation is provided. Two drama critics, Birdboot and
Moon, are covering the premiere of a thriller, written in a
broad parody of the style of Agatha Christie. At curtain rise,
there is a male corpse onstage. Stoppard unconvincingly
maintains that when the play was half finished he still didn't
know the dead man's name or the murderer's identity. (How
did he find out? "There is a God," Stoppard says when he is
asked this question, "and he looks after English playwrights.") Toward the end, the two critics implausibly leave
their seats and join in the action. In the dénouement, Moon,
who is the second-string critic for his paper, is killed onstage

by the envious third-string critic, who, posing as an actor in
the play within a play, has previously slain the first-string
critic (the curtain-rise corpse) and rigged the evidence to
frame Moon. (A general rule about Stoppard may be stated
thus: The shorter the play, the harder it is to summarize the
plot without sounding unhinged.) People sometimes say that
Stoppard, for all his brilliance, is fundamentally a leech, drawing the lifeblood of his work from the inventions of others.
In *Rosencrantz and Guildenstern*, he battens on Shakespeare,
in *Inspector Hound* on Christie, in *Jumpers* on the logical
positivists, in *Travesties* on Wilde, James Joyce, and Lenin.
The same charge, of course, has been levelled against other
and greater writers; in 1592, for example, the playwright and
pamphleteer Robert Greene accused Shakespeare of artistic
thievery, calling him an "upstart crow, beautified with our
feathers."

Allegations of this kind do not ruffle Stoppard's feathers.
"I can't invent plots," he admitted in a public discussion of
his work which was held in Los Angeles earlier this year.
"I've formed the habit of hanging my plays on other people's
plots. It's a habit I'm trying to kick." Apropos of borrowings,
I may as well reveal my suspicion that a hitherto undetected
influence on *Inspector Hound* is that of Robert Benchley.
At one point, when the stage is empty, a phone rings, and the
critic Moon gets up to answer it. Surely this calls to mind the
legendary moment during a Broadway premiere when a phone
rang on an empty stage and the critic Benchley, remarking,
"I think that's for me," rose and left the theatre. Nor is
Stoppard's play the first in which a drama critic has been
seen dead onstage. Back in 1917, seeking material for a newspaper article, a writer lately employed as the drama critic of
Vanity Fair played the role of a corpse in *The Thirteenth
Chair*. His name, guessably, was Robert Benchley.

Jumpers, produced in 1972, was the next milestone in
Stoppard's career; but something should first be said of his
work for radio, a medium he has used more resourcefully than

any other contemporary English playwright. In *Albert's Bridge* (1967) and *Artist Descending a Staircase* (1972), both written for the BBC, he explores two of his favorite themes. The first is the relativity of absolutely everything. (It all depends on where you're sitting.) The second is the definition of art. (Is it a skill or a gift? Is it socially useful? Or does that, too, depend on where you're sitting?) Albert, in the earlier play, is painting a lofty railway bridge that will have to be repainted as soon as he has finished painting it. Despite the repetitious and mechanical nature of his job, he loves it, because it has a symmetry and coherence that are lacking in his life on the ground. He is joined by Fraser, a would-be suicide, who has climbed the bridge in order to jump off. The world below, Fraser explains, is doomed:

> Motor-cars nose each other down every street, and they are beginning to breed, spread, they press the people to the walls by their knees, and there's no end to it, because if you stopped making them, thousands of people would be thrown out of work, and they'd have no money to spend, the shopkeepers would get caught up in it, and the farms and factories, and all the people dependent on them, with their children and all. There's too much of everything, but the space for it is constant. So the shell of human existence is filling out, expanding, and it's going to go bang.

After a while, however, he changes his mind. Seeing it all from above, at a distance, he finds order in the chaos. "Yes," he says, "from a vantage point like this, the idea of society is just about tenable." So he descends; but shortly afterward he returns, convinced that he was right the first time. The bridge finally collapses, with both men on it, when a massed phalanx of assistant painters marches across it without breaking step. It is a fine catastrophe, but also a neat escape hatch for Stoppard, who is thus absolved from the responsibility of telling us which view of life we should espouse—the long shot or the closeup.

Artist Descending a Staircase has a plot that starts out backward and then goes forward. I shall not take up the challenge to summarize it, except to say that it concerns the careers and beliefs of three artists, one of whom is dead and may have been murdered by either of the others, or by both working in cahoots. The title derives from Marcel Duchamp's painting "Nude Descending a Staircase," and the play contains plenty of evidence that self-cannibalism is not alien to Stoppard. For example:

> The artist is a lucky dog. . . . In any community of a thousand souls there will be nine hundred doing the work, ninety doing well, nine doing good, and one lucky dog painting or writing about the other nine hundred and ninety-nine.

Slightly compressed, this superb speech reappears in *Travesties*; and there are references to Lenin and Tristan Tzara (and their joint sojourn in Zurich during the First World War) which look forward to the same play. Stoppard leaves us in no doubt about his attitude toward twentieth-century art in its more extreme manifestations, which he calls "that child's garden of easy victories known as the avant-garde." Again:

> Skill without imagination is craftsmanship and gives us many useful objects such as wickerwork picnic baskets. Imagination without skill gives us modern art.

He also takes a sharp sideswipe at an artist who, having gone through a period of making ceramic food, realizes that this will not help to fill empty bellies. The artist decides instead to sculpture edible art out of sugar. One of his colleagues says, "It will give Cubism a new lease of life." I think we can take it that Stoppard is expressing his own feelings in the following definition, which recurs unchanged in *Travesties*:

An artist is someone who is gifted in some way that
enables him to do something more or less well which
can only be done badly or not at all by someone who
is not thus gifted.

I once told Stoppard that, impressive though his dictum
sounded, it could equally well be applied to a jockey. He
wandered out of the room for a full minute, presumably to
ponder, and then wandered back. "That's exactly what I
meant," he said. "In other words, a chap who claims to be a
jockey and wears a jockey's cap *but sits facing the horse's tail*
is not a jockey."

During the four years that separate *Inspector Hound* from
Jumpers, the total of new work by Stoppard consisted of
three one-acters and a short play for television. This apparent
unproductiveness was due partly to distracting upheavals in
his private life (the collapse of his first marriage, the
cementing of his new relationship with Miriam) and partly
to an ingrained habit of preparing for his major enterprises
with the assiduity of an athlete training for the Olympics.
Or, to use Derek Marlowe's simile: "For Tom, writing a play
is like sitting for an examination. He spends ages on research,
does all the necessary cramming, reads all the relevant books,
and then gestates the results. Once he's passed the exam—
with the public and the critics—he forgets all about it and
moves on to the next subject." Moreover, the second play is
always a high hurdle. Although *Inspector Hound* came after
Rosencrantz and Guildenstern, it didn't really count, being a
lightweight diversion, staged in a commercial theatre. The
real test, as Stoppard knew, would be his second play *at the
National*.

Early in 1970, he told me, over lunch, that he had been
reading the logical positivists with fascinated revulsion. He
was unable to accept their view that because value judgments
could not be empirically verified they were meaningless.
Accordingly, he said, he was toying with the idea of a play

whose entire first act would be a lecture in support of moral philosophy. This led us into a long debate on morality—specifically, on the difference between the Judeo-Christian tradition (in which the creator of the universe also lays down its moral laws, so that the man who breaks them is committing an offense against God) and the Oriental tradition represented by Zen Buddhism (in which morality is seen as a man-made convention, quite distinct from God or cosmogony). Only with Stoppard or Vaclav Havel can I imagine having such a conversation about a play that was intended to be funny. A few days later, Stoppard sent me a letter in which he said that our chat had "forced me to articulate certain ideas, to their immense hazard, which I suppose is useful," and went on, "All that skating around makes the ice look thin, but a sense of renewed endeavour prevails—more concerned with the dramatic possibilities than with the ideas, for it is a mistake to assume that plays are the end-products of ideas (which would be limiting): the ideas are the end-products of the plays."

The theatrical image that triggered *Jumpers* came from an exchange in *Rosencrantz and Guildenstern,* when Rosencrantz says, "Shouldn't we be doing something—constructive?" and Guildenstern replies, "What did you have in mind? A short, blunt human pyramid?" Stoppard subsequently told an interviewer:

> I thought, How marvellous to have a pyramid of people on a stage, and a rifle shot, and one member of the pyramid just being blown out of it, and the others imploding on the hole as he leaves. . . . Because of the success of "Rosencrantz" it was on the cards that the National Theatre would do whatever I wrote, if I didn't completely screw it up. . . . It's perfectly true that having shot this man out of the pyramid, and having him lying on the floor, I didn't know who he was or who had shot him or why or what to do with the body. Absolutely not a clue.

Cf. Stoppard's virtually identical and identically unper-
suasive statement about a similar situation in *Inspector
Hound*. However, play it again, Tom:

> At the same time, there's more than one point of
> origin for a play, and the only useful metaphor I can
> think of for the way I think I write my plays is con-
> vergences of different threads. . . . One of the threads
> was the entirely visual image of the pyramid of acrobats,
> but while thinking of that pyramid I knew I wanted to
> write a play about a professor of moral philosophy. . . .
> There was a metaphor at work in the play already be-
> tween acrobatics and mental acrobatics, and so on.

In December, 1970, I got a note from Stoppard saying that
the new piece would not be ready until the following
autumn. In the late summer of 1971, I called him and begged
him to give us some idea of its substance, since within a
couple of weeks we had to fix our plans for the forthcoming
season. He replied that, although he had nearly finished the
first draft, he could not possibly get it typed so soon. Might
he therefore read it to us himself? Acting on this suggestion,
I arranged a singular audition at my house in Kensington.
The audience consisted of Laurence Olivier, John Dexter
(then associate director of the National Theatre), and me.
The time was late afternoon, and Olivier had come straight
from an exhausting rehearsal. Stoppard arrived with the text
and a sheaf of large white cards, each bearing the name of
one of the characters. We had a few glasses of wine, after
which Stoppard announced that he would read the play
standing at a table, holding up the appropriate card to indicate who was speaking. What ensued was a gradual descent
into chaos. *Jumpers* (which was then called *And Now the
Incredible Jasmin Jumpers*) is a complex work with a big cast,
and before long Stoppard had got his cards hopelessly mixed
up. Within an hour, Olivier had fallen asleep. Stoppard
gallantly pressed on, and I have a vivid memory of him,

desperate in the gathering dusk, frantically shuffling his precious pages and brandishing his cards, like a panicky magician whose tricks are blowing up in his face. After two hours, he had got no farther than the end of Act I. At that point, Olivier suddenly woke up. For about thirty seconds, he stared at the ceiling, where some spotlights I had recently installed were dimly gleaming. Stoppard looked expectantly in his direction: clearly, Olivier was choosing his words with care. At length, he uttered them. "Ken," he said to me ruminatively, "where did you buy those lights?" Stoppard then gave up and left. Next day, it took all the backslapping of which Dexter and I were capable to persuade him that the play was worth saving.

Jumpers turned out to be something unique in theatre: a farce whose main purpose is to affirm the existence of God. Or, to put it less starkly, a farcical defense of transcendent moral values. At the same time, it is an attack on pragmatic materialism as this is practiced by a political party called the Radical Liberals, who embody Stoppard's satiric vision of socialism in action. They have just won an election (the time, unspecified, seems to be the near future), and no sooner are the votes counted than they take over the broadcasting services, arrest the newspaper proprietors, and appoint a veterinary surgeon Archbishop of Canterbury. A prominent Rad-Lib—and the villain of Stoppard's piece—is Sir Archie Jumper, vice-chancellor of an English university and an all-round bounder, who holds degrees in medicine, philosophy, literature, and law, and diplomas in psychiatry and gymnastics. Archie encourages the philosophers of his staff (mostly logical positivists) to be part-time athletes, and it is they who form the human pyramid, perforated by a bullet, with which the action begins.

The killing takes place during a party thrown at the home of George Moore, professor of moral philosophy—a middle-aged word-spinner and resolute nonacrobat, who is implacably opposed to Archie's values, or lack of them. This is Stoppard's hero, and it is not the least of his problems that he bears the same name as the world-famous English philosopher (d. 1958) who wrote *Principia Ethica*. However, being one of Stoppard's unsinkable eccentrics, he does not let this mischievous coincidence get him down. On hearing that the veterinarian Clegthorpe is the new Primate, he ironically observes, "Sheer disbelief hardly registers on the face before the head is nodding with all the wisdom of instant hindsight. 'Archbishop Clegthorpe? Of course! The inevitable capstone to a career in veterinary medicine!' " (The use of a rare word like "capstone" instead of the more obvious "keystone" or "climax" is typical of Stoppard. Nabokov, another exile with a taste for verbal surprises, might have made the same choice.) George's role, one of the longest in the English comic repertoire, is devoted mainly to the composition of a hilarious, interminable, outrageously convoluted lecture designed to prove that moral absolutes exist—and closely analogous, as I've said, to the address dictated by Dr. Huml in Havel's *The Increased Difficulty of Concentration*. Theatrically, it disproves the philistine maxim that intellectual comedy can never produce belly laughs.

Seeking to demonstrate that purely rational arguments do not always make sense, George cites the Greek philosopher Zeno, who concluded that "since an arrow shot towards a target first had to cover half the distance, and then half the remainder, and then half the remainder after that, and so on *ad infinitum*, the result was . . . that though an arrow is always approaching its target, it never quite gets there, and Saint Sebastian died of fright." To underline his point, George actually uses a bow and arrow, just as he employs a trained tortoise and a trained hare (both of which escape) to refute another of Zeno's famous paradoxes, "which showed in every way but experience . . . that a tortoise given a head start in a race with, say, a hare, could never be overtaken." Hare, tortoise, arrow, and bow come together at the play's climax, which is one of the supreme—tragicomic is not quite the word, let us say tragi-farcical—moments in modern theatre.

George sums up his beliefs in a discussion with Archie:

> When I push *my* convictions to absurdity, *I* arrive at God. . . . All I know is that I think that I know that I know that nothing can be created out of nothing, that my moral conscience is different from the rules of my tribe, and that there is more in me than meets the microscope—and because of *that* I'm lumbered with this incredible, indescribable and definitely shifty *God*, the trump card of atheism.

He dismisses Archie's supporters as "simplistic scoresettlers." George versus Archie is Stoppard's dazzling dramatization of one of the classic battles of our time. Cyril Connolly gives a more dispassionate account of the same conflict in *The Unquiet Grave*, his semiautobiographical book of confessions and aphorisms:

> The two errors: We can either have a spiritual or a materialist view of life. If we believe in the spirit then we make an assumption which permits a whole chain of them, down to a belief in fairies, witches, astrology, black magic, ghosts and treasure-divining. . . . On the other hand, a completely materialistic view leads to its own excesses, such as a belief in Behaviourism, in the economic basis of art, in the social foundation of ethics, and the biological nature of psychology, in fact to the justification of expediency and therefore ultimately to the Ends-Means fallacy of which our civilisation is perishing. If we believe in a supernatural or superhuman intelligence creating the universe, then we end by stocking our library with the prophecies of Nostradamus, and the calculations on the Great Pyramid. If instead we choose to travel via Montaigne and Voltaire, then we choke amid the brimstone aridities of the Left Book Club.

In that great debate there is no question where Stoppard stands. He votes for the spirit—although he did not state his position in the first person until June of this year, when, in the course of a book review, he defined himself as a supporter of "Western liberal democracy, favouring an intellectual elite and a progressive middle class and based on a moral order derived from Christian absolutes."

The female principle in the George-Archie struggle is represented by George's wife, Dotty. Some ten years his junior, she is a star of musical comedy who has suffered a nervous breakdown (and gone into premature retirement) because the landing of men on the moon has destroyed her romantic ideals. She says:

> Not only are we no longer the still centre of God's universe, we're not even uniquely graced by his footprint in man's image. . . . Man is on the moon, his feet on solid ground, and he has seen us whole . . . and all our absolutes, the thou-shalts, and the thou-shalt-nots that seemed to be the very condition of our existence, how did *they* look to two moonmen with a single neck to save between them?

We already know the answer. Captain Scott, the first Englishman to reach the moon, has a damaged spaceship that may not make it back to earth. To reduce the weight load, he has kicked Astronaut Oates off the ladder to the command module, thereby condemning him to death. What is moral has been sacrificed in favor of what is practical. Remember that we are still dealing with a high—a very high —comedy. In this context, Geoffrey Reeves's opinion is worth quoting:

> "Rosencrantz" is a beautiful piece of theatre, but "Jumpers" is *the* play, without any doubt. The ironic tone perfectly matches the absurd vision. It's far more than an exercise in wit; it ends up making a fierce

statement. Not necessarily one that I would agree with
—politically and philosophically. Tom and I have very
little in common. But it's a measure of his brilliance
that in the theatre I suspend rational judgment. He
simply takes my breath away. People sometimes say he
has a purely literary mind. That's not true of "Jumpers."
It uses the stage *as* a stage, not as an extension of TV
or the novel.

Jumpers went into rehearsal at the Old Vic in November,
1971. Diana Rigg played Dotty, and Michael Hordern, as
George, had the part of his life: quivering with affronted
dignity, patrolling the stage like a neurotic sentry, his face
infested with tics, his fists plunging furiously into his cardigan
pockets, he was matchlessly silly and serious at the same
time. Ten days before the premiere, however, the play was
still running close to four hours. I begged Olivier for permission to make cuts. He told me to approach the director,
Peter Wood, who said he was powerless without the author's
approval. Stoppard felt that alterations at this stage would
upset the actors. Faced with this impasse, I took unilateral
action. The next afternoon, just after the lunch break, I
nipped into the rehearsal room ahead of the director and
dictated to the cast a series of cuts and transpositions which
reduced the text to what I considered manageable length.
They were accepted without demur, and the matter, to my
astonished relief, was never raised again. *Jumpers* opened in
February, 1972, to resounding acclaim. B. A. Young, of the
Financial Times, spoke for most of his colleagues when he
wrote, "I can't hope to do justice to the richness and sparkle
of the evening's proceedings, as gay and original a farce as
we have seen for years."

Two months later, the London *Sunday Times*, whose
regular critic had given a rhapsodic account of the first night,
unexpectedly published a second review of the play—written
by Sir Alfred Ayer, Wykeham Professor of Logic at Oxford
and, by general consent, the foremost living English

philosopher. He had made his name (which was then plain
A. J. Ayer) in the nineteen-thirties as the precocious author
of *Language, Truth and Logic,* probably the most masterly
exposition in English of the principles of logical positivism.
Thus, Ayer represented, in its most Establishment form, the
philosophical tradition that Stoppard had set out to under-
mine. George tells us in the play that his next book will be
entitled *Language, Truth and God,* and Dotty summarizes
the archfiend Archie's views on morality in a speech that
might have been borrowed from Ayer:

> Things and actions, you understand, can have any
> number of real and verifiable properties. But good and
> bad, better and worse, these are not real properties of
> things, they are just expressions of our feelings about
> them.

It seemed on the cards that Ayer-Archie would resent being
cast as Stoppard's villain. But nothing of the sort: he
"enormously enjoyed" the evening, and "came away feeling
the greatest admiration for its author and for the actor
Michael Hordern, who takes the leading part." If he identified
himself with any of the characters, it was not Archie but
George, in whom "I thought, perhaps conceitedly, that I
occasionally caught echoes of my own intonations"—though
not, needless to say, of his ideas. He analyzed the play's
philosophical content with detached but devastating aplomb:

> The argument is between those who believe in
> absolute values, for which they seek a religious sanction,
> and those, more frequently to be found among con-
> temporary philosophers, who are subjectivists or relativists
> in morals, utilitarians in politics, and atheists or at least
> agnostics. . . .
> George needs not one but two Gods, one to create the
> world and another to support his moral values, and is
> unsuccessful in obtaining either of them. For the creator
> he relies on the first-cause argument, which is notoriously

fallacious, since it starts from the assumption that everything must have a cause and ends with something that lacks one. As for the view that morals can be founded on divine authority, the decisive objection was beautifully put by Bertrand Russell: "Theologians have always taught that God's decrees are good, and that this is not a mere tautology; it follows that goodness is logically independent of God's decrees." This argument also shows that even if George had been able to discover his second God it would not have been of any service to him. It would provide a utilitarian motive for good behaviour, but that was not what he wanted. It could, more respectably, provide an object for emulation, but for that imaginary or even actual human beings could serve as well. . . .

The moral of the play, in so far as it has one, seemed to be that George was humane, and therefore human, in a way the others were not. This could have been due to his beliefs, but it did not have to be. Whatever Kant may have said, morality is very largely founded on sympathy and affection, and for these one does not require religious sanctions. Even logical positivists are capable of love.

After reading Ayer's review, Stoppard invited him to lunch, and the two men became close friends.

We now flash forward to an entry in my journal for October 19, 1976, when Stoppard and I motored to New College, Oxford, to be Ayer's guests for dinner at High Table. An English drama critic once said, "Stoppard, who never went to a university, writes more like a University Wit than any graduate dramatist now practising." The trip to New College would be Stoppard's initiation into Oxford life, and he would be going in off the top board, since, of all the dons currently teaching at the university, Ayer is the reigning superstar:

En route to Oxford, Tom and I lunch at the Waterside Inn, plush French restaurant forty minutes west of London by car. The Thames idles past our table, visible through plate glass and weeping willows. Tom talks of how, earlier this year, he lunched with the Queen at Buckingham Palace: "Everything you touch is beautiful, and the food is superb. The other guests were writers, athletes, accountants—all kinds of people. Don't expect me to knock occasions like that. I'm very conservative. As a foreigner, I'm more patriotic than anyone else in England except William Davis." (Davis is the German-born editor of *Punch*.) I ask whether there's any living person he especially longs to meet. Three names cross his mind: Marlon Brando, Alexander Solzhenitsyn, and Sugar Ray Robinson. We discuss his view of politics in general and British politics in particular: "I don't lose any sleep if a policeman in Durham beats somebody up, because I know it's an exceptional case. It's a sheer perversion of speech to describe the society I live in as one that inflicts violence on the underprivileged. What worries me is not the bourgeois exception but the totalitarian norm. Of all the systems that are on offer, the one I don't want is the one that denies freedom of expression—no matter what its allegedly redeeming virtues may be. The only thing that would make me leave England would be control over free speech." Of his plays he says, "My characters are all mouthpieces for points of view rather than explorations of individual psychology. They aren't realistic in any sense. I write plays of ideas uneasily married to comedy or farce." Has he got any manuscripts hidden away in a bottom drawer? He grins and answers, "No—with me everything is top drawer." We talk about James Joyce's exuberantly erotic letters to his wife, which have recently been published for the first time. If Tom had read them before writing *Travesties*, in which Joyce is a leading character, would he have made use of them? "I wouldn't have dreamed of it. I'm interested in Joyce the author of *Ulysses*, not Joyce the husband. Nor, by the way, do I think of him as a biochemical parcel consumed by worms. I believe there is something of him that is still around, still capable of suffering because of the revelations made public by Faber & Faber."

After lunch, coffee at the large nondescript Victorian house that Tom bought four years ago in the nearby village of Iver, in Buckinghamshire. The garden, though spacious, is a bit too close for comfort to a traffic roundabout. In his book-upholstered study, he shows me his most prized possessions, among them a first edition of Hemingway's *In Our Time* and a framed letter, written in January, 1895, at the Albemarle Hotel, London, in response to an insolent request for an interview, a photograph, and a job as the addressee's literary agent:

> Sir,—I have read your letter and I see that to the brazen everything is brass.
>
> Your obedient servant,
> OSCAR WILDE

What would Tom do if he found a gold mine under his garden and never needed to work again? "Nothing spectacular. I love books—nonfiction for preference. If I had a gigantic windfall of bullion, I'd take a six-month sabbatical, pluck out of my shelves the two or three hundred books I haven't opened, and just read. The secret of happiness is inconspicuous consumption." For such a wealthy writer, he leads a comparatively simple life. He employed his first secretary only a year ago ("I got the idea from Harold Pinter") and knows little about his financial affairs, which are handled by his brother, a professional accountant.

Thence to Oxford, an hour's drive away, and the back quad of New College, where Freddie Ayer, scholastically gowned, gives us sherry in his rooms. A busy, bright-eyed man, short of stature and formidably alert, he tells me that C. S. Lewis, the great critic, novelist, and Christian apologist, described him after their first meeting as "a cross between a rodent and a firefly." He shares Tom's passion for cricket. "I

used to captain the New College Senior Common Room
XI," he says proudly. "The first time I played for the team,
I was fifty-three years old and I scored seventy-five"—a highly
respectable total. We then pass through the ritual stages
of an Oxford banquet.

Phase I: We meet the Warden of the College at his
lodgings, where the other dons and their guests are assembled,
making about forty in all. More sherry is consumed, with
champagne as the alternative option. "My taste in theatre
is mainly classical," Freddie says, adding that the twentieth-
century playwrights he most admires are Pirandello, Coward,
Maugham, and Sartre. "I vastly prefer Sartre's plays to his
philosophy. Existentialism works much better in the theatre
than in theory."

Phase II: We march in procession to take our place at
High Table, set on a dais overlooking hundreds of already
seated undergraduates. Tom and I sit on either side of
Freddie. Food forgettable; wines exceptional (hock, Burgundy, Sauternes). "Tom is the only living dramatist whose
work I would go to see just because he wrote it," Freddie
says. "There was a time when I would have said the same
about John Osborne, but now—well, let's say I would wait
to be taken by other people. With John, the rhetoric runs
away with the context. Tom plays with words and makes
them dance. John uses them as a sledgehammer."

Phase III: We move on to a panelled, candlelit chamber
and are seated at tables where port, Madeira, and Moselle
are circulated. Tom tells me a story of how he attended a
performance of *Travesties*, at the Aldwych Theatre, in
London, in order to be introduced to the proposed French
translator of the play. In the intermission, he presented himself at the manager's office, where a group of people were
sipping drinks. Before long, they were joined by a foreign-
looking stranger with flaring nostrils. Taking the newcomer
into a corner, Tom embarked on a detailed explanation of
the major linguistic problems posed by the text. The man
seemed a little perplexed, but he nodded politely, and Tom

pushed ahead for fully five minutes. Suddenly, a thought shot through his mind: What an odd coincidence that I should have a French translator who looks exactly like Rudolf Nureyev. At that moment, there was a knock on the door, and in came a little man in a beret, smoking a Gauloise. . . .

Phase IV: We end up in a common room for coffee and/or brandy. Here Tom amazes me. Either he has put himself through a refresher course (which is by no means impossible) or he is even cleverer than I suspected. He shows himself splendidly equipped to hold his own with Freddie and his colleagues in philosophical debate. With scintillating skill, he defends such theses as the following: (a) that Wagner's music is not as good as it sounds, and (b) that there are *fewer* things in heaven and earth than are dreamed of in philosophy. I am also impressed by his ability, under whatever pressure, to quote Bertrand Russell verbatim, especially after five hours of steady alcoholic intake. At one point, I interject a tentative reference to Eastern philosophies, but Freddie pooh-poohs them with Hegelian vehemence, dismissing Taoism, Confucianism, Hinduism, and Buddhism in a single barking laugh. "They have some psychological interest, but nothing more than that," he adds. "For the most part, they're devices for reconciling people to a perfectly dreadful earthly life. I believe there were one or two seventh-century Indians who contributed a few ideas to mathematics. But that's about all." I expect Tom would agree.

By 1972, the year of *Jumpers*, the voice of Vaclav Havel had been efficiently stifled. The ban on Czech productions of his work had remained in operation since 1969. Censorship had returned to the press and the broadcasting stations as well as to the theatre and the cinema; and in January, 1969, Gustav Husak (Dubcek's successor as Communist Party Secretary) made an ominous speech in which he said that the time had come to "strengthen internal discipline." He issued a strong warning to those who held "private meetings in their

apartments for inventing campaigns" against the regime.
Havel and Jan Nemec, the film director, at once sent a
courageous telegram to President Ludvik Svoboda, protesting
against Husak's threats and predicting (with melancholy
accuracy) that the next step would be police interrogations
and arrests. Later in 1969, Havel received an American
foundation grant that would enable him to spend a year
in the United States. The Czech government responded by
confiscating his passport. Productions of his plays outside
Czechoslovakia had been effectively forbidden, because the
state literary agency, through which all foreign contracts
had to be negotiated, refused to handle Havel's work, on the
ground that it gave a distorted picture of Czechoslovakian
life. This meant that thenceforward there was no officially
sanctioned way for anything by Havel to be performed anywhere in the world. The authorities, however, were far from
satisfied. What irked them was that they could drum up no
evidence on which to bring him to court. He had engaged
in no antistate activities, and nothing in his plays could be
construed as seditious. They recognized in him a stubborn
naysayer, a noncollaborator; but dumb insolence was not a
criminal offense. One of the archetypes of Czech literature is
the hero of Jaroslav Hasek's novel *The Good Soldier
Schweik*, who drives his superior officers to distraction by
practicing passive resistance beneath a mask of pious conformity. Like many Czech dissidents before him, Havel had
learned from Schweik's example.

He continued to write. In 1971, the first draft of his latest
play, *Conspirators*, translated by Vera Blackwell, reached my
desk at the National Theatre. It is set in an unnamed country,
conceivably South American, where a corrupt dictatorship
has just been overthrown and replaced by a cautious and in-
decisive democratic government. A group of five staunch
patriots (including the chief of police and the head of the
general staff) hear rumors of a conspiracy to reinstate the
deposed tyrant, now living in exile. Fearful that the new
regime will be too weak to prevent a coup, they plan a

countercoup of their own. One of them says, "In order to preserve democracy, we shall have to seize power ourselves." Their plot necessitates the use of violence, but whenever they meet they learn that their opponents are preparing to commit acts of comparable, if not greater, ferocity. This compels them to devise even more bloodthirsty countermeasures. The process of escalation continues until we suddenly realize what is actually happening. The rumors they hear about the exiled conspirators are in fact quite accurate accounts of their own conspiracy—reported by a government spy in their midst and then fed back to them by one of their own agents in the Secret Service. In other words, as Havel put it in a letter to me, "they have been plotting to save the country from themselves." He warned me not to suppose that because the play dealt with politics it was a political play:

> I am not trying either to condemn or to defend this or that political doctrine. . . . What I am concerned with is the general problem of human behavior in contemporary society. Politics merely provided me with a convenient platform. . . . All the political arguments in the play have a certain plausibility, and in some circumstances they might even be valid. . . . The point is that one cannot be sure. For truth is not only what is said: it depends on who says it, and why. Truth is guaranteed only by the full weight of humanity behind it. Modern rationalism has led people to believe that what they call "objective truth" is a freely transferable commodity that can be appropriated by anyone. The results of this divorce between truth and human beings can be most graphically observed in politics.

I was ready to recommend the play for inclusion in the National Theatre's repertoire as a pirated, unauthorized production (thereby keeping Havel legally in the clear), but the script needed extensive revision, and the author, trapped in his homeland, could not come to London to work on it. For this reason, we decided regretfully to shelve the project.

Around this time, his German publishers (coincidentally, the same as Stoppard's) decided to thwart the Czech veto by acting as his agents in the Western world. The state literary agency retaliated by intercepting and withholding all royalties sent to Havel by Western producers of his work. As far as I know, *Conspirators* remains unrevised and unperformed.

In 1974, Havel's savings began to run out, and he took the only employment he could find—a post in a brewery at Trutnov, about eighty miles from Prague. Apart from the income it provided, he welcomed the opportunity of meeting Czech citizens who were not members of the secret police. Havel's job consisted of stacking empty beer barrels. This period of his life yielded two short plays, both of them patently autobiographical. In *Audience*, thinly disguised under the name of Ferdinand Vanek, he is summoned to an interview with the head maltster of the brewery, a chain drinker and experienced compromiser, who jovially offers him a chance to better himself. Wouldn't it be more seemly for an intellectual like him to have a post in the stock-checking department, where no manual labor would be involved? All that Vanek has to do to be thus upgraded is to submit a weekly report on his thoughts and activities, and to bring a certain actress (much admired by the maltster) to an office party. Vanek is quite happy to invite the actress, but he politely explains that he cannot see his way to informing on himself. This provokes the maltster into a self-pitying alcoholic tirade against intellectuals and their so-called principles: "The thing is, you can live on your flipping principles! But what about me? All I can expect is a kick in the pants if I so much as *mention* a principle." And so on. Vanek gravely lets the storm pass over his head. The maltster then falls into a stupor, from which, a few moments later, he briskly recovers. Having erased the confessional outburst from his memory, he starts the interview over again as if nothing had happened.

Audience is Havel's vignette of life among the workers. *Private View*, its companion piece, takes a similarly ironic look at life among the intelligentsia. Vanek/Havel is invited to dinner by a sophisticated middle-class couple who are eager to show off their newly redecorated apartment, with its stereo deck, its costly clutter of modern and antique furniture, and its crates of bourbon, picked up on a trip to the States. All this *douceur de vivre*, they point out, could be his. Why does he insist on burying himself in a brewery? If only he would stop associating with people who criticize the regime ("Communists," his hostess disdainfully calls them), he could easily get a well-paid job in a publishing house. Like the maltster, the couple feel personally affronted (and accused) by his perverse reluctance to make the few small adjustments that could gain him such shining privileges. "You're an egoist!" his hostess shrieks. "Disgusting, unfeeling, inhuman egoist! Ungrateful, stupid, bloody traitor!" But her diatribe, like the maltster's, ends as abruptly as it began, and when the curtain falls she and her husband are entertaining their guest with the very latest pop single from New York. (The two plays were broadcast on BBC radio in April, 1977. The role of Vanek was played by Harold Pinter.)

In 1974, the year Havel started stacking beer barrels, Stoppard's third major work, *Travesties*, opened at the Aldwych Theatre, presented by the Royal Shakespeare Company and directed (as *Jumpers* had been) by Peter Wood. The play had its origin in Stoppard's discovery that James Joyce, Lenin, and Tristan Tzara, the founder of Dadaism, had all lived in Zurich during the First World War—a conjunction of expatriates that made instant comic connections in his mind. In addition, he had long wanted to write a leading role for his friend John Wood, a tall aquiline actor who had a matchless capacity for delivering enormous speeches at breakneck speed with crystalline articulation. From Richard Ellmann's biography of Joyce, Stoppard learned that during his stay in Zurich Joyce had been the business manager of a semiprofessional troupe of English actors, whose inaugural production was *The Importance of*

Being Earnest. The part of Algernon Moncrieff was played
by a young man named Henry Carr, who held a minor post
at the British consulate. Carr bought a new pair of trousers
to embellish his performance, and later sued Joyce for reim-
bursement. Joyce counterclaimed that Carr owed him the
price of five tickets for the show, and, for good measure,
accused him of slander. Stoppard sought to link this story,
true but implausible, with the hypothesis, plausible but untrue, that Joyce, Tzara, and Lenin had known one another
in Zurich. He hit on the idea of filtering the action through
the faulty memory of Henry Carr in old age, a querulous
eccentric in whose mind fact and fantasy were indissolubly
blended. With Henry myopically at the wheel, Stoppard
was off to the races. Clive James said of the play in *Encounter*:

> Before John Wood was halfway through his opening
> speech I already knew that in Stoppard I had en-
> countered a writer of my generation whom I could
> admire without reserve. It is a common reaction to
> "Travesties" to say that seeing it is like drinking
> champagne. But not only did I find that the play tasted
> like champagne—I found that in drinking it I felt like
> a jockey. Jockeys drink champagne as an everyday tipple,
> since it goes to the head without thickening the waist.
> "Travesties" to me seemed not an exotic indulgence, but
> the stuff of life. Its high speed was not a challenge but
> a courtesy; its structural intricacy not a dazzling pattern
> but a perspicuous design; its fleeting touch not of a
> feather but of a fine needle.

There were many such panegyrics, not only in London but
on Broadway, where the play won Stoppard his second Tony
award. (The first had been for *Rosencrantz and Guildenstern*.) I gladly concede that the grotesque rhetorical ram-
blings of Henry Carr, whether in soliloquy or in his long
first-act confrontation with Tzara, are sublimely funny; but

at the heart of the enterprise something is sterile and arbitrary. As Ronald Hayman, a devout Stoppard fan, put it, "there is no internal dynamic." Stoppard imposes the plot of Wilde's play, itself thoroughly baroque, upon his own burlesque vision of life in wartime Zurich, which is like crossbreeding the bizarre with the bogus. Following Wilde's blueprint, he gives Carr (Algernon) and Tzara (Jack Worthing) a Cecily and a Gwendolen with whom, respectively, to fall in love; while James Joyce stands unconvincingly in for Lady Bracknell. In an interview with Hayman, Stoppard said he was particularly proud of the scene in the first act between Joyce and Tzara:

> It exists almost on three levels. On one it's Lady Bracknell quizzing Jack. Secondly, the whole thing is actually structured on [the eighth] chapter in *Ulysses*, and thirdly, it's telling the audience what Dada is, and where it comes from.

All of which is undeniable, and the well-read playgoer will happily consume such a layer cake of pastiche. But cake, as Marie Antoinette discovered too late, is no substitute for bread. To change the metaphor, the scene resembles a triple-decker bus that isn't going anywhere. What it lacks, in common with the play as a whole, is the sine qua non of theatre; namely, a narrative thrust that impels the characters, whether farcically or tragically or in any intermediate mode, toward a credible state of crisis, anxiety, or desperation. (Even the two derelicts in *Waiting for Godot*, so beloved of Stoppard, are in a plight that most people would consider desperate.) In *Rosencrantz and Guildenstern*, *Inspector Hound*, and *Jumpers*, acts of homicide are committed—acts insuring that a certain amount of pressure, however factitious, is exerted on the characters. They are obviously in trouble; they may be killed, or, at least, be accused of killing. Trying, as Stoppard does in *Travesties*, to make a play without the magic ingredient of pressure toward desperation is—to lift a phrase from *Jumpers*—"tantamount to constructing a Gothic arch out of junket."

The opening speech, for instance, is made up of words that Tristan Tzara has silently cut out of an unidentified newspaper and drawn from a hat. He arranges them at random, and recites them in the form of a limerick. It concludes:

Ill raced alas whispers kill later nut east.
Noon avuncular ill day Clara.

To French-speaking members of the audience, the lines sound roughly the same as:

Il reste à la Suisse parce qu'il est un artiste.
"Nous n'avons que l'art," il déclara.

Which means, roughly Englished:

He lives in Switzerland because he is an artist.
"We have only art," he declared.

No translation or explanation, however, is offered in the text. Nonspeakers of French are thus left in outer darkness, while French-speakers who have not read the published version are unaware that what they have just heard is a linguistic joke. The result is that nobody laughs. This seems to me unadulterated junket.

As for the arbitrary element in the play, I once asked Stoppard what he would have done if Joyce's company of actors had chosen to present Maxim Gorky's *The Lower Depths* instead of Wilde's comedy. He breezily replied that he would probably have based his plot on Gorky. I have since fed into his mind what I regard as a perfectly corking scenario. During the Second World War, Arnold Schönberg, Swami Prabhavananda, and W. C. Fields were simultaneously

working in Hollywood. Cast that trio in *The Lower Depths*,
and who knows what monument of junket you might come
up with?

The hard polemic purpose of *Travesties* is to argue that art
must be independent of the world of politics. Carr says to
Tzara, "My dear Tristan, to be an artist *at all* is like living
in Switzerland during a world war." Tzara is the target for
Stoppard's loathing of the avant-garde. He is made to describe himself as "the natural enemy of bourgeois art" (which
Stoppard cherishes) and as "the natural ally of the political
left" (which Stoppard abhors). By lending his support to
the antibourgeois forces, Tzara has pledged himself to the
destruction of art. At one point, he rounds on Joyce and says:

> Your art has failed. You've turned literature into a
> religion and it's as dead as all the rest, it's an overripe
> corpse and you're cutting fancy figures at the wake. It's
> too late for geniuses!

What's needed, the zealous Dadaist goes on, is vandalism
and desecration. Having set up Tzara in the bowling alley,
Stoppard proceeds to knock him down with a speech by
Joyce, which was not in the original script (it was suggested
by the director) but which Stoppard now regards as "the
most important . . . in the play." Joyce begins by dismissing
Tzara as "an overexcited little man, with a need for self-
expression far beyond the scope of your natural gifts." This,
he says, is not discreditable, but it does not make him an
artist: "An artist is the magician put among men to gratify
—capriciously—their urge for immortality." If the Trojan
War had gone unrecorded in poetry, it would be forgotten by
history. It is the artists who have enriched us with its legends
—above all, with the tale of "Ulysses, the wanderer, the most
human, the most complete of all heroes." He continues,
"It is a theme so overwhelming that I am almost afraid to
treat it. And yet I with my Dublin Odyssey will double that

immortality, yes by God *there's* a corpse that will dance for some time yet and *leave the world precisely as it finds it.*"

So much for any pretensions that art might have to change, challenge, or criticize the world, or to modify, however marginally, our view of it. For that road can lead only to revolution, and revolution will mean the end of free speech, which is defined by Lenin, later in the play, as speech that is *"free from bourgeois anarchist individualism."* Stoppard's idol—the artist for art's sake, far above the squalid temptations of politics—is, unequivocally, Joyce. The first act ends with Henry Carr recounting a dream in which he asked Joyce what he did in the Great War. " 'I wrote *Ulysses,*' he said. 'What did you do?' "

The implication of all this—that Joyce was an apolitical dweller in an ivory tower—is, unfortunately, untrue. He was a professed socialist. And this is where Stoppard's annexation of the right to alter history in the cause of art begins to try one's patience. (A minor symptom of the same sin occurs when Carr says that Oscar Wilde was "indifferent to politics" —a statement that will come as a surprise to readers of Wilde's propagandist handbook *The Soul of Man under Socialism.*) In a recent essay in the *New York Review of Books,* Richard Ellmann has pointed out that Joyce's library in Trieste was full of works by leftist authors; that the culmination of his political hopes was the foundation of the Irish Free State; and that Leopold Bloom, in *Ulysses,* is a left-winger of long standing who annoys his wife by informing her that Christ was the first socialist. Moreover, Ellmann quotes a speech from the quasi-autobiographical first draft of A *Portrait of the Artist* in which Joyce addresses the people of the future with oratorical fervor:

> Man and woman, out of you comes the nation that is to come, the lightening of your masses in travail, the competitive order is arrayed against itself, the aristocracies are supplanted, and amid the general paralysis of an insane society, *the confederate will* issues in action.

The phrase I've italicized can only mean, as Ellmann says, "the will of like-minded revolutionaries." It is all very well for Stoppard to claim that he has mingled "scenes which are self-evidently documentary . . . with others which are just as evidently fantastical." The trouble with his portrait of Joyce is that it is neither one thing nor the other, neither pure fantasy nor pure documentary, but is simply based on a false premise. When matters of high importance are being debated, it is not pedantic to object that the author has failed to do his homework.

The second act of *Travesties* is dominated by Lenin. Stoppard quotes him fairly and at length but cannot fit him into the stylistic framework of the play. Somerset Maugham once said that sincerity in society was like an iron girder in a house of cards. Lenin is the girder that topples *Travesties*. Stoppard fleetingly considered making him the equivalent of Miss Prism, the governess in *The Importance*—"but that," he wisely concluded, "would have killed the play because of the trivialization." On the other hand, he did think it would be funny to start Act II with a pretty girl (Cecily) delivering a lecture on Lenin. "And indeed it *was* funny," he told an interviewer, "except that I was the only person laughing." (I wonder, incidentally, what he found so comic about the idea of a pretty girl taking Lenin seriously.) At all events, the lecture stayed in, funny or not, together with the ensuing scenes, which deal with Lenin and his plans for revolution. Too frail a bark to bear such weighty cargo, the play slowly capsizes and sinks.

A footnote from Derek Marlowe: "With Tom, words always precede thoughts. Phrases come first, ideas later. The Stoppard you find in *Travesties* doesn't sound any older than the Stoppard of *Rosencrantz and Guildenstern*. You'd think that nothing had happened to him in the intervening seven years. But, by God, a great deal has."

After *Travesties*, a literary circus of a play in which historical figures jumped through hoops at the flick of Stoppard's

whim, it was clear that he had spent long enough in the
library. The time had come to turn his attention to events
in the outside world. Not unexpectedly, the field he chose to
explore was the treatment of political dissidents in Eastern
Europe and the Soviet Union. First, however, he had to
fulfill an obligation to Ed Berman. Berman is an expatriate
American, bursting with bearded enthusiasm, who came to
London in 1968 and set up a cooperative organization called
Inter-Action, which presents plays in schools, remand
homes, youth clubs, mental hospitals, community centers,
and the streets. Inter-Action also runs a thriving farm in the
dingy heart of a London suburb and launched the Almost
Free Theatre, in Soho, where the price of admission is whatever you think the show will be worth. Berman produced
the world premiere of two one-acters by Stoppard (*After
Magritte*, in 1970, and *Dogg's Our Pet*, the following year),
and not long afterward Stoppard, learning that Berman had
applied for British citizenship, promised to give him a new
play if the application was successful. It was, and *Dirty Linen*,
Stoppard's deadpan farce about sexual misconduct in the
House of Commons, opened at the Almost Free Theatre in
April, 1976. It was an instant hit. The Czech émigré had
done honor to his American counterpart, welcoming him to
membership in the Western European club.

Simple chronology may be the best way to set out the
convergence that subsequently developed between the lives,
and careers, of Stoppard and Vaclav Havel.

August, 1976: Stoppard addresses a rally in Trafalgar
Square sponsored by the Committee Against Psychiatric
Abuse, from which he joins a march to the Soviet Embassy.
There he attempts to deliver a petition denouncing the use
of mental homes as punishment camps for Russian dissidents.
"The chap at the door wouldn't accept it," he told me after-
ward, "so we all went home."

October 5, 1976: Havel celebrates his fortieth birthday at
the converted farmhouse, ninety miles from Prague, where

he and his wife live. The next day, he is officially ordered to quit the place, on the ground, patently false, that it is unfit for human habitation.

January 11, 1977: *Dirty Linen* opens on Broadway, to generally favorable reviews. Walter Kerr, in his Sunday column in the *New York Times*, sounds one of the few discordant notes:

> Intellectually restless as a hummingbird, and just as incapable of lighting anywhere, the playwright has a gift for making the randomness of his flights funny. . . . Busy as Mr. Stoppard's mind is, it is also lazy; he will settle for the first thing that pops into his head. . . . Wide-ranging as his antic interests are, delightful as his impish mismatches can occasionally be, his management of them is essentially slovenly.

One speech that gets an unfailing ovation, however, is the following tribute to the American people, paid by a senior British civil servant:

> They don't stand on ceremony. . . . They make no distinction about a man's background, his parentage, his education. They say what they mean, and there is a vivid muscularity about the way they say it. . . . They are always the first to put their hands in their pockets. They press you to visit them in their own home the moment they meet you, and are irrepressibly good-humoured, ambitious and brimming with self-confidence in any company. Apart from all that I've got nothing against them.

On the thirteenth of the month, Stoppard flies from New York to the West Coast, where he is to undergo a sort of Southern California apotheosis. At the Mark Taper Forum, which is the fountainhead of theatrical activity in Los Angeles, *Travesties* and *The Importance of Being Earnest* are being staged in repertory for the first time. *Inspector*

Hound is about to open at a new theatre in Beverly Hills. And the University of California at Santa Barbara is holding "a Tom Stoppard Festival, during which I will be carried through the streets and pelted with saffron rice," Stoppard has told me in a letter, adding, "That is if I haven't gone out of fashion by then." I hasten to southern California. Stoppard, whisked from the airport to a press conference at the Mark Taper, where I join him, fields every question with effortless charm. For example, "I suspect I am getting more serious than I was, though with a redeeming streak of frivolity." And "We get our moral sensibility from art. When we have a purely technological society, it will be time for mass suicide." What American playwrights does he admire? Sam Shepard, for one; and Edward Albee, "especially for *The Zoo Story* and *A Delicate Balance*. But my favorite American play is *The Front Page*—though I might have to admit, if extremely pressed, that it wasn't *quite* as fine as *Long Day's Journey into Night*."

January 14, 1977: Vaclav Havel is arrested in Prague and thrown into jail. The real, though unacknowledged, reason for his imprisonment is that he is one of three designated spokesmen for a document called Charter 77, signed by over three hundred leading Czech writers and intellectuals, which urges the government to carry out its promises, made in the Helsinki accords of 1975, to respect human rights, especially those relating to free speech.

On the same day, leaving Los Angeles at dawn, I drive Stoppard to the Santa Barbara campus, which is preposterously pretty, palm-fringed, and moistened by ocean breakers. A silk scarf is knotted round his neck, and he wears flashy cowboy boots. We are met by Dr. Homer Swander, professor of English. A bronzed, gray-haired fan, he proudly informs Stoppard that no fewer than four of his plays will be presented at the university within the next week. In addition, there will be mass excursions to L.A. to see *Inspector Hound, The Importance*, and *Travesties*. During the morning, Tom discusses his work with a class of drama students. "I'm a very conventional artist," he says when someone quizzes him about Dadaism. "I have no sympathy at all with Tristan Tzara. The trouble with modern art, from my point of view, is that there's nothing left to parody."

A girl asks him, "Which of your plays do you think will be performed in fifty years' time?"

He replies, "There is no way I can answer that question without sounding arrogant to the point of mania or modest to the point of nausea."

Lunch with the top brass of the faculty is followed by a tour of the campus. The Mark Taper Forum has paid Tom's round-trip air fare from New York; a thousand dollars is his reward for spending the day at Santa Barbara. His lecture that evening fills a nine-hundred-seat auditorium to over-flowing. Dr. Swander introduces him as an author in whom Santa Barbara has long taken a proprietary interest. (This is his second visit to the place in two years.) "We claim him as our own," Dr. Swander declares, to applause, "and I personally acclaim him as the most Shakespearean writer in English drama since Webster."

Stoppard lopes into sight, detaches the microphone from its stand to gain mobility, and lights a cigarette. "I've been brought ten thousand miles to talk to you about theatre," he says, "which I find only slightly more plausible than coming here on a surfing scholarship." Solid laughter. "I should explain that my technique when lecturing is to free-associate within an infinite regression of parentheses. Also, it's only fair to confess that what you are about to hear is in the nature of an ego trip." To illustrate the problems of dramatic composition, he has brought along two dozen drafts of the blast of invective that Tzara launches against Joyce in *Travesties*. He reads them out, from the first attempt, which begins, "You blarney-arsed bog-eating Irish pig," to the final version, which starts, "By God, you supercilious streak of

Irish puke!" What isn't commonly understood, he adds, is
that "all this takes *weeks.*" He paces for a while, and then
notices a heavy glass ashtray that has been thoughtfully
placed on a table in front of him. "Writing a play," he continues, "is like smashing that ashtray, filming it in slow
motion, and then running the film in reverse, so that the
fragments of rubble appear to fly together. You start—or at
least *I* start—with the rubble."

Strolling back and forth across the stage, meditatively
puffing on his cigarette, he says, "Whenever I talk to intelligent students about my work, I feel nervous, as if I were
going through customs. 'Anything to declare, sir?' 'Not really,
just two chaps sitting in a castle at Elsinore, playing games.
That's all.' 'Then let's have a look in your suitcase, if you
don't mind, sir.' And, sure enough, under the first layer of
shirts there's a pound of hash and fifty watches and all kinds
of exotic contraband. 'How do you explain this, sir?' 'I'm
sorry, Officer, I admit it's there, but I honestly can't remember packing it.' " He says he has addressed only one American
campus audience apart from the present assembly; that was
at Notre Dame, in 1971, and the occasion did not get off to
an auspicious start. "I began my talk by saying that I had not
written my plays for purposes of discussion," he recalls in
Santa Barbara. "At once, I felt a ripple of panic run through
the hall. I suddenly realized why. To everyone present, *discussion was the whole point of drama.* That was why the
faculty had been endowed—that was why all those buildings
had been put up! I had undermined the entire reason for their
existence."

There are questions from the floor.

> Q.: May I say, Mr. Stoppard, that I think you are
> less slick this time than you were two years ago?
> STOPPARD: Oh, good. Or—I'm sorry. Depending on
> your point of view.
> Q.: Why don't you try directing your own work? Or
> acting in it?

STOPPARD: Look, I spend only about three and a half percent of my life writing plays. I'm trying very hard to build it up to four and a half percent. That's all I can handle at the moment.

(Tom's modesty is a form of egoism. It is as if he were saying, "See how self-deprecating I can be and still be self-assertive.")

His act has a strong finish. For an hour and a half, he says, he has shared his thoughts with us and answered many of our questions. But what is the real dialogue that goes on between the artist and his audience? By way of reply, he holds the microphone close to his mouth and speaks eight lines by the English poet Christopher Logue:

> Come to the edge.
>   We might fall.
> Come to the edge.
>   It's too high!
> **COME TO THE EDGE!**
>   And they came
> and he pushed
>   and they flew.

A short silence. Then a surge of applause. In imagination, these young people are all flying.

February 11, 1977: Stoppard has an article in the *New York Times* about the new wave of repression in Prague. It starts:

> Connoisseurs of totalitarian double-think will have noted that Charter 77, the Czechoslovak document which calls attention to the absence in that country of various human rights beginning with the right of free expression, has been refused publication inside Czechoslovakia on the grounds that it is a wicked slander.

Of the three leading spokesmen for Charter 77, two were merely interrogated and released—Jiri Hajek, who had been

Foreign Minister under Alexander Dubcek in 1968, and Jan Patocka, an internationally respected philosopher. (Patocka, however, was later rearrested, and, after further questioning, suffered a heart attack and died in hospital.) Havel alone was charged under the subversion laws, which carry a maximum sentence of ten years. "Clearly," Stoppard says, "the regime had decided, finally and after years of persecution and harassment, to put the lid on Vaclav Havel."

February 27, 1977: Stoppard travels to Moscow with a representative of Amnesty International and meets a number of the victimized Soviet nonconformists, in support of whom he writes a piece for the London *Sunday Times*.

May 20, 1977: After four months' imprisonment in a cell seven feet by twelve, which he shared with a burglar, Havel is released. The subversion indictment is dropped, but he must still face trial on a lesser charge, of damaging the name of the state abroad, for which the maximum prison term is three years. He agrees not to make "any public political statements" while this new case is *sub judice*. The state attempts to make it a condition of his release that he resign his position as spokesman for Charter 77. He rejects the offer. Once outside the prison gates, however, he unilaterally announces that, although he remains an impenitent supporter of Charter 77, he will relinquish the job of spokesman until his case has been settled in court. He returns, together with his wife, to the farmhouse from which they were evicted the previous fall. (In October, when Havel's case came up for trial, he received a fourteen-month suspended sentence.)

June 18, 1977: By now, Stoppard has recognized in Havel his mirror image—a Czech artist who has undergone the pressures that Stoppard escaped when his parents took him into exile. After thirty-eight years' absence (and two weeks before his fortieth birthday), Stoppard goes back to his native land. He flies to Prague, then drives ninety miles north to Havel's home, where he meets his *Doppelgänger* for the first time. They spend five or six hours together, conversing

mainly in English. Stoppard tells me later that some of the
Marxist signatories of Charter 77 regard Havel primarily as
a martyr with celebrity value, and didn't want him as their
spokesman in the first place. "But they didn't go to jail,"
Stoppard adds. "He did. He is a very brave man."

Like Stoppard, Havel asks only to be allowed to work
freely, without political surveillance. But that in itself is a
political demand, and the man who makes it on his own
behalf is morally bound to make it for others. Eleven years
earlier, Stoppard's hero Lord Malquist said, undoubtedly
echoing his author's views, "Since we cannot hope for order,
let us withdraw with style from the chaos." Stoppard has
moved from withdrawal to involvement. Some vestige of
liberty may yet be reclaimed from the chaos, and if Stoppard
has any hand in the salvage operation we may be sure that it
will be carried out with style.

Nothing that he writes, however, is likely to give comfort
to those who are not content to delegate the administration
of liberty to "an intellectual elite and a progressive middle
class"—the phrase, as I've already noted, that Stoppard has
recently used to indicate where his deepest loyalties lie. He
is not a standard-bearer for those who seek to create, anywhere in the world, a society like that which permitted the
Prague Spring of 1968 to put forth its prodigious, poly-
morphous flowering. For that was a socialist society, and, of
the many artists who flourished in it, Vaclav Havel was
almost alone in not being a socialist. I wonder—or, rather, I
doubt—whether Stoppard would seriously have relished living in the libertarian socialist Prague whose suppression by
the Soviets he now so eloquently deplores.

July 1, 1977: World premiere, at the Festival Hall, in
London, of Stoppard's latest piece, Every Good Boy De-
serves Favour, acted by members of the Royal Shakespeare
Company (including John Wood) and accompanied by the
London Symphony Orchestra. Its subject: the use of pseudo-
psychiatry to brainwash political dissenters in Soviet mental

hospitals. With few exceptions, the reviews are eulogistic.
Michael Billington writes in the *Guardian*:

> Stoppard brilliantly defies the theatrical law that says
> you cannot have your hand on your heart and your
> tongue in your cheek at the same time. . . . An extraor-
> dinary work in which iron is met with irony and rigidity
> with a relaxed, witty defiance.

Bernard Levin, in the London *Sunday Times*, pulls out
all the stops:

> Although this is a profoundly moral work, the argu-
> ment still undergoes the full transmutation of art, and
> is thereby utterly changed; as we emerged, it was the fire
> and glitter of the play that possessed us, while its eternal
> truth, which is that the gates of hell shall not prevail,
> was by then inextricably embedded in our hearts. . . .
> I tell you this man could write a comedy about
> Auschwitz, at which we would sit laughing helplessly
> until we cried with inextinguishable anger.

What is Stoppard's picture of happiness? Work and
domesticity, of course, enlivened by friendship and the admiration of his artistic peers. But of the thing itself—pure,
irresponsible joy—his work gives us only one glimpse. It is an
image summoned up from childhood and scarred by the
passage of years. In *Where Are They Now?*, a radio play he
wrote in 1969, a middle-aged man attends a class reunion
at his public school and recalls a single moment of unalloyed
delight. He was seven years old at the time:

> I remember walking down one of the corridors,
> trailing my finger along a raised edge along the wall,
> and I was suddenly totally happy, not elated or par-
> ticularly pleased, or anything like that—I mean I
> experienced happiness as a state of being: everywhere I
> looked, in my mind, *nothing was wrong.* You never get

that back when you grow up; it's a condition of maturity that almost *everything* is wrong, *all the time,* and happiness is a borrowed word for something else—a passing change of emphasis.

[1977]

Fifteen years
of the salto mortale
⊢JOHNNY CARSON

J ULY 14, 1977: There is a dinner party tonight at the
Beverly Hills home of Irving Lazar, doyen of agents and
agent of doyens. The host is a diminutive potentate, as bald
as a doorknob, who was likened by the late screenwriter
Harry Kurnitz to "a very expensive rubber beach toy." He
has represented many of the top-grossing movie directors
and best-selling novelists of the past four decades, not always
with their prior knowledge, since speed is of the essence in
such transactions; and Lazar's flair for fleet-footed deal-
clinching—sometimes on behalf of people who had never
met him—has earned him the nickname of Swifty. On this
occasion, at his behest and that of his wife, Mary (a sleek
and catlike sorceress, deceptively demure, who could pass for
her husband's ward), some fifty friends have gathered to
mourn the departure of Fred de Cordova, who has been the
producer of NBC's "Tonight Show" since 1970; he is about
to leave for Europe on two weeks' vacation. A flimsy pretext,
you may think, for a wingding; but, according to Beverly

Hills protocol, anyone who quits the state of California for more than a long weekend qualifies for a farewell party, unless he is going to Las Vegas or New York, each of which counts as a colonial suburb of Los Angeles. Most of the Lazars' guests tonight are theatre and/or movie people; e.g., Elizabeth Ashley, Tony Curtis, Gregory Peck, Sammy Cahn, Ray Stark, Richard Brooks. And even Fred de Cordova spent twenty years working for the Shuberts, Warner Brothers, and Universal before he moved into television. The senior media still take social precedence in the upper and elder reaches of these costly hills.

One of the rare exceptions to this role is the male late-comer who now enters, lean and dapper in an indigo blazer, white slacks, and a pale-blue open-necked shirt. Apart from two months in the late nineteen-fifties (when he replaced Tom Ewell in a Broadway comedy called *The Tunnel of Love*), Johnny Carson has never been seen on the legitimate stage; and, despite a multitude of offers, he has yet to appear in his first film. He does not, in fact, much like appearing *anywhere* except (a) in the audience at the Wimbledon tennis championships, which he and his wife recently attended, (b) at his home in Bel Air, and (c) before the NBC cameras in Burbank, which act on him like an addictive and galvanic drug. Just how the drug works is not known to science, but its effect is witnessed—ninety minutes per night, four nights per week, thirty-seven weeks per year—by upward of fourteen million viewers; and it provoked the actor Robert Blake, while he was being interviewed by Carson on the "Tonight Show" in 1976, to describe him with honest adulation as "the ace comedian top-dog talk artist of the universe." I once asked a bright young Manhattan journalist whether he could define in a single word what makes television different from theatre or cinema. "For good or ill," he said, "Carson."

This pure and archetypal product of the box shuns large parties. Invitations from the Lazars are among the few he accepts. Tonight, he arrives alone (his wife, Joanna, has stopped off in New York for a few days' shopping), greets his host with the familiar smile, cordially wry, and scans the assembly, his eyes twinkling like icicles. Hard to believe, despite the pewter-colored hair, that he is fifty-one: he holds himself like the midshipman he once was, chin well tucked in, back as straight as a poker. (Carson claims to be five feet ten and a half inches in height. His pedantic insistence on that extra half inch betokens a man who suspects he looks small.) In repose, he resembles a king-sized ventriloquist's dummy. After winking impassively at de Cordova, he threads his way across the crowded living room and out through the ceiling-high sliding windows to the deserted swimming pool. Heads discreetly turn. Even in this posh peer group, Carson has cynosure status. Arms folded, he surveys Los Angeles by night—"glittering jewel of the Southland, gossamer web of loveliness," as Abe Burrows ironically called it. A waiter brings him a soft drink. "He looks like Gatsby," a young actress whispers to me. On the face of it, this is nonsense. Fitzgerald's hero suffers from star-crossed love, his wealth has criminal origins, and he loves to give flamboyant parties. But the simile is not without elements of truth. Gatsby, like Carson, is a midwesterner, a self-made millionaire, and a habitual loner, armored against all attempts to invade his emotional privacy. "He had come a long way to this blue lawn," Fitzgerald wrote of Gatsby—as far as Carson has come to these blue pools, from which steam rises on even the warmest nights.

"He doesn't drink now." I turn to find Lazar beside me, also peeking at the man outside. He continues, "But I remember Johnny when he was a *blackout* drunk." That was before the "Tonight Show" moved from New York to Los Angeles, in 1972. "A couple of drinks was all it took. He could get very hostile."

I point out to Lazar that Carson's family tree has deep Irish roots on the maternal side. Was there something atavistic in his drinking? Or am I glibly casting him as an ethnic ("black Irish") stereotype? At all events, I now begin to see in him—still immobile by the pool—the lineaments of a magnified leprechaun.

"Like a lot of people in our business," Lazar goes on, "he's a mixture of extreme ego and extreme cowardice." In Lazar's lexicon, a coward is one who turns down starring roles suggested to him by Lazar.

Since Carson already does what nobody has ever done better, I reply, why should he risk his reputation by plunging into movies or TV specials?

Lazar concedes that I may be right. "But I'll tell you something else about him," he says, with italicized wonder. "*He's celibate.*" He means "chaste." "In his position, he could have all the girls he wants. It wouldn't be difficult. But he never cheats."

It is thirty minutes later. Carson is sitting at a table by the pool, where four or five people have joined him. He chats with impersonal affability, making no effort to dominate, charm, or amuse. I recall something that George Axelrod, the dramatist and screenwriter, once said to me about him: "Socially, he doesn't exist. The reason is that there are no television cameras in living rooms. If human beings had little red lights in the middle of their foreheads, Carson would be the greatest conversationalist on earth."

One of the guests is a girl whose hobby is numerology. Taking Carson as her subject, she works out a series of arcane sums and then offers her interpretation of his character. "You are an enormously mercurial person," she says, "who swings between very high highs and very low lows."

His eyebrows rise, the corners of his lips turn down: this is the mock-affronted expression he presents to the camera when a baby armadillo from some local zoo declines to respond to his caresses. "This girl is great," he says to de Cordova. "She makes me sound like a cross between Spring Byington and Adolf Hitler."

Before long, he departs as unobtrusively as he came.

Meeting him a few days afterward, I inquire what he thought of the party. He half grins, half winces. "Torturous?" he says.

Within a month, however, I note that he is back in the same torture chamber. Characteristically, although he is surrounded by the likes of Jack Lemmon, Roger Vadim, Michael Caine, James Stewart, and Gene Kelly, he spends most of the evening locked in NBC shoptalk with Fred de Cordova. De Cordova has just returned from his European safari, which has taken him through four countries in half as many weeks. The high point of the trip, de Cordova tells me, was a visit to Munich, where his old friend Billy Wilder was making a film. This brings to mind a recent conversation I had with Wilder in this very living room. He is a master of acerbic put-downs who has little time for TV pseudostars, and when I mentioned the name of Carson I expected Wilder to dismiss him with a mordant one-liner. What he actually said surprised me. It evolved in the form of a speech. "By the simple law of survival, Carson is the best," he said. "He enchants the invalids and the insomniacs as well as the people who have to get up at dawn. He is the Valium and the Nembutal of a nation. No matter what kind of dead-asses are on the show, he has to make them funny and exciting. He has to be their nurse and their surgeon. He has no conceit. He does his work and he comes prepared. If he's talking to an author, he has read the book. Even his rehearsed routines sound improvised. He's the cream of middle-class elegance, yet he's not a mannequin. He has captivated the American bourgeoisie without ever offending the highbrows, and he has never said anything that wasn't liberal or progressive. Every night, in front of millions of people, he has to do the *salto mortale*"—circus parlance for an aerial somersault performed on the tightrope. "What's more"—and here Wilder leaned forward, tapping my knee for emphasis—"he does it without a net. No rewrites. No retakes. The jokes must work tonight."

Since a good deal of what follows consists of excerpts from the journal of a Carson-watcher, I feel bound to declare a financial interest, and to admit that I have derived pecuniary benefit from his activities. During the nineteen-sixties, I was twice interviewed on the "Tonight Show." For each appearance I received three hundred and twenty dollars, which was then the minimum payment authorized by AFTRA, the TV and radio performers' union. (The figure has since risen to four hundred and twenty-seven dollars.) No guest on the show, even if he or she does a solo spot in addition to just chatting, is paid more than the basement-level fee. On two vertiginous occasions, therefore, my earning power has equalled that of Frank Sinatra, who in November, 1976, occupied the hot seat on Carson's right for the first time. (A strange and revealing encounter, to which we'll return.) Actually, "hot" is a misnomer. To judge from my own experience, "glacial" would be nearer the mark. The other talk shows in which I have taken part were all saunas by comparison with Carson's. Merv Griffin is the most disarming of ego strokers; Mike Douglas runs him a close second in the ingratiation stakes; and Dick Cavett creates the illusion that *he* is *your* guest, enjoying a slightly subversive private chat. Carson, on the other hand, operates on a level of high, freewheeling, centrifugal banter that is well above the snow line. Which is not to say that he is hostile. Carson treats you with deference and genuine curiosity. But the air is chill; you are definitely on probation.

Mort Sahl, who was last seen on the "Tonight Show" in 1968, described to me not long ago what happens when a guest fails to deliver the goods. "The producer is crouching just off camera," he said, "and he holds up a card that says, 'Go to commercial.' So Carson goes to a commercial, and the whole team rushes up to his desk to discuss what went wrong. It's like a pit stop at Le Mans. Then the next guest comes in, and—I promise you this is true—she's a girl who says straight out that she's a practicing lesbian. The card goes up again, only this time it means, 'Come in at once,

your right rear wheel is on fire.' So we go to another commercial. . . ." Sahl is one of the few performers who is willing
to be quoted in dispraise of Carson. Except for a handful of
really big names, people in show business need Carson more
than he needs them; they hate to jeopardize their chance of
appearing on the program that pays greater dividends in
publicity than any other. "Carson's assumption is that the
audience is dumb, so you mustn't do difficult things," Sahl
continued. "He never takes serious risks. His staff will only
book people who'll make him look artistically potent. They
won't give him anyone who'll take him for fifteen rounds.
The whole operation has got lazy."

When an interviewer from *Playboy* asked Robert Blake
whether he enjoyed doing the "Tonight Show," he gave a
vivid account of how it feels to face Carson. He began by
confessing that "there's a certain enjoyment in facing death,
periodically." He went on:

> There's no experience I can describe to you that
> would compare with doin' the "Tonight Show" when
> *he's* on it. It is so wired, and so hyped, and so up. It's
> like Broadway on opening night. There's nothing
> casual about it. And it's not a talk show. It's some other
> kind of show. I mean, he has such energy, you got like
> six minutes to do your thing. . . . And you better be
> good. Or they'll go to the commercial after two minutes.
> . . . They are highly professional, highly successful,
> highly dedicated people. . . . The producer, all the
> *federales* are sittin' like six feet away from that couch.
> And they're right on top of you, man, just watchin' ya.
> And when they go to a break, they get on the phone.
> They talk upstairs, they talk to—Christ, who knows?
> They talk all over the place about how this person's
> going over, how that person's going over. They whisper
> in John's ear. John gets on the phone and he talks. And
> you're sittin' there watchin', thinkin', What, are they
> gonna hang somebody? . . . And then the camera
> comes back again. And John will ask you somethin' else
> or he'll say, "Our next guest is . . ."

Carson's office suite at Burbank is above the studio in which, between 5:30 and 7 P.M., the show is taped. Except for his secretary, the rest of the production team occupies a crowded bungalow more than two hundred yards away, outside the main building. "In the past couple of months," a receptionist in the bungalow said to me not long ago, "I've seen Mr. Carson in here just once." Thus the king keeps his distance—not merely from his colleagues but from his guests, with whom he never fraternizes either before or after the taping. Or hardly ever: he may decide, if a major celebrity is on hand, to bend the rule and grant him or her the supreme privilege of prior contact. But such occasions are rare. As Orson Welles said to me, "he's the only invisible talk host." A Carson guest of long standing, Welles continued, "Once, before the show, he put his head into my dressing room and said hello. The effect was cataclysmic. The production staff behaved the way the stagehands did at the St. James's Theatre in London twenty-five years ago when Princess Margaret came backstage to visit me. They were in awe! One of Carson's people stared at me and said, 'He actually came to *see* you!'" (Gust of Wellesian laughter.) Newcomers like me are interviewed several days in advance by one of Carson's "talent coordinators," who makes a list of the subjects on which you are likely to be eloquent or funny. This list is in Carson's head as you plunge through the rainbow-hued curtains, take a sharp right turn, and just avoid tripping over the cunningly placed step that leads up to the desk where you meet, for the first time, your host, interrogator, and judge. The studio is his native habitat. Like a character in a Harold Pinter play, or any living creature in a Robert Ardrey book, you have invaded his territory. Once you are on Carson's turf, the onus is on you to demonstrate your right to stay there; if you fail, you will decorously get the boot. You feel like the tourist who on entering the Uffizi Gallery, in Florence, was greeted by a guide with the minatory remark, "Remember, Signore, that here it is not the pictures that are on trial." Other talk hosts flatter their visitors with

artificial guffaws; Carson laughs only when he is amused.
All I recall of my first exposure to the Carson ordeal is
that (a) I had come to discuss a controversial play about
Winston Churchill, (b) the act I had to follow was the TV
debut of Tiny Tim, who sang "Tip Toe Through the
Tulips," (c) Carson froze my marrow by suddenly asking my
opinion not of Churchill, but of General de Gaulle, and (d)
from that moment on, fear robbed me of saliva, so that my
lips clove to my gums, rendering coherent speech impossible.
The fault was mine, for not being the sort of person who can
rise to Carson's challenge—i.e., a professional performer.
There is abundant evidence that comedians, when they are
spurred by Carson, take off and fly as they cannot in any
other company. David Brenner, who has been a regular
Carson guest since 1971, speaks for many young entertainers
when he says, "Nowhere is where I'd be without the 'Tonight
Show.' It's a necessary ingredient. . . . TV excels in two
areas—sports and Carson. The show made my career."

October 1, 1977, marked Carson's fifteenth anniversary
as the star of a program he recently called "NBC's answer to
foreplay." For purposes of comparison, it may be noted that
Steve Allen, who was the show's host when it was launched,
in September, 1954, lasted only two years and four months.
The mercurial and thin-skinned Jack (Slugger) Paar took
over from Allen in the summer of 1957, after a six-month
interregnum during which doomed attempts were made to
turn the "Tonight Show" into a nocturnal TV magazine,
held together by live contributions from journalists in New
York, Chicago, and Los Angeles. Paar's tenure of office seems
in retrospect longer than it was, perhaps because of the
emotional outbursts that kept his name constantly in the
headlines; it actually ended after four years and eight months.
On March 29, 1962, having resigned for positively the last
time, he took his final bow on the program, his face a
cascade of tears. "*Après le déluge, moi*" is the thought that
should have passed through Carson's mind, though there is

no evidence that it did. He was then in his fifth years as m.c. of "Who Do You Trust?" an ABC quiz show that had become, largely because of his verbal dexterity, the hottest item on daytime television. A few months before Paar's farewell, Carson had turned down a firm offer from NBC to replace its top banana. The gulf between chatting with unknown contestants for half an hour every afternoon and matching wits with celebrities for what was then an hour and forty-five minutes every night seemed unnervingly wide, and he doubted his ability to bridge it. However, when the job had been rejected by a number of possible candidates— among them Bob Newhart, Jackie Gleason, Joey Bishop, and Groucho Marx—either because they wanted too much money or because they were chary of following Paar, NBC came back in desperation to Carson. This time, he asked for two weeks to consider the proposition. Coolly, he weighed the size of his talent against the size of his ambition, decided that the scales approximately balanced, and told NBC that his answer was yes. The only snag was that his contract with ABC did not run out until September. Undismayed, NBC agreed to keep the "Tonight Show" supplied with guest hosts (they included Merv Griffin, Mort Sahl, and Groucho) throughout the summer. On October 1, 1962, Carson took command. His announcer and second banana, transplanted from "Who Do You Trust?" was Ed McMahon, who was already in great demand as the owner of the most robust and contagious laugh in television. The guests were Rudy Vallee, Tony Bennett, Mel Brooks (then a mere comedy writer, though he nowadays insists that he gave a dazzling impersonation of Fred Astaire on that October evening), and Joan Crawford.

Any qualms that NBC may have had about its new acquisition were soon allayed. Star performers lined up to appear with Carson. Even his fellow comedians, a notoriously paranoid species, found that working with him was a stimulus rather than a threat. "He loves it when you score," Woody Allen said, "and he's witty enough to score himself."

Mel Brooks has explained to me, "From the word go, Carson could tell when you'd hit comic gold, and he'd help you to mine it. He always knew pay dirt when he saw it. The guys on other talk shows didn't." There were one or two dissenters. Jackie Mason enjoyed his first session with Carson but reported that during his second appearance he was treated with "undisguised alienation and contempt," and went on to say, "I'd never go back again, even if he asked me." The press reaction to Carson was enthusiastic, except for a blast of puritanism from John Horn of the *Herald Tribune*, who wrote of Carson, "He exhibits all the charm of a snickering small boy scribbling graffiti on a public wall." He added, in one of those phrases that return to haunt critics in their declining years, that Carson had "no apparent gift for the performing arts."

With the public, Carson's triumph was immediate and nonpareil. Under the Paar regime, the show had very seldom been seen by more than seven and a half million viewers. (One such occasion was March 7, 1960, when the unruly star came back to his post after walking out in a fit of pique, brought on by the network's decision to delete a mildly scatological joke and protracted for several well-publicized weeks.) Under Carson, the program *averaged* seven million four hundred and fifty-eight thousand viewers per night during its first six months. The comparable figure for the same period in 1971–72 was eleven million four hundred and forty-one thousand, and it is currently being seen by seventeen million three hundred thousand. Over fifteen years, therefore, Carson has more than doubled his audience—a feat that, in its blend of staying power and mounting popularity, is without precedent in the history of television. (Between April and September, the numbers dip, but this reflects a seasonal pattern by which all TV shows are affected. A top NBC executive explained to me, with heartless candor, "People who can afford vacations go away in the summer. It's only the poor people who watch us all the year round.") By network standards, the ultimate test is not so much the size of the audience as the share it represents of the total viewing public in the show's time slot. Here, after some early ups and downs, the Carson trend has been consistently upward; for example, from twenty-eight percent in the third quarter of 1976 to thirty percent in the second quarter of 1977. Moreover, his percentage seems to rise with the temperature; for example, in the four weeks that ended on July 15, 1977—a period during which guest hosts frequently stood in for Carson, whose absence from the show normally cuts the audience by about one-sixth—NBC chalked up thirty-two percent of the late-night viewers, against twenty-four percent registered by CBS and twenty-three percent by ABC. These, of course, are national figures. The happiness of Fred de Cordova, as producer, is incomplete unless Carson not only leads the field nationwide but beats the combined opposition (ABC plus CBS) in the big cities, especially New York and Los Angeles. He is seldom unhappy for long. On peak nights, when Carson rakes in a percentage of fifty or more from the key urban centers, de Cordova is said to emit an unearthly glow, visible clear across the Burbank parking lot.

For his first year on the show, making five appearances per week, Carson was paid just over a hundred thousand dollars. His present contract (the latest of many), which comes into force this spring, guarantees him an annual salary of two and a half million dollars. For twenty-five weeks of the year his performances, which were long since reduced from five to four, will further dwindle, to three; and his vacation period will stay at fifteen weeks—its duration under several previous contracts. These details, which were announced by NBC last December, leave no doubt that Carson qualifies for admission to what the late Lucius Beebe called "the mink-dust-cloth set." Whether they tell the whole story is less certain. Carson's earlier agreements with NBC contained clauses that both parties were forbidden to disclose, reportedly relating to such additional rewards as large holdings in RCA stock and a million-dollar life-insurance policy at the network's expense. Concerning Carson's total earnings, I cannot do better than quote from one of his employers, who told me, months before the new contract was signed, "If someone were to say in print that Johnny takes home around four million a year, I doubt whether anyone at NBC would feel an overpowering urge to issue a statement denying it." And even this figure excludes the vast amounts he makes from appearances at resort centers—preeminently Las Vegas— and from Johnny Carson Apparel, Inc., a thriving menswear business, founded in 1970, whose products he models on the show. David Tebet, the senior vice-president of NBC, who is revered in the trade as a finder, keeper, and cosseter of talent, and is described in his publicity handout as being "solely in charge of the Johnny Carson show," said to me recently, "For the past four or five years, Johnny has made more money per annum than any other television performer ever has. And he has also made more money per *week* than anyone else—except, maybe, for a very rare case like Sinatra, where you can't be sure, because Sinatra will sell you a special through his own company and you don't know how much he's personally taking out of the deal." Despite the high cost of Carson, he remains a bargain. The network's yearly income from the show is at present between fifty and sixty million dollars. "As a money-maker," de Cordova says, "there's nothing in television close to it." In 1975, a sixty-second commercial on the program cost twenty-six thousand dollars. In 1977, that sum had risen by half.

I dwell on these statistics because they are unique in show business. Yet there is a weird disproportion between the facts and figures of Carson's success and the kind of fame he enjoys. To illustrate what I mean, let me cite a few analogies. Star tennis players are renowned in every country on earth outside China, and the same is true of top heavyweight boxers. (A probable exception in the latter category is Muhammad Ali, who must surely be known inside China as well.) At least fifty living cricketers are household names throughout the United Kingdom, the West Indies, Australia,

South Africa, India, and Pakistan. Movie stars and pop singers command international celebrity; and Kojak, Starsky, Hutch, Columbo, and dozens more are acclaimed (or, at any rate, recognized) wherever the TV programs that bear their names are bought and transmitted. Outside North America, by contrast, Johnny Carson is a nonentity: the general public has never heard of him. The reason for his obscurity is that the job at which he excels is virtually unexportable. (O. J. Simpson is a parallel case, illustrious at home and *nada* abroad; and if the empire of baseball had not reached out and annexed Japan, Reggie Jackson would be in the same plight.) The TV talk show as it is practiced by Carson is topical in subject matter and local in appeal. To watch it is like dropping in on a nightly family party, a conversational serial, full of private jokes, in which a relatively small and regularly rotated cast of characters, drawn mainly from show business, turn up to air their egos, but which has absolutely no plot. Sometimes the visitors sing. Sometimes, though less often nowadays than in the past, they are people of such worldwide distinction that their slightest hiccup is riveting. But otherwise most of what happens on the show would be incomprehensible or irrelevant to foreign audiences, even if they were English-speaking. This drives yet another nail into the coffin lid, already well-hammered down, of Marshall McLuhan's theory that TV has transformed the world into a global village. (Radio is, as it has long been, the only medium that gives us immediate access to what the rest of the planet is doing and thinking, simply because every country of any size operates a foreign-language service.) Only for such events as moon landings and Olympiads does TV provide live coverage that spans the globe. The rest of the time, it is obstinately provincial, addressing itself to a village no bigger than a nation. Carson, in his own way, is what Gertrude Stein called Ezra Pound—a village explainer.

He has spent almost all of his life confined, like his fame, to his country of origin. He served in the Navy for three years, beginning in 1943, and was shipped as far west as

Guam. Thereafter, his travels abroad indicate no overwhelming curiosity about the world outside his homeland. Apart
from brief vacations in Mexico, and a flying visit to London
in 1961, when he appeared in a TV special starring Paul
Anka, he has left the United States only on three trips: in
1975, to the ultrasmart Hotel du Cap in Antibes (at the
instigation of his wife, Joanna, who had been there before);
in 1976, to see the tennis at Wimbledon; and in 1977, when
he threw caution to the winds and went to both Wimbledon
and the Hotel du Cap. He was recognized in neither place,
except by a handful of fellow-Americans. This, of course,
was the purpose of the exercise. Carson goes to foreign parts
for the solace of anonymity. But enough is enough: he is soon
impatient to return to the cavernous Burbank Studio, where
his personality burgeons in high definition, and where he
publicly discloses as much of his private self as he has ever
revealed to anyone, except (I assume, though even here I
would not care to bet) his parents, siblings, sons, and wives.

"Johnny Carson on TV," one of his colleagues confided
to me, "is the visible eighth of an iceberg called Johnny
Carson." The remark took me back to something that Carson
said of himself ten years ago, when, in the course of a
question-and-answer session with viewers, he was asked,
"What made you a star?" He replied, "I started out in a
gaseous state, and then I cooled." Meeting him tête-à-tête is,
as we shall see later, a curious experience. In 1966, writing
for *Look*, Betty Rollin described Carson off camera as
"testy, defensive, preoccupied, withdrawn, and wondrously
inept and uncomfortable with people." Nowadays, his off-
camera manner is friendly and impeccably diplomatic. Even
so, you get the impression that you are addressing an
elaborately wired security system. If the conversation edges
toward areas in which he feels ill at ease or unwilling to
commit himself, burglar alarms are triggered off, defensive
reflexes rise around him like an invisible stockade, and you
hear the distant baying of guard dogs. In addition to his
childhood, his private life, and his income, these no-trespass-

ing zones include all subjects of political controversy, any
form of sexual behavior uncountenanced by the law, and such
matters of social concern as abortion and the legalization of
marijuana. His smile as he steers you away from forbidden
territory is genial and unfading. It is only fair to remember
that he does not pretend to be a pundit, employed to express
his own opinions; rather, he is a professional explorer of other
people's egos. In a magazine article that was published with
annotations by Carson, Fred de Cordova wrote, "He's reluctant to talk much about himself because he is essentially
a private person." To this Carson added a marginal gloss,
intended as a gag, that had an eerie ring of truth: "I will not
even talk to myself without an appointment." He has asked
all the questions and knows all the evasive, equivocal answers.
When he first signed to appear on the "Tonight Show," he
was quizzed by the press so relentlessly that he refused after
a while to submit to further interrogation. Instead, he issued
a list of replies that journalists could append to any questions
of their choice:

1. Yes, I did.
2. Not a bit of truth in that rumor.
3. Only twice in my life, both times on Saturday.
4. I can do either, but I prefer the first.
5. No. Kumquats.
6. I can't answer that question.
7. Toads and tarantulas.
8. Turkestan, Denmark, Chile, and the Komandorskie
   Islands.
9. As often as possible, but I'm not very good at it yet.
   I need much more practice.
10. It happened to some old friends of mine, and it's a
    story I'll never forget.

Extract from Carson-watching journal, January, 1976:
There is such a thing as the pleasure of the expected.
Opening routine of "Tonight Show" provides it; millions
would feel cheated if the ceremony were changed. The close

shot of Big Ed McMahon as his unctuous baritone takes off on its steeply ascending glissando "Heeeeeeeere's Johnny!" Stagehands create gap in curtain. Carson enters in his ritual Apparel, style of which is Casual Square. Typical outfit: checked sports coat with two vents, tan trousers, pale-blue shirt with neat but ungaudy tie. Not for him the blue-jeaned, open-necked, safari-jacketed Hollywood ensemble: that would be too Casual, too Californian. On the other hand, no dark suits with vests: that would be too Square, too Eastern Seaboard. Carson must reflect what de Cordova possessively calls "our bread-basket belt"—the Midwest, which bore him (on October 23, 1925, in Corning, Iowa), and which he must never bore.

On his lips as he walks toward applauding audience is the only unassuming smirk in show business. He halts and swivels to the right (upper part of body turning as rigid vertical unit, like that of man in plaster cast) to acknowledge Big Ed's traditional act of obeisance, a quasi-Hindu bow with fingertips reverently joined. Then the leftward rotation, to accept homage from Doc Severinsen—lead trumpet and musical director, hieratically clad in something skintight and ragingly vulgar—which takes more bizarrely Oriental form: the head humbly bowed while the hands orbit each other. Music stops; applause persists. In no hurry, Carson lets it ride, facially responding to every nuance of audience behavior; e.g., shouts of greeting, cries of "Hi-yo!" When the ecstasy subsides, the exordium is over, and Carson begins the monologue, or address to the faithful, which must contain (according to one of his writers) between sixteen and twenty-two sure-fire jokes.

Tone of monologue is skeptical, tongue-in-cheek, ironic. Manner: totally relaxed, hitting bull's-eyes without seeming to take aim, TV's embodiment of *Zen in the Art of Archery*. In words uttered to me by the late screenwriter Nunnally Johnson, "Carson has a delivery like a Winchester rifle." Theme: implicitly liberal, but careful to avoid the stigma of leftism. The unexpected impromptus with which he rescues himself from gags that bomb, thereby plucking triumph from disaster, are also part of the expected pleasure. "When it comes to saving a bad line, he is the master"—to quote a tribute paid in my presence by George Burns. Carson registers a gag's impact with instant, seismographical finesse. If the laugh is five percent less than he counted on, he notes the failure and reacts to it ("Did they clear the hall? Did they have a drill?") before any critic could, usually garnering a double-strength guffaw as reward. Whatever spoils a line— ambiguous phrasing, botched timing, faulty enunciation—he is the first to expose it. Nobody spots flaws in his own work more swiftly than Carson, or capitalizes on them more effectively. Query: Is this becoming a dangerous expertise? In other words, out from under how many collapsed jokes can you successfully climb?

This evening's main attraction is Don (The Enforcer) Rickles, not so much the court jester of TV as the court hit man. Carson can cope superbly with garrulous guests who tell interminable stories (whether ponderously, owing to drink or downers, or manically, owing to uppers or illicit inhalations). Instead of quickly changing the subject, as many hosts would, he slaughters the offenders with pure politesse. Often, he will give them enough rope to hang themselves, allowing them to ramble on while he affects attentive interest. Now and then, however, he will let the camera catch him in the act of half-stifling a yawn, or raising a baffled eyebrow, or aiming straight at the lens a stare of frozen, I-think-I-am-going-mad incredulity. He prevents us from being bored by making his own boredom funny—a daring feat of comic one-upmanship. The way in which he uses the camera as a silent conspirator is probably Carson's most original contribution to TV technique. There is a lens permanently trained on him alone—a private pipeline through which he transmits visual asides directly to the viewer, who thus becomes his flattered accomplice. Once, talking to me on a somewhat tattered theme, the difference between stage and screen acting, Paul Newman made a remark that seemed obvious at the time but

grows in wisdom the more I ponder it. "On the stage, you
have to seek the focus of the audience," he said. "In movies,
it's given to you by the camera." Among the marks of a star
on television, as in the cinema, is his or her ability to grasp
this truth and act on it. Seek, and you shall not find; grab,
and it shall not be given unto you. Carson learned these rules
early and is now their master practitioner.

Even the best-planned talk shows, however, run into
doldrums; e.g., the guest who suffers from incontinent
sycophancy, or whose third marriage has brought into his
life a new sense of wonder plus three gratingly cute anecdotes
about the joys of paternity, or who is a British comedian on
his first, tongue-tied trip to the States, or whose conversational
range is confined to plugging an upcoming appearance at
Lake Tahoe. On such occasions, the ideal solution is: Bring
on Rickles, king of icebreakers, whose chosen weapon is the
verbal hand grenade. Rickles is an unrivalled catalyst (though
I can already hear him roaring, "What do you mean, I'm a
catalyst? I'm a Jew!"). Squatly built, rather less bald than
Mussolini, his bulbous face running the gamut from jovial
contempt to outright nausea, he looks like an extra in a crowd
scene by Hieronymus Bosch. No one is immune from his
misanthropy; he exudes his venom at host and guests alike.
In a medium ruled by the censorious Superego, Rickles is the
unchained Id. At his best, he breaks through the bad-taste
barrier into a world of sheer outrage where no forbidden
thought goes unspoken and where everything spoken is
anarchically liberating. More deftly than anyone else, Carson
knows how to play matador to Rickles's bull, inciting him to
charge, and sometimes getting gored himself. At one point
during this program, Rickles interrupts a question from
Carson with an authentic conversation-stopper. "Your left
eye is dancing!" he bellows, leaning forward and pointing a
stubby finger. "That means you're self-conscious. Ever since
you stopped drinking, your left eye dances." Even Carson is
momentarily silenced. (I did not fully understand why

until, at a subsequent meeting, Carson told me that there
was one symptom by which he could infallibly recognize a
guest who was on the brink of collapse, whether from fear,
stimulants, or physical exhaustion. He called it "the dancing-
eyeball syndrome." A famous example from the early nineteen-sixties: Peter O'Toole appeared on the show after
forty-eight sleepless hours, spent filming and flying, and
could not utter a coherent sentence. Carson ushered him offstage during the first commercial. "The moment he sat down,
I could see his eyeballs were twitching," Carson said to me.
"I recognized the syndrome at once. He was going to bomb.")

Testimony of a Carson colleague:

My witness is Pat McCormick, who has been supplying
Carson with material on and off for eighteen years and was a
staff writer on the show from 1972 to 1977. Regarded as one
of the most inventive gagmen in the business, he has also
worked for Red Skelton, Danny Kaye, and others of note.
McCormick, at forty-seven, is a burly, diffident man with hair
of many colors: a reddish thatch on top, a gray mustache, and
patches of various intermediate tints sprouting elsewhere on
his head and face. Suitably resprayed, he might resemble a
cross between Teddy Roosevelt and Zero Mostel. I have it
on Ed McMahon's authority that McCormick takes the
occasional drink, and that he once turned up at a script
conference declaring, "I have lost my car, but I have tire
marks on my hands." He gives me his account of a typical
day on the "Tonight Show." "The writers—there are usually
five of us—arrive at the studio around 9:30 A.M.," he says.
"We've read the morning papers and the latest magazines.
Once a week, we all get together for an ideas meeting, but
most days we work separately, starting out with the monologue. I tend to specialize in fairly weird, uninhibited stuff.
Johnny enjoys that kind of thing, and I just let it pour out.
Like a line I came up with not long ago: 'If you want to
clear your system out, sit on a piece of cheese and swallow

a mouse.' Johnny finds his own ways of handling bum gags. When he's in a bad situation, I always wonder how the hell he'll get out of it, and he always surprises me."

Always? I remind McCormick of an occasion two days earlier, when a series of jokes had died like flies, and Carson had got a situation-saving laugh by remarking, "I now believe in reincarnation. Tonight's monologue is going to come back as a dog." That sounded to me like *echt* McCormick.

With a blush matching some of his hair, he admits to authorship of the line. He continues, "All the monologue material has to be on Johnny's desk by three o'clock. He makes the final selection himself. One of his rules is: Never tell three jokes running on the same subject. And, of course, he adds ideas of his own. He's a darned good comedy writer, you know."

One sometimes detects a vindictive glint in Carson's eye when a number of gags sink without risible trace, but McCormick assures me that this is all part of the act and causes no outbreaks of cold sweat among the writing team. "After the monologue," he goes on, "we work on the desk spot with Ed McMahon, which comes next in the show, or on sketches that need polishing, or on material for one of Johnny's characters."

Accustomed to thinking of Carson the host, we forget the range of Carson the actor-comedian. His current incarnations include the talkative crone Aunt Blabby (Whistler's mother on speed); the bungling turbanned clairvoyant named Carnac the Magnificent; Art Fern, described by McCormick as "the matinee-movie m.c. with patent-leather hair who'll sell *anything*"; and—a newer acquisition—Floyd Turbo, the man in the red shirt who speaks for the silent majority, rebutting liberal editorials with a vehemence perceptibly impaired by his inability to read from a TelePrompTer at more than dictation speed. Fans will recall Turbo's halting diatribe against the antigun lobby: "If God didn't want man to hunt, he wouldn't have given us plaid shirts. . . . I only kill in self-defense. What would *you* do if a rabbit pulled a knife on you? . . . Always remember: you can get more with a smile and a gun than you can with just a smile."

Everything for the evening's show must be rehearsed and ready for taping by five-thirty, apart from the central, imponderable element, on which all else depends: Carson's handling of the guests. Briefed by his aides, he knows the visitors' backgrounds, recent achievements, and immediate plans, and during the commercials he will listen to tactical suggestions from confreres like Fred de Cordova; but when the tape is running, he is the field commander, and his intuitions dictate the course of events. As he awaits his entrance cue, he is entitled to reflect, like Henry V on a more earthshaking occasion, "The day, my friends, and all things stay for me." McCormick, who now and then appears as a guest on the show, has this to say of Carson the interviewer: "He leans right in and goes with you, instead of leaning back and worrying about what the viewers are thinking. He never patronizes you or shows off at your expense. If you're getting a few pockets of laughter from the studio audience, he'll encourage you and feed you. He's an ideal straight man as well as a first-rate comedian, and that's a unique combination. Above all, there's a strand of his personality that is quite wild. He can do good bread-and-butter comedy any day of the week—like his Vegas routines or his banquet speeches— but he has this crazy streak that keeps coming through on the show, and when it does it's infectious. You feel anything could happen."

Example of Carson when the spirit of pure, eccentric play descends upon him and he obeys its bidding, wherever it may lead: During the monologue on May 11, 1977, he finds, as sometimes happens, that certain words are emerging from his mouth in slightly garbled form. He wrinkles his brow in mock alarm, shrugs, and presses on to the next sentence: "*Yetserday*, U.S. Steel announced . . ." He pauses, realizing what he has said, turns quizzically to McMahon, and observes, " 'Yesterday' is not a hard word to say." Facing the camera again, he goes on, "Yesterday—all my troubles seemed

so far away . . ." Only now he is *singing*—singing, unac-
companied, the celebrated standard by John Lennon and
Paul McCartney: "Now it looks as though they're here to
stay. Oh, I believe in yesterday." By this time, the band,
which was clearly taken by surprise, has begun to join in,
at first raggedly, but soon improvising a respectable accom-
paniment. Warming to his berserk task, Carson does not
stop until he has reached the end of the chorus. He
resumes the monologue: "Now, what was I talking about?
Oh, yes. Yesterday . . ." But no sooner has the word passed
his lips than Doc's combo, determined not to let him off the
hook, strikes up the melody again. Undaunted, Carson
plunges into the second chorus. Having completed it, he
silences the musicians with a karate chop. There is loud
applause, followed by an extended pause. Where can he go
from here? Cautiously feeling his way, he continues, "*About
twelve hours ago*, U.S. Steel announced . . ." And successfully
finishes the gag. Everyone in the studio is laughing, not so
much at the joke as the sight of Carson on the wing.
Grinning, he addresses McMahon.

> CARSON: That's what makes this job what it is.
> McMAHON: What is it?
> CARSON (*frowning, genuinely puzzled*): I don't know.

McCormick on Carson the private man: "Don't believe
those iceberg stories. Once, when I was going through a bad
divorce and feeling pretty low, I was eating alone in a
restaurant and Johnny came in with a bunch of people. I'm
not one of his intimate friends, but as soon as he saw me he
left his guests and sat with me for more than half an hour,
giving me all kinds of comfort and advice."

Further notes of a Carson-watcher (random samplings
from October and November, 1976):
Where other performers go home to relax after the show,
Carson goes to the show to relax. The studio is his den, his

living space—the equivalent in the show-business world of an exclusive salon in the world of literature. He instantly reacts to any untoward off-camera occurrence—a script inadvertently dropped, a guitar string accidentally plucked, a sneeze from a far corner of the room—as most of us would react to comparably abnormal events in the privacy of our homes. *Mutatis* very much *mutandis,* the show could be seen as a TV version of "The Conning Tower," Franklin P. Adams's famous column in the *Tribune,* which was launched in 1914 and consisted mainly of anecdotes, aphorisms, and verses contributed by F.P.A.'s friends and correspondents. "The Conning Tower," like the "Tonight Show," was a testing ground for new talents, and many of the people it introduced to the public went on to become celebrities.

October 1: Traditional two-hour retrospective to mark the fourteenth anniversary of Carson's enthronement as NBC's emperor of causerie. Choice of material is limited to the period since 1970, for, with self-destructive improvidence, the company erased all the earlier Carson tapes, including Barbra Streisand's first appearance as his guest and Judy Garland's last. Host's debonair entry is hailed with fifty-second ovation, which sounds unforced. I note the digital mannerisms (befitting one who began his career as a conjurer) that he uses to hold our attention during his patter. The right index finger is particularly active, now stabbing downward as if pressing computer buttons, now rising to flick at his ear, to tickle or scratch one side of his nose: constantly in motion, never letting our eyes wander. Thus he stresses and punctuates the gags, backed always by Big Ed's antiphonal laughter.

Well-loved bits are rerun. The portly comic Dom DeLuise attempts a feat of legerdemain in which three eggs are at risk, and carries it off without breakage. But the sight of unbroken eggs—and others on standby—provokes Carson to a spell of riot. He tosses the original trio at DeLuise, who adroitly juggles with them and throws them back; Carson retaliates with more eggs, aiming a few at McMahon for good measure. Before long, in classic slapstick style, he has expressionlessly cracked an egg over DeLuise's head and dropped another inside the front of his trousers, smashing it as it falls with a kindly pat on the belly. "You're insane!" the victim cries. "You guys are bananas!" He gives Carson the same treatment; McMahon joins in; and by the end, the floor and the three combatants are awash with what Falstaff would have called "pullet sperm." Looking back on the clip, Carson puckishly observes, "There's something about eggs. I went ape." The whole impromptu outburst would not have been funny if it had been initiated by someone like Buddy Hackett; it worked because of its incongruity with Carson's persona—that of a well-nurtured midwestern lad, playful but not vulgar. ("Even though he's over fifty," Fred de Cordova once said to me, "there's a Peck's Bad Boy quality that works for Johnny, never against him.")

 Other oddities from the program's past: Carson diving onto a mattress from a height of twenty feet; splitting a block of wood with his head on instructions from a karate champion; tangling with a sumo wrestler; cuddling a cheetah cub; permitting a tarantula to crawl up his sleeve. We also see Carson confronted by guests with peculiar skills—the bird mimic whose big items are the mallard in distress and the cry of the loon, for instance, and the obsessive specialist whose act (one of the most memorable stunts ever recorded in a single take) consists of seven thousand dominoes arranged on end in a convoluted, interwoven pattern, involving ramps and tunnels, so that the first, when it is pushed, sets off a chain reaction that fells the remaining six thousand nine hundred and ninety-nine, which spell out—among other things—the DNA symbol and Carson's name. In addition, we get the parody of "Dragnet," that triumph of alliterative tongue-twisting in which Jack Webb, investigating the theft of a school bell, sombrely elicits from Carson the information that kleptomaniac Claude Cooper copped the clean copper clappers kept in the clothes closet. Best of all are the snippets from Carson's interviews with people aged ninety and upward, whom he addresses as exact equals, with care and without condescension, never patronizing them, and never afraid to laugh when they get a sentence back to front or forget the punch line of a joke; one such encounter is with a woman of a hundred and three years, who is still a licensed driver. (Paul Morrissey, the movie director, who is watching the program with me, remarks, "Nobody else on TV treats old people with the perfect tact and affection of Carson. He must have a very loving relationship with his parents.") An NBC spokesman chips in with a resounding but meretricious statistic. The Carson show, he says, has already been seen by more than four times the population of our planet. This presumably means that one person who has watched the program a hundred times counts as a hundred people. Either that or NBC is laying claim to extraterrestrial viewers. The ratings war being what it is, anything is possible.

November 12: After days of spot announcements and years of coaxing by the network, Frank Sinatra makes his debut on the show. Received like visiting royalty, he gives the impression of swaggering even when seated. For once, the host seems uneasy, overawed, too ready to laugh. Don Rickles is hurried on unannounced to dissipate the atmosphere of obsequiousness, which he does by talking to the singer like Mafia subaltern reporting to Godfather; at least this is better than treating him as God. (I get memory flash of cable sent to me by Gore Vidal when he agreed to accept my younger daughter as godchild: "Always a godfather, never a god." For many people in entertainment business, Sinatra is both.) When conversation again falters, Rickles declares to world at large, "I'm a Jew, and he's an Italian, and *here*"—he thrusts at Carson a face contorted with distaste, like diner finding insect in soup—"*here* we have . . . *what?*" Rickles wraps up interview by saying that he truly admires Sinatra, because "he stimulates excitement, he stimulates our industry, and"—fixing Carson with glare of malign relish—"*he . . . makes . . . you . . . nervous.*"

Not long afterward, Carson had his revenge. While acting

as guest host on the show, Rickles broke the cigarette box on Carson's desk by striking it with his clenched fist when a gag fell flat. The next night, Carson returned. As soon as he sat down, he noticed the damage. "That's an heirloom," he said. "I've had it for nine years." Informed that Rickles was the culprit, he picked up the debris and rose, telling one of the cameras to follow him. (None of this was rehearsed.) He then left the "Tonight Show" studio, crossed the corridor outside, and, ignoring the red warning lights, marched into the studio opposite, where Rickles was at that moment halfway through taping the next episode of his comedy series "CPO Sharkey." Walking straight into the middle of a shot, Carson held out his splintered treasure to Rickles and sternly demanded both restitution and an apology. The Enforcer was flabbergasted, as were his supporting cast, his producer, and his director. Carson was impenitent. "I really shook him," he said to me later with quiet satisfaction. "He was speechless."

Testimony from the two NBC associates who are closest to Carson:

These are Fred de Cordova and Ed McMahon. De Cordova, who has been Carson's producer for the past seven years, talks to me in the "Tonight Show" bungalow at Burbank. He is a large, looming, beaming man with horn-rimmed glasses, an Acapulcan tan, and an engulfing handshake that is a contract in itself, complete with small print and an option for renewal on both sides. Now in his mid-sixties, he looks like a cartoon of a West Coast producer in his early fifties. His professional record, dating back to 1933, is exceptional: Ten years in theatre with the Shubert organization, followed by a decade making movies in Hollywood. Thence into TV, where he worked (directing and/or producing) with Burns and Allen, George Gobel, Jack Benny, and the Smothers Brothers. In the magazine piece he wrote which appeared with notations by Carson, he said he now had "the last great job in show business," because the Carson program was "spontaneous" and "instantaneous." He explained that it wasn't technically live, in that taping preceded transmission; nevertheless, "practically speaking, we are the only continuing live show left." (For accuracy's sake, this phrase should be amended to read, "the only continuing nationwide nighttime quasi-live talk show left, apart from Merv Griffin's.") He went on to compare the program to a ballgame, played "in front of a jammed grandstand night after night." "To me," Carson noted in the margin, "it's like a salmon going up the Columbia River." Trying to define Carson's appeal, de Cordova wrote, "He's somebody's son, somebody's husband, somebody's father. He combines them all." Which sounds very impressive until you reflect that it applies to most of the adult male population. Carson circled this passage and made it slightly narrower in scope by adding to the first sentence, "and several people's ex-husband." De Cordova's most telling point, at which no one could cavil, came later in the article. "We have no laugh track," he said. "We're naked." In an age when canned hilarity has all but usurped the viewer's right to an autonomous sense of humor, it is reassuring to read a statement like that.

On the wall behind de Cordova's desk hangs a chart showing the lineup of guests for weeks, and even months, ahead. Perennial absentees, long sought, never snared, include Elton John and Robert Redford. When de Cordova is asked why the list is so sparsely dotted with people of much intellectual firepower, he reacts with bewilderment: "That just isn't true. We've had some of the finest minds I know—Carl Sagan, Paul Ehrlich, Margaret Mead, Gore Vidal, Shana Alexander, Madalyn Murray O'Hair." This odd aggregation of names sprang from the lips of many other "Tonight Show" employees to whom I put that question, almost as if they were contractually bound to commit it to memory. Nobody, however, denied that there have been few latter-day guests with the political weight of Nelson Rockefeller, Hubert Humphrey, and John and Robert Kennedy, all of whom appeared with Carson in his earlier years. De Cordova continues, "I've heard it said that Johnny is intimidated by witty, intellectual women. Well, just who *are* these women? Apart from people like Shana, who've had a lot of TV experience, they tend to freeze on camera. We've so often been fooled by witty cocktail talkers who simply didn't transfer to television." Carson, he points out, is no numbskull; he reads extensively, with special emphasis on politics, and has more than an amateur knowledge of astronomy. Also of sports: "Ilie Nastase, Chris Evert, and Dwight Stones have all been very effective guests." But there are, he admits, certain categories of people who are unlikely to receive the summons to Burbank: "We don't have an official blacklist, but Johnny wouldn't have Linda Lovelace on the show, for example. Or anyone mixed up in a sexual scandal, like Elizabeth Ray. And no criminals, except reformed criminals—we turned down Clifford Irving, the guy who forged the Howard Hughes memoirs. Johnny prefers to look for noncelebrities who'll make human-interest stories. We subscribe to fifty-seven newspapers from small towns and cities all over the country, and that's where we find some of our best material." He goes on to say, "In the monologue, Johnny will attack malfeasance, illiberal behavior, constitutional abuses. But then compassion sets in. He was the first person to *stop* doing anti-Nixon jokes." (Ten years ago, Henry Morgan said of Carson, "He believes that justice is some kind of entity that is palpable. He talks about it as if he were talking about a chair.") Does the monologue suffer from network censorship? "The problem doesn't come up, because Johnny has an in-built sense of what his audience will take," de Cordova says. "He's the best self-editor I've ever known." This, as we shall see, was a somewhat disingenuous reply.

Lunch with the bulky, eternally clubbable McMahon in the Polo Lounge of the Beverly Hills Hotel. Born in Detroit, Big Ed is now in his midfifties, and has worked with Carson for two decades, including five years as his announcer on "Who Do You Trust?" NBC gives him eight weeks' annual vacation with full pay, and he makes a great deal of money

on the side from nightclub appearances, real-estate invest-
ments, and commercials for a variety of products, chief
among them beer and dog food. Even so, he is well aware
that, as he says to me, "the 'Tonight Show' is my staple diet,
my meat and potatoes—I'm realistic enough to know that
everything else stems from that." In 1972, when the show
moved from New York to Los Angeles, McMahon left his
wife and four children, after twenty-seven years of marriage,
to go with it. (Divorce followed soon afterward; McMahon
remarried in 1976.) He has known his place, and kept to it
without visible resentment, since 1965, when the notorious
Incident of the Insect Repellent showed him exactly where
he stood. "Johnny was demonstrating an antimosquito
spray," he says, "and just before using it he said he'd heard
that mosquitoes only went for really passionate people.
Acting on instinct, I stuck out my arm and slapped it. It
wrecked Johnny's gag, and I had to apologize to him during
the next break. That taught me never to go where he's
going. I have to get my comedy in other areas. Before the
show, I do the audience warmup, and even there I have to
avoid any topical material he might be using in the monologue."

This being a show day, McMahon eats and drinks frugally
(cold cuts and beer). Both he and Carson have drastically
reduced their alcoholic intake over the past few years. On
camera, Carson sips coffee and cream (no sugar), and Mc-
Mahon makes do with iced tea. McMahon denies the rumor
that Carson has become antisocial because of his abstinence:
"If it's a big affair, you'll maybe find him in a corner, talking
one to one, but in a small group he can be the life of the
party, doing tricks, killing everybody." One of the unauthorized biographies of Carson contains a story about a
surprise birthday party to which his second wife, Joanne,
invited all his close friends. "There were about eight people
there," an unnamed guest is quoted as saying, "and I think it
was a shock to all of us." Pooh-poohing this yarn, McMahon
counters by telling me about a surprise party he gave for

Carson in 1962: "I built it up by pretending it was being held in his honor by *TV Guide* and he really had to go. He finally gave in. I said I'd drive him down there, and he began bitching as soon as he got in the car. So I suggested stopping off at my place for a preliminary drink, and he agreed. I'd arranged for the other cars to be parked out of sight, in case he recognized them. What happened was that he walked straight into the arms of about fifty friends and relatives who'd come from all over to see him. He had tears in his eyes. That was the first time I saw him touched."

Professionally, McMahon most enjoys the tête-à-tête at Carson's desk which follows the monologue: "Sometimes he develops a real resistance to bringing out the first guest. I see something goofy in his eyes. It means that he wants us to go on rapping together, so we play back and forth, getting wilder and wilder, until maybe the guest has gone home and it's time for the first commercial."

I read to him some remarks made by the columnist Rex Reed, who described Carson as "the most over-rated amateur since Evelyn and her magic violin" and continued, "The most annoying thing about Carson is his unwillingness to swing, to trust himself or his guests. . . . He never looks at you; he's too busy (1) watching the audience to see if they are responding, and (2) searching the face of his producer for reassurance."

McMahon finds these comments inexplicable. "Johnny can get absolutely spellbound by his guests," he says. "You'll see him lean his chin on his hand and really drink them in. And as for that stuff about not swinging—did the guy ever watch him with Tony Randall or Buck Henry or Orson Bean? He's always going off into unplanned areas and uncharted places. Other people have clipboards full of questions and use them like crutches. Johnny never uses any. And he loves meeting new comics and feeding them lines, the way he did with Steve Martin and Rodney Dangerfield when hardly anyone had heard of them. Naturally, he likes to get laughs himself. That's part of the job. A few nights ago, Tony

Bennett was on the show, talking about his childhood and how his family hoped he'd achieve fabulous things when he grew up. Johnny listened for a long while and then said, quite deadpan, 'My parents wanted me to be a sniper.' Another time, he asked Fernando Lamas why he'd gone into movies, and Lamas said, 'Because it was a great way to meet broads.' I loved Johnny's comeback. He just nodded and said, 'Nietzsche couldn't have put it more succinctly.' And, of course, there are the famous ad-libs that everyone remembers, like when Mr. Universe was telling him how important it was to keep fit—'Don't forget, Mr. Carson, your body is the only home you'll ever have'—and Johnny said, 'Yes, my home *is* pretty messy. But I have a woman who comes in once a week.' " McMahon confirms my impression that Carson was daunted by Sinatra. He adds, "And he's always been a little bit overawed by Orson Welles. But there was one time when we were both nervous. I came on as a guest to plug a film I'd just made, and we had a rather edgy conversation. When the interview was over, Johnny came out from behind his desk to shake hands and revealed to the world that he had no pants on. I was so anxious to get off that I didn't even notice." How long, I ask, will Carson stay with the show? "He'll still be there in 1980," says McMahon confidently.

The year 1977, for Carson-watchers, was one in which the "Tonight Show," while retaining all its sparkle and caprice, gained not an inch in intellectual stature. It is one thing to say, as Carson often does, that he is not a professional controversialist. It is quite another to avoid controversy altogether.

February 2: Appearance of Alex Haley to talk about *Roots*. (During the previous night's monologue, Carson used a curiously barbed phrase to account for the success of ABC's televised adaptation of Haley's best-seller. "Give the people what they want," he said. "Hatred, violence, and sex." It was difficult to tell whether the gibe was aimed at the rival network or at the book itself. One wondered, too, why he thought it amusing to add, "My great-great-great-great-grandfather was a runaway comedian from Bangladesh.") In 1967, when Haley was working for *Playboy*, he conducted a lengthy interview with Carson. In the course of it, Carson attacked the CIA for hiring students to compile secret reports on campus subversives, condemned "the kind of corporate espionage and financial hanky-panky that goes on in business," supported the newly insurgent blacks in demanding "equality for all," and said, "It's ludicrous to declare that it's wrong to have sex with anyone you're not married to." Moreover, he summed up the war in Vietnam as "stupid and pointless." He seldom voiced these opinions with much vehemence on the show. Ten years later, with the war safely over, he welcomed Jane Fonda as his guest and congratulated her on having lived to see her views on Vietnam fully justified by history. With considerable tact Ms. Fonda not only resisted the temptation to address her host as Johnny-come-lately, but refrained from reminding him that when she most needed a television outlet for her ideas the doors of the "Tonight Show" studio were closed to her.

To return to February 2: Haley takes the initiative by asking Carson how far back he can trace his own roots. He replies that he knows who his grandparents were, and was personally very close to his father's parents, both of whom survived into their nineties. Of his pedigree before that, he confesses total ignorance. Haley thereupon shakes him by producing a heavy, leather-bound volume with a golden inscription on the cover: "Roots of Johnny Carson—A Tribute to a Great American Entertainer." Haley has signed the flyleaf, "With warm best wishes to you and your family from the family of Kunta Kinte." Carson is obviously stirred. "I was tremendously moved that Alex had found time to do all this research in the middle of his success," he said to me afterward, and I learned from McMahon that this was only the second occasion on which he had seen the boss tearful. Although Haley was the instigator, the work was in fact carried out by the Institute of Family Research, in Salt Lake

City. The people there first heard of the project on the evening of Saturday, January 29, when Haley called them up and told them that the finished book had to be ready for presentation to Carson in Los Angeles the following Wednesday. "That gave us two working days to do a job that would normally take us two months," a spokesman for the Institute told me. "What's more, we had to do it in absolute secrecy, without any access to the person involved." A task force of fifteen investigators toiling round the clock for forty-eight hours just managed to beat the deadline. The result of their labors—consisting of genealogical charts going back to the sixteenth century, biographical sketches of Carson's more prominent forebears, and anecdotes from the family's history —ran to more than four hundred pages. The gesture cost Haley (or his publishers) approximately five thousand dollars. Carson lent me the book, a massive quarry of data, from which I offer a few chippings:

(1) Earliest known Carson ancestor: Thomas Kellogg, on the paternal side of the family, born c. 1521 in the English village of Debdon, Essex. The first Kelloggs to cross the Atlantic were Daniel (born 1630) and his wife, Bridget, who settled in Connecticut. By the early nineteenth century, we find offshoots of the clan widely dispersed in Indiana and Nebraska, and it was Emiline, of the Nebraska Kelloggs, who married Marshall Carson, great-grandfather of Johnny. Marshall (born c. 1833) was allured by gold, and staked a profitless claim in the western part of Nebraska. Along with Emiline, he moved to Iowa where by dying in 1922 he narrowly failed to become a nonagenarian. That was the year in which his grandson Homer Loyd Carson married a girl named Ruth Hook. John William Carson (born 1925) was the second child of this union, flanked by an elder sister, Catherine, and a younger brother, Dick.

(2) On his mother's side, Carson's first authenticated forebear is Thomas Hooke, a seventh great-grandfather, who sailed from London to Maryland in 1668. Most of his maternal roots, however, lead back to Ireland, whence two of

his fifth great-grandfathers embarked for the States in the middle years of the eighteenth century.

(3) His family tree is laden with hardworking farmers. Decennial census sheets from 1840 to 1900 show Carson progenitors tilling the land in Maine, Ohio, Indiana, Nebraska, and Iowa.

(4) As far as anyone knows, Johnny and Kit Carson are no more closely related than Edward and Bonwit Teller. Johnny's background nonetheless contains two figures of some regional celebrity. One is Captain James Hook (maternal branch), who is reputed, but not proved, to have served with Washington at Valley Forge. In a private quarrel, Captain Hook lost a sliver of his ear to a man who pulled a knife on him. Being unarmed, Hook riposted by tearing off a much larger piece of his assailant's ear with his teeth. (Carson, of course, is in the business of bending people's ears, but not dentally.) The other Carson ancestor of note is Judge James Hardy (paternal branch), a whimsical but beloved dispenser of justice in midnineteenth-century Iowa.

(5) Judge Hardy's son Samuel, who died in 1933, at the age of eighty-five, was a skilled amateur violinist. Otherwise, in all the four previous centuries of the Carson family saga, there is no sign of anyone with an interest in the arts or a talent for entertainment.

February 10: Significant how many of the failed gags in Carson's monologues miss their target because they are based on the naive assumption that the studio audience has read the morning papers. One often gets the feeling that Carson is doubly insulated against reality. Events in the world outside Burbank and Bel Air impinge on him only when they have been filtered through magazines and newspapers and then subjected to a second screening by his writers and researchers. Hence his uncanny detachment, as of a man sequestered from the everyday problems with which most of us grapple. In fifteen years, barely a ripple of emotional commitment has disturbed the fishpond smoothness of his professional style. We are watching an immaculate machine. Some find the spectacle inhuman. "He looks plastic," said Dorothy Parker in 1966. On the other hand, Shana Alexander told me with genuine admiration, "He's like an astronaut, a Venusian, a visitor from another planet, someone out of 'Star Trek.' "

Two reflections on tonight's monologue. First, drawing on the latest Nielsen report, Carson informs us that during the icebound month of January the average American family watched television for seven hours and sixteen minutes per day. A fearsome statistic. No wonder they have so little time for newspapers. Second, he knocks the Senate for allowing its members' salaries to be raised to fifty-seven thousand five hundred dollars a year. The joke gives off a whiff of bad taste, coming, as it does, from a man who earns more than that every week. Whatever Carson's failings may be, they do not include a lack of chutzpah.

April 1: Nice to hear Ethel Merman on the show, blasting out "Ridin' High" as if calling the cattle home across the sands of D-flat major. But I wonder whether Carson would (or could) have done what Merv Griffin, of all people, did earlier in the evening; namely, devoted most of a ninety-minute program to a conversation with Orson Wells, which was conducted on what by talk-show standards was a respectably serious level. In 1962, when Carson took over the stewardship of the "Tonight Show," America was about to enter one of the grimmest and most divisive periods in its history, marked by the assassinations of the Kennedy brothers and Martin Luther King, the ghetto insurrections, the campus riots, the Vietnam war. Is it arguable that during this bad time Carson became the nation's chosen joker because, in Madison Avenue terms, he was guaranteed to relieve nervous strain and anxiety more swiftly and safely (ask your doctor) than any competing brand of wag? Now that the country's headaches have ceased to throb so painfully, its viewers may be ready for a more substantial diet than any that Carson, at the moment, cares to provide.

April 7: Characteristic but in no way exceptional duologue between Carson and Buck Henry, the screenwriter and occasional actor. Whenever they meet on the show, their exchanges are vagrant, ethereal, unhurried, as if they were conversing in a limbo borrowed from a play by Samuel Beckett.

CARSON: Do you believe in plastic surgery?

HENRY: Absolutely. It's important, I think, to move things about judiciously.

CARSON: They're talking about freezing people and then reviving them in hundreds of years' time.

HENRY (*nods for a while, until a thought strikes him*): But suppose you died of freezing to death? (*Pause.*) I think it would be frightening to come back.

CARSON: If you could come back as somebody else, who would it be?

HENRY (*unhesitatingly*): Miss Teenage America.

CARSON: Where do you get ideas for your work?

HENRY: Oh, everyday places. Looking through keyholes.

CARSON: Eugene O'Neill got his ideas from his family.

HENRY: I expect to get a short monograph out of mine. (*Pause.*)

CARSON: You have a strange turn of mind.

Carson brings up a newspaper story about a California woman who was recently interred, in accordance with a clause in her will, at the wheel of her Ferrari.

HENRY: Yes. It's reasonable to be married—or I may mean buried—in a Ferrari.

CARSON: How do you want to go?

HENRY (*very slowly*): Very slowly. With a jazz band playing in the background. I want to be extremely old. I want to be withered beyond recall.

CARSON: But if you lived to be a hundred and fifty, how would you kill time for the last seventy years?

HENRY (*contemplatively*): You'd read a lot. I don't know what the real fun things to do would be after a hundred and twenty. I think the normal activities that come to mind would probably cripple you.

There was also some adagio talk about quarks and their relationship to other subatomic particles, but Henry declined to expand on the subject, perhaps feeling that it might be over our heads.

May 11: Advice from Carson on longevity: "If you must smoke, don't do it orally." And, more cryptically: "You can add years to your life by wearing your pants backward."

June 15: He chats with someone who has attained longevity. Clare Ritter, an impoverished widow from Florida in her late seventies, discloses that her life's ambition is to make a trip to Egypt. In order to achieve it, she sells waste aluminum, which she collects by ransacking garbage cans.

> CARSON: How much is this trip going to cost?
> MRS. RITTER: Three thousand dollars.
> CARSON: And how much have you saved so far?
> MRS. RITTER: About half of it.

Carson volunteers to give her the rest himself. A graceful (and I am assured, unpremeditated) gesture.

July 19: Seated at the desk with McMahon, Carson says, "If you decide to ban your kids from watching TV, here's what they can do instead." He picks up a sheaf of humorous suggestions submitted by his writers, scans the first page, shows by his reaction that he finds it unfunny, and drops it on the floor. (This, like what ensues, is unplanned and impromptu.) He inspects page 2, raises his eyebrows, shows it to McMahon, drops *that* on the floor; goes on to page 3, gives McMahon a glimpse of it, whereupon both men shake their heads, and it, too, ends up on the floor. At this point, Carson starts to chuckle to himself. "How about *this*?" he says, and page 4 is tossed away, to be joined in rapid succession by a dozen, by *two* dozen more pages, falling faster and faster (the chuckle is by now uncontrollable), in a blizzard of rejection that does not stop until he has discarded every sheet of what was obviously planned as a solid five-minute comedy routine. On network TV, this is just not done. You do not throw away an expensive script in full view of a national audience unless you can ad-lib something funnier to take its place. Carson offers us nothing in exchange except what he alone can supply: the spectacle of Carson being Carson, acting on impulse, surrendering to whim, and, as ever, getting away with it. (No claim is made for the above escapade as archive material, or as anything more than a specimen of Carson in average form on an average night. I record it to illustrate how, in the right hands, pure behavior becomes pure television. Like Shakespeare's Parolles, Carson can say, "Simply the thing I am shall make me live.")

Later in this show, Albert Finney, an actor who has temporarily turned his hand to lyric-writing and his voice to singing, plugs his first LP, declaring with brooding self-satisfaction that his songs derive from "the spring well" of personal experience. The number with which he favors us constitutes more of a threat to English grammar ("What has become of you and I?") than to Charles Aznavour, who seems to be Finney's model. The last guest is Madeline Kahn, who discusses the psychological ups and downs of her career as an actress. Carson responds with a rare flash of self-revelation. "I've had a little therapy myself," he says, "to cut down the hills and get out of the valleys."

August 4: President Carter has recommended that it should not be a criminal offense to be found in possession of an ounce or less of marijuana.

> CARSON: The trouble is that nobody in our band knows what an ounce or less means.
> DOC SEVERINSEN: It means you're about out.

January 18, 1977: My first solo encounter with Carson. We are to meet at the Beverly Hills Hotel for an early luncheon in the Polo Lounge. I prepare for my date by looking back on Carson's pre-"Tonight Show" career. It is not a story of overnight success. At the time of his birth in Corning, Iowa, his father was a lineman for an electricity company. It was a peripatetic job, and the family moved with him through several other Iowa hamlets. When Johnny was eight, they settled in Norfolk, Nebraska, a town of some ten thousand, where Carson senior got a managerial post with the local light-and-power company. "When one meets Johnny's parents, one understands him," Al Capp has said. "They're almost the definitive Nebraska mother and father. Radiantly decent, well spoken. The kind that raised their kids to have manners. Of all the television hosts I've faced, Carson has the most old-fashioned manners." By contemporary standards, he had a strict—even rigorous—upbringing, not calculated to encourage extrovert behavior. His brother Dick (now director of the "Merv Griffin Show") was once quoted as saying, "Put it this way—we're not Italian. Nobody in our family ever says what they really think or feel to anyone else." Except, I would add, in moments of professional crisis, when Johnny Carson can express himself with brusque and unequivocal directness. In 1966, for instance, the first three nights of a cabaret engagement he played in Miami were spoiled by a backstage staff too inexperienced to handle the elaborate sound effects that his act required. Carson accused his manager, Al Bruno, who had looked after his business affairs for almost ten years, of responsibility for the fiasco, and fired him on the spot. Again, there was the case of Art Stark, who described himself to an interviewer in 1966 as "Johnny's best friend." He had every reason to think so: for nearly a decade he had been Carson's producer, first on "Who Do You Trust?" and then on the "Tonight Show." He was the star's closest confidant, and when, in 1967, Carson embarked on a legal struggle with NBC for control of the show, including the right to hire and fire, he repeatedly assured Stark that, whatever the outcome, Stark's job would be safe. Having won the battle, however, Carson summoned Stark to his apartment and announced without preamble that he wanted another producer, unconnected with NBC. Dumbfounded, Stark asked when he would have to quit. "Right now," said Carson.

When Carson was twelve, he picked up, at a friend's house,

a conjuring manual for beginners called *Hoffman's Book of Magic*. Its effect on him has been compared to the impact on the youthful Keats of Chapman's Homer. ("Chapman hit it in the bottom of the ninth to tie the game against Milwaukee," said the man who made the comparison, a former Carson writer. "Little Johnny Keats was standing behind the center-field fence and the ball landed smack on his head.") Carson immediately wrote off for a junior magician's kit. He worked hard to master the basic skills of the trade, and, having tried out his tricks on his mother's bridge club, he made his professional debut, billed as The Great Carsoni, before a gathering of Norfolk Rotarians. For this he received three dollars—the first of many such fees, for the kid illusionist was soon in demand at a variety of local functions, from firemen's picnics to county fairs. As a student at Norfolk High, he branched out into acting and also wrote a comic column for the school newspaper.

Digressive flash forward: In 1976, Carson was invited back to Norfolk to give the commencement address. Immensely gratified, he accepted at once. He took great pains over his speech, and when he delivered it, on May 23, the school auditorium was packed to the roof. In the front row, alongside his wife, brother, and sister, sat his parents, to whom he paid tribute for having "backed me up and let me go in my own direction." He also thanked one of his teachers, Miss Jenny Walker, who had prophetically said of him in 1943, "You have a fine sense of humor and I think you will go far in the entertainment world." In case anyone wondered why he had returned to Norfolk, he explained, "I've come to find out what's on the seniors' minds and, more important, to see if they've changed the movie at the Granada Theatre" (where, I have since discovered, Carson was working as a part-time usher when the manager interrupted the double feature to announce that the Japanese had bombed Pearl Harbor). He went on to recall that he had been chosen to lead the school's scrap-metal drive: "Unfortunately, in our zeal to help the war effort, we sometimes appropriated metal and brass from people who did not know they were parting with it." He continued, "I was also a member of the Thespians. I joined because I thought it meant something else. Then I found out it had to do with acting." In the manner expected of commencement speakers, he offered a little advice on coping with life in the adult world. Though his precepts were homespun to the point of platitude, they were transparently sincere and devoid of conventional pomposity. The main tenets of the Carson credo were these: (1) Learn to laugh at yourself. (2) Never lose the curiosity of childhood: "Go on asking questions about the nature of things and how they work, and don't stop until you get the answers." (3) Study the art of compromise, which implies a willingness to be convinced by other people's arguments: "Stay loose. In marriage, above all, compromise is the name of the game. Although"—and here he cast a glance at his third wife—"you may think that my giving advice on marriage is like the captain of the Titanic giving lessons on navigation." (4) Having picked a profession, feel no compulsion to stick to it: "If you don't like it, stop doing it. Never continue in a job you don't enjoy." (On the evidence, it would be hard to fault Carson for failing to practice what he preached.) A question-and-answer session then took place, from which I append a few excerpts:

Q: How do you feel about Norfolk nowadays?
CARSON: I'm very glad I grew up in a small community. Big cities are where alienation sets in.
Q: Has success made you happy?
CARSON: I have very high ups and very low downs. I can all of a sudden be depressed, sometimes without knowing why. But on the whole I think I'm relatively happy.
Q: Who do you admire most, of all the guests you've interviewed.
CARSON: People like Carl Sagan, Paul Ehrlich, Margaret Mead . . . (*He recites the official list, already quoted, of Most Valued Performers.*)
Q: In all your life, what are you proudest of?

CARSON: Giving a commencement address like this
has made me as proud as anything I've ever done.

The applause at the end was so clamorous that Carson
felt compelled to improvise a postscript. "If you're happy in
what you're doing, you'll like yourself," he said. "And if you
like yourself, you'll have inner peace. And if you have that,
along with physical health, you will have had more success
than you could possibly have imagined. I thank you all very
much." He left the stage to a further outburst of cheers,
having established what may be a record for speakers on
such occasions: throughout the evening, he had made no
reference to the deity, the flag, or the permissive society; nor
had he used the phrase "this great country of ours."

After graduating from Norfolk, in 1943, Carson enrolled
in the Navy's V-12 program, but training did not start until
the fall, so he filled in time by hitchhiking to California.
There, in order to gain access to the many entertainments
that were offered free of charge to servicemen, he stopped
off at an Army-Navy store and prematurely bought himself
a naval cadet's uniform. Thus attired, he danced with
Marlene Dietrich at the Hollywood Stage Door Canteen.
Later, he traveled south to see Orson Welles give a display
of magic in San Diego, where he responded to the maestro's
request for a volunteer from the audience and ecstatically
permitted himself to be sawed in half. That night, he was
arrested by two M.P.s and charged with impersonating a
member of the armed forces—an offense that cost him fifty
dollars in bail. After induction, he attended the midship-
men's school at Columbia University and served in the
Pacific aboard the battleship *Pennsylvania*. Never exposed to
combat, he had plenty of time to polish his conjuring skills.
In 1946, discharged from the Navy, he entered the University
of Nebraska, where he majored in English and moonlighted
as a magician, by now earning twenty-five dollars per appearance. In need of an assistant, he hired a girl student
named Jody Wolcott; he married her in 1948. (To dispose,

as briefly as possible, of Carson's marital history: The liaison with Jody produced three sons—Chris, Ricky, and Cory—and was finally dissolved, after four years of separation, in 1963. "My greatest personal failure," Carson has said, "was when I was divorced from my first wife." In August, 1963, he married Joanne Copeland, aged thirty, a diminutive, dark-haired model and occasional actress. They parted company in 1970 but were not legally sundered until two years later, when the second Mrs. Carson was awarded a settlement of nearly half a million dollars, in addition to an annual hundred thousand in alimony. She had by then moved from New York to Los Angeles. Shortly afterward, Carson migrated to the West Coast, bringing the show with him. Between these two events she discerns a causal connection. She has also declared that when, at a Hollywood party, Carson first met his next wife-to-be, "she was standing with her back to him, and he went right up to her, thinking it was me." On matters such as this, Carson's lips are meticulously sealed. All we know—or need to know—is that on September 30, 1972, during a gaudy celebration at the Beverly Hills Hotel in honor of his tenth anniversary on the "Tonight Show," he stepped up to the microphone and announced that at one-thirty that afternoon he had married Joanna Holland. Of Italian lineage, and a model by profession, she was thirty-two years old. They are still together. It is difficult to see how Carson could have mistaken her, even from behind, for her predecessor. She could not be sanely described as diminutive. Dark-haired, yes; but of medium height and voluptuous build. The third Mrs. Carson is the kind of woman, bright and *molto simpatica*, whom you would expect to meet not in Bel Air but at a cultural soirée in Rome, where—as like as not—she would be more than holding her own against the earnest platonic advances of Michelangelo Antonioni.)

Carson's post-college career follows the route to success traditionally laid down for a television—What? Personality-cum-comedian-cum-interviewer? No single word yet exists to epitomize his function, though it has had many practitioners, from Steve Allen, the archetypal pioneer, to the hosts of the latest and grisliest giveaway shows. In Carson's case, there are ten steps to stardom. (1) A multipurpose job (at forty-seven dollars and fifty cents a week) as disc jockey, weather reporter, and reader of commercials on an Omaha radio station, where he breaks a precedent or two; e.g., when he is required to conduct pseudo interviews, consisting of answers prerecorded by minor celebrities and distributed to small-town d.j.s with a list of matching questions, he flouts custom by ignoring the script. Instead of asking Patti Page how she began performing, he says, "I understand you're hitting the bottle pretty good, Patti—when did you start?," which elicits the taped reply, "When I was six, I used to get up at church socials and do it." (2) A work-hunting foray, in 1951, to San Francisco and Los Angeles, which gets him nowhere except back to Omaha. (3) A sudden summons, later in the same year, from a Los Angeles television station, KNXT, offering him a post as staff announcer, which he accepts, at a hundred and thirty-five dollars a week. (4) A Sunday afternoon show of his own ("KNXT *cautiously* presents 'Carson's Cellar' "), produced on a weekly budget of twenty-five dollars, plus fifty for Carson. It becomes what is known as a cult success (a golden phrase, which unlocks many high-level doors), numbering among its fans—and subsequently its guests—such people as Fred Allen, Jack Benny, and Red Skelton. (5) Employment, after thirty weeks of "Carson's Cellar," as a writer and supporting player on Skelton's CBS-TV show. (6) The Breakthrough, which occurs in 1954 and is brought about, in strict adherence to the "Forty-second Street" formula, by an injury to the star: Skelton literally knocks himself out while rehearsing a slapstick routine, and Carson, at roughly an hour's notice, triumphantly replaces him. (7) The Breakdown: CBS launches "The Johnny Carson Show," a half-hour program that goes through seven directors, eight writers, and thirty-nine weeks of worsening health before expiring, in the spring of 1956. (8) Carson picks self up, dusts self off, starts all over again. On money borrowed from his father, he moves from the West Coast to New York, where he joins the Friars Club, impresses its show-business membership with his cobra-swift one-liners, makes guest appearances on TV, and generally repairs his damaged reputation until (9) he is hired by ABC, in 1957, to run its quiz program "Who Do You Trust?" on which he spends the five increasingly prosperous years that lead him to (10) the "Tonight Show," and thence to the best table in the Polo Lounge, where he has been waiting for several minutes when I arrive, precisely on time.

He is making copious notes on a pad. I ask what he is writing. He says he has had an idea for tonight's monologue. In Utah, yesterday, the convicted murderer Gary Gilmore, who had aroused national interest by his refusal to appeal against the death sentence passed upon him, got his wish by facing a firing squad—Utah being a state where the law allows condemned criminals to select the method by which society will rid itself of them. Thus, the keepers of the peace have shot a man to death at his own urgent request. Carson's comment on the macabre situation takes the form of black comedy. Since justice must be seen to be done, why not let the viewing public in on the process of choice? Carson proposes a new TV show, to be called "The Execution Game." It would work something like this: Curtains part to reveal the death chamber, in the middle of which is an enormous wheel, equipped with glittering lights and a large golden arrow, to be spun by the condemned man to decide the nature of his fate. For mouth-watering prizes—ranging from a holiday for two in the lovely Munich suburb of Dachau to a pair of front-row seats at the victim's terminal throes—members of the audience vie with one another to guess whether the arrow will come to rest on the electric chair, the gas chamber, the firing squad, the garrote, or the noose.

This routine seems to me apt and mordant, and I tell Carson that I look forward to seeing it developed this evening. (Footnote: I looked in vain. The January 18 edition of the "Tonight Show" contained no mention of Gary Gilmore's execution apart from a terse and oddly sour sentence—"Capital punishment is a great deterrent to monologues"—inserted without buildup or comic payoff in Carson's opening spiel. A couple of nights later, one of his guests was Shelley Winters, who burst into an attack on the death penalty, using the Gilmore case as her springboard. Carson showed a distinctly nervous reluctance to commit himself; indeed, he shied away from the subject, and cut the discussion short by saying, "There are no absolutes." Yet I had seen him writing a piece that implied fairly bitter opposition to the process of judicial killing. What had happened? I called up Fred de Cordova, who admitted, after some hesitation, that he had disliked the "Execution Game" idea and that the network had backed him up. There had been a convulsive row with Carson, but in the end "Johnny saw reason" and the item was dropped. Hence his remark, meaningless except to insiders, about capital punishment's being "a great deterrent to monologues"; and so much for de Cordova's description of Carson as a supreme "self-editor" who never needed censorship.)

A believer in eating only when one is hungry, Carson orders nothing more than a salad and some mineral water. "I gave up drinking a couple of years ago," he says. "I couldn't handle it." He adds that we can chat until two o'clock when he must be off to Burbank. He doesn't know who is lined up to appear tonight. This prompts an obligatory question: Which guests has he coveted and failed to corral? "Cary Grant, of course. But straight actors often get embarrassed on the show. They say they feel naked. Their business is to play other people, and it bugs them to have to speak as themselves. Naturally, I'd be glad to have Henry Kissinger. And it was a great sorrow to me when Charles Laughton, whom we'd been after for ages, died a few days before he was scheduled to appear. But on the whole I'm pretty content to have had a list of guests like Paul Ehrlich, Gore Vidal, Carl Sagan, Madalyn Murray O'Hair . . ." He flips through the familiar roster. "And it gives me a special kick to go straight from talking to that kind of person into an all-out slapstick routine." He runs over his rules for coping with fellow comedians on the program: "You have to lay back and help them. Never compete with them. I learned that from Jack Benny. The better they are, the better the show is." (In more immature days, Carson's technique was less self-effacing. The late Jack E. Leonard told a reporter in 1967, "You say a funny line on Griffin, and he laughs and says, 'That's brilliant.' Carson repeats it, scavenging, hunting all over for the last vestiges of the joke, trying desperately to pull a laugh of his own out of it.") Carson continues, "When people get outrageous, you have to capitalize on their outrageousness and go along with it. The only absolute rule is: Never lose control of the show."

To stay in control is the hardest trick of all, especially when the talk veers toward obscenity; you have to head it off, preferably with a laugh, before it crashes through the barrier of public acceptance. At times, you have to launch a preemptive strike of salaciousness in order to get an interview started. "Not long ago, a movie starlet came on the show with gigantic breasts bulging out of a low-cut dress," Carson says. "The audience couldn't look at anything else. If I'd ignored them, nobody would have listened to a word we said. There was only one thing to do. As soon as she sat down, I stared straight at her cleavage and said, 'That's the biggest set of jugs I ever saw.' It got a tremendous laugh. 'Now that we've got that out of the way,' I said, 'let's talk.'"

High on his list of favorite guests is Don Rickles, though he feels that Rickles has sadly mishandled his own TV career: "He went in for situation comedy and tried to be lovable. He failed every time. What he needed—and I've told him this over and over again—was a game show called something like 'Meet Don Rickles,' where he could be himself and insult the audience, the way Groucho did on 'You Bet Your Life.'" Although Carson himself is less acid than he used to be, he is still capable of slapping down visitors who get uppish with him. "There was one time," he recalls, "when we had Tuesday Weld on the program, and she started behaving rather snottily. I finally asked her something innocuous about her future plans, and she said she'd let me know 'when I'm back on the show next year.' I was very polite. I just said that I hadn't scheduled her again quite that soon." Beyond doubt, Carson's least beloved subjects are British comedians, of whom he says, "I find them unfunny, infantile, and obsessed with toilet jokes. They're lavatory-minded." (It is true that British comics sometimes indulge, on TV, in scatological—and sexual—humor that would not be permitted on any American network; but this kind of liberty, however it may be abused, seems to me infinitely preferable to the restrictiveness that prevented Buddy Hackett, Carson's principal guest on February 1, 1977, from completing a single punch line without being bleeped.) I throw into the conversation my own opinion, which is that to shrink from referring to basic physical functions is to be truly infantile; to make good jokes about them, as about anything else, is evidence of maturity. It is depressing to reflect that if Rabelais were alive today he would not be invited to appear on the "Tonight Show."

Carson once said, "I've never seen it chiselled in stone tablets that TV must be uplifting." I ask him how he feels about his talk-show competitor Dick Cavett. His answer is brisk: "The trouble with Dick is that he's never decided what he wants to be—whether he's going for the sophisticated, intellectual viewer or for the wider audience. He falls between two stools. It gets so that you feel he's apologizing if he makes a joke." In reply to the accusation that his own show is intellectually jejune, Carson has this to say: "I don't want to get into big debates about abortion, homosexuality, prostitution, and so forth. Not because I'm afraid of them but because we all know the arguments on both sides, and they're circular. The fact is that TV is probably not the ideal place to discuss serious issues. It's much better to read about them." With this thought—self-serving but not easily refutable—he takes his leave.

February 10, 1977: The Hasty Pudding Club at Harvard has elected Carson its Man of the Year. There have been ten previous holders of the title, among them Bob Hope, Paul Newman, Robert Redford, James Stewart, Dustin Hoffman, and Warren Beatty. Delighted by the honor, because it is untainted by either lobbying or commercialism, Carson will fly to Harvard in two weeks' time to receive his trophy. While he is there, he will attend the opening night of "Cardinal Knowledge," the hundred and twenty-ninth in the series of all-male musicals presented by Hasty Pudding Theatricals, which claims to be the oldest dramatic society in the United States. I am to travel with Carson on what will be his first trip to Harvard. To give me details of the program of events that the Pudding people have prepared for him, he asks me to his home in Bel Air, where I present myself at 11 A.M. It is roughly five minutes by car from the Beverly Hills Hotel, and was built in 1950 for the director Mervyn LeRoy. Carson bought it five years ago, and, like many places where West Coast nabobs dwell, it is about as grand as a house can be that has no staircase. When you turn in at the driveway, a voice issuing from the wall sternly inquires your name and business; if your reply pacifies it, iron gates swing open to admit you.

I am welcomed by Joanna Carson's secretary, a lively young woman named Sherry Fleiner, part of whose job consists of working with Mrs. C. for a charitable organization known as SHARE—Share Happily And Reap Endlessly—which raises funds for the mentally retarded. (Other than a married couple who act as housekeepers, the Carsons have no live-in servants.) Proffering Carson's apologies, Miss Fleiner says that he is out on the tennis court behind the house, halfway through a closely fought third set. While awaiting match point, I discreetly case the joint, which has (I learn from

Miss Fleiner) six bedrooms. Except where privacy is essential, the walls are mainly of glass, and there is window-to-window carpeting with a zebra-stripe motif. Doors are infrequent. In accordance with local architectural custom, you do not leave one room to enter another, you move from one living area to the next. In the reading area (or "library") I spot a photograph of four generations of Carsons, the eldest being my host's grandfather, Christopher Carson, who died two years ago at the age of ninety-eight, and I recall Carson's saying to me, in that steely survivor's voice of his, "One thing about my family—we have good genes." On a wall nearby hangs a portrait of Carson by Norman Rockwell, the perfect artist for this model product of Middle American upbringing. Other works of art, scattered through the relaxing, ingesting, and greeting areas, reveal an eclectic, opulent, but not barbarously spendthrift taste; e.g., a well-chosen group of paintings by minor Impressionists; a camel made out of automobile bumpers by John Kearney and (an authentic rarity) a piece of sculpture by Rube Goldberg; together with statues and graphic art from the Orient and Africa. Over the fireplace in the relaxing area, a facile portrait of Mrs. Carson, who deserves more eloquent brushwork, smilingly surveys the swimming pool.

Having won his match, Carson joins me, his white sporting gear undarkened by sweat, and leads me out of the house to a spacious octagonal office he has built alongside the tennis court. This is his command module. It contains machinery for large-screen TV projection, and a desk of presidential dimensions, bristling with gadgets. On a built-in sofa lies a cushion that bears the embroidered inscription "IT'S ALL IN THE TIMING." Coffee is served, and Carson offers me one of his cigarettes, which I refuse. He says that most people, even hardened smokers, do the same, and I do not find this surprising, since the brand he favors is more virulent and ferociously unfiltered than any other on the market. He briefs me on the impending Harvard visit—a day and a half of sightseeing, speechmaking, banquets, conferences, seminars, and receptions that would tax the combined energies of Mencken, Mailer, and Milton Berle—and then throws himself open to me for further questioning.

Q: When you're at home, whom do you entertain?

CARSON: My lawyer, Henry Bushkin, who's probably my best friend. A few doctors. One or two poker players. Some people I've met through tennis, which is my biggest hobby right now—though I'm still interested in astronomy and scuba diving. And, of course, a couple of people who work on the show. But the point is that not many of my friends are exclusively show business.

Q: Why do you dislike going to parties?

CARSON: Because I get embarrassed by attention and adulation. I don't know how to react to them in private. Swifty Lazar, for instance, sometimes embarrasses me when he praises me in front of his friends. I feel much more comfortable with a studio audience. On the show, I'm in control. Socially, I'm not in control.

Q: On the show, one of the things you control most strictly is the expression of your own opinions. Why do you keep them a secret from the viewers?

CARSON: I hate to be pinned down. Take the case of Larry Flynt, for example. [Flynt, the publisher of the sex magazine *Hustler*, had recently been convicted on obscenity charges.] Now, I think *Hustler* is tawdry, but I also think that if the First Amendment means what it says, then it protects Flynt as much as anyone else, and that includes the American Nazi movement. As far as I'm concerned, people should be allowed to read and see whatever they like, provided it doesn't injure others. If they want to read pornography until it comes out of their ears, then let them. But if I go on the "Tonight Show" and defend *Hustler*, the viewers are going to tag me as that guy who's into pornography. And that's going to hurt me as an entertainer, which is what I am.

Q: In private life, who's the wittiest man you've ever known?

CARSON: The wittiest would have to be Fred Allen. He appeared on a show I had in the fifties, called "Carson's

Cellar," and I knew him for a while after that—until he died, in 1956. But there's an old vaudeville proverb—"A comic is a man who says funny things, and a comedian is a man who says things funny." If that's a valid distinction, then Fred was a comic, whereas Jonathan Winters and Mel Brooks are comedians. But they make me laugh just as much.

Before I go, Carson takes me down to a small gymnasium beneath the module. It is filled with gleaming steel devices, pulleys and springs and counterweights, which, together with tennis, keep the star's body trim. In one corner stands a drum kit at which Buddy Rich might cast an envious eye. "That's where I work off my hostilities," Carson explains. He escorts me to my car, and notices that it is fitted with a citizens-band radio. "I had one of those damned things, but I ripped it out after a couple of weeks," he says. "I just couldn't bear it—all those sick anonymous maniacs shooting off their mouths."

I understand what he means. Most of what you hear on CB radio is either tedious (truck drivers warning one another about speed traps) or banal (schoolgirls exchanging notes on homework), but at its occasional—and illegal—worst it sinks a pipeline to the depths of the American unconscious. Your ears are assaulted by the sound of racism at its most rampant, and by masturbation fantasies that are the aural equivalent of rape. The sleep of reason, to quote Goya's phrase, brings forth monsters, and the anonymity of CB encourages the monsters to emerge. Not often, of course; but when they do, CB radio becomes the dark underside of a TV talk show. No wonder Carson loathes it.

February 24, 1977: Morning departure from Los Angeles Airport of flight bearing Boston-bound Carson party, which consists of Mr. and Mrs. C., Mr. and Mrs. Henry Bushkin, and me. Boyish-looking, with an easy smile, a soft voice, and a modest manner, Bushkin, to whom I talked a few days earlier, is a key figure in Carson's private and professional

life. "Other stars have an agent, a personal manager, a business manager, a P.R. man, and a lawyer," he told me. "I
serve all those functions for Johnny." Bushkin was born in
the Bronx in 1942. He moved to the West Coast five years
ago and swiftly absorbed the ground rules of life in Beverly
Hills; e.g., he is likely to turn up at his desk in a cardigan and
an open-necked shirt, thus obeying the precept that casual-
ness of office attire increases in direct ratio to grandeur of
status. He first met Carson through a common friend in
1970, when he was working for a small Manhattan law firm
that specialized in show-business clients. At that time, Carson
lived at the United Nations Plaza, where one of his neighbors
was David (Sonny) Werblin, formerly the driving force
behind the Music Corporation of America and (until 1968)
the president of the New York Jets. In 1969, Werblin had
drawn up a plan whereby he and Carson would form a
corporation, called Raritan Enterprises, to take over the entire
production of the "Tonight Show," which would then be
rented out to NBC for a vast weekly fee. Rather than risk
losing Carson, the network caved in and agreed to Raritan's
terms. "As the tax laws were in the late sixties, when you
could pay up to ninety percent on earned income, the Raritan
scheme had certain advantages," Bushkin explained to me.
"But there were handicaps that Johnny hadn't foreseen.
Werblin had too many outside interests—for one thing, he
owned a good-sized racing stable—and Johnny found himself
managing the company as well as starring in the show, because his partner wasn't always there. When a major problem
came up, he'd suddenly discover that Werblin had taken off
for a month in Europe and couldn't be reached. Around 1972,
Johnny decided that the plan wasn't working, and that's when
he asked me to represent him. Not to go into details, let's
just say that Werblin was painlessly eliminated from the
setup. By that time, the maximum tax on earned income
was down to fifty percent, and that removed the basic motive
for the corporate arrangement. So the show reverted to being
an NBC operation. But Johnny went back with a much better

financial deal than he had in 1969." When Bushkin came to
Beverly Hills, in 1973, his life already revolved around
Carson's. "It took about three years for our relationship to
get comfortable, because Johnny isn't easy to know," he
went on. "But now we're the best of friends, and so are our
wives. The unwritten rule for lawyers is: Don't get too
friendly with clients. But this is an unusual situation. This is
Carson, and Carson's my priority."

Ed McMahon, I remarked, had predicted that Carson
would stay with the "Tonight Show" until 1980. "I'll bet you
that he's still there in 1984," Bushkin said.

If Carson can hold on as long as that, it would be churlish
of NBC to unseat him before he reaches retiring age, in 1990.

5:30 P.M.: We land at Boston. Frost underfoot. Carson,
following President Carter's example, totes his suit (presumably the tuxedo required for tomorrow's festivities) off
the plane. He murmurs to me, "If someone could get Billy
Carter to sponsor a carry-off suitcase, they'd make a fortune."
He walks through popping flashbulbs and a fair amount of
hand-held-camera work to be greeted by Richard Palmer and
Barry Sloane, undergraduate co-producers of the Hasty
Pudding show, who look bland, businesslike, and utterly un-
theatrical; i.e., like co-producers. Waiting limos take Carsons
and Bushkins to the Master's Residence at Eliot House,
where they are to spend the night. I repair to my hotel.

8:30 P.M.: Pudding people give dinner for Carson and his
entourage at waterfront restaurant called Anthony's Pier 4.
When I announce destination, my cabdriver says, "That's
the big Republican place. Gold tablecloths. Democrats like
checked tablecloths. They go to Jimmy's Harbor Side." Decor
at Anthony's features rustic beamery and period prints. Tablecloths definitely straw-colored, though cannot confirm that
this has political resonance. Carson (in blue sports jacket,
white shirt, and discreetly striped tie) sits beside wife (in
brown woollen two-piece, with ring like searchlight on left
hand) at round table with Bushkins, Pudding officials, and
short, heavily tanned man with vestigial hair, dark silk suit,

smoke-tinted glasses, and general aspect of semi-simian elegance. This, I learn, is David Tebet, the senior vice-president of NBC, whose suzerainty covers the Carson show, and who in May, 1977, will celebrate his twenty-first anniversary with the network. Of the three men who wield influence over Carson (the others being Bushkin and Fred de Cordova), Tebet is ultimately the most powerful. "It's a terrible thing to wish on him," Frank Sinatra once said of Tebet, "but it's too bad he's not in government today." In 1975, Robert D. Wood, then president of CBS-TV, described Tebet as "the ambassador of all NBC's good will—he sprinkles it around like ruby dust." With characteristic effusiveness, de Cordova has declared that the dust-sprinkler's real title should be "vice-president in charge of caring." In 1965, Carson came to the conclusion that he had to quit the "Tonight Show," because the daily strain was too great, but Tebet persuaded him to stay; what tipped the scale was the offer of an annual paid vacation of six weeks. Ten years later, Carson said he had a feeling that when he died a color TV set would be delivered to his graveside and "on it will be a ribbon and a note that says, 'Have a nice trip. Love, David.' "

During dinner, although wine is served, Carson drinks only coffee. He talks about "Seeds," a Wasp parody of *Roots*, dealing with history of orthodox midwestern family, which was recently broadcast on the "Tonight Show." Concept was his, and he is pleased with how it came out, though he regrets loss of one idea that was cut; viz., scene depicting primitive tribal ceremony at which the hyphen is ritually removed from Farrah Fawcett-Majors.

"He looks so mechanical," mutters a Pudding person on my right. "Like a talking propelling pencil." Same fellow explains to me that the club is divided into social and theatrical compartments. Former was founded in 1795; latter did not develop until 1844, when first show was presented, establishing an annual tradition that has persisted—apart from two inactive years in each of the world wars—ever since. Pudding performers have included Oliver Wendell Holmes, William

Randolph Hearst, Robert Benchley (star of *Below Zero*,
1912), and Jack Lemmon. Tomorrow's production, which is to
play a month at Pudding theatre, followed by quick tour
to New York, Washington, and Bermuda, will cost a hundred
thousand dollars. Revenue from box office and from program
advertising, plus aid from wealthy patrons, will insure that it
breaks even. (Undergraduates provide words, music, and cast;
direction, choreography, and design are by professionals.)
Publicity accruing from Carson's presence will boost ticket
sales; thus, his visit amounts to unpaid commercial for show.

Another Pudding functionary tells me that club also be-
stows award on Woman of the Year—has, in fact, been
doing so since 1951. First recipient was Gertrude Lawrence,
Bette Midler got the nod in 1976, and last week Elizabeth
Taylor turned up to collect the trophy for 1977. "She is
genuinely humble," my informant gravely whispers. After
dinner, Carson and wife are interviewed in banqueting salon
of restaurant by local TV station. Mrs. C. is asked, "Did you
fall in love with the private or the public Johnny Carson?"
She replies, "I fell in love with both." Before further secrets
of the confessional can be extracted, camera runs out of
tape, to her evident relief.

February 25, 1977: Dining hall of Eliot House is crowded
at 8:45 A.M. University band, with brass section predominant,
lines up and plays "Ten Thousand Men of Harvard" as
Carson (black-and-white checked sports jacket) leads his
party in to breakfast. His every move is followed, as it will be
all day, by television units, undergraduate film crew, and
assorted press photographers. Asked by TV director whether
sound system is to his liking, Carson says he has no com-
plaints, "except I thought the microphone under the bed was
pushing it a bit." Member of Harvard band achieves minor
triumph of one-upmanship by conning Carson into inscribing
and autographing autobiography of Dick Cavett.

Fast duly broken, party embarks on walking tour of
Harvard Yard and university museums. Hundreds of undergraduates join media people in the crush around Carson, and

police cars prowl in their wake to protect the star from terrorist assaults or kidnap attempts. Weather is slate-clouded and icy; Mrs. Carson and Mrs. Bushkin both wear mink coats. Climax of tour is meeting with John Finley, internationally eminent classical scholar and treasure of Harvard campus, Eliot Professor of Greek Literature Emeritus and Master of Eliot House Emeritus, whose study is in the Widener Library. (During previous week, I called Professor Finley to find out how he felt about forthcoming encounter with Carson. "At first, I thought it was an asinine idea," he said. "I've never seen the man on television—as a matter of fact, I've spent most of my life with my nose plunged into classical texts. But, after all, how important is one's time, anyway?") Carson is properly deferential in the presence of this agile septuagenarian. Eavesdropping on their conversation, I hear Professor Finley say, "Writing is like an artesian well that we sink to find the truth." He talks about Aristotle, getting little response, and then tries to clarify for Carson the distinction drawn by Lionel Trilling between sincerity and authenticity, in literature and in life. "President Carter is an example of sincerity," he explains. "But whether he has authenticity—well, that's another matter. I'm not sure that Trilling would have been much impressed." Cannot imagine what Carson is making of all this.

12:30 P.M.: Luncheon in Carson's honor at the A.D. Club, described to me by reliable source as "the second-stuffiest in Harvard." (First prize goes, by general consent, if not by acclamation, to the Porcellian Club. Choice of venue today is dictated by fact that co-producers of Pudding show are members of A.D. and not of Porcellian.) Atmosphere is robustly patrician enough to warm heart of late Evelyn Waugh: sprigs of Back Bay dynasties sprawl in leather armchairs beneath group photographs of their forebears. Club clearly deserves title of No. 2; it could not conceivably try harder. Members cheer as Carson enters, flanked by Bushkin and Tebet. (This is a strictly stag sodality.) About twenty guests present, among them Professor Finley and Robert

Peabody, son of former governor of Massachusetts and vice-president of Pudding Theatricals—a bouncing two-hundred-and-fifty-pound lad much cherished by Pudding enthusiasts for his comic talent in drag. Carson, still rejecting grape in favor of bean, wears blue sweater, dark slacks, and burgundy patent-leather shoes. When meal is consumed, he makes charming speech of thanks, in which he regrets that life denied him the opportunity of studying under Prof. Finley. (Later, rather less lovably, he is to tell drama students at Pudding Club that from his lunchtime chat with Finley "I learned a hell of a lot more about Aristotle than I wanted to know.")

2 P.M.: Carson is driven to Pudding H.Q. on Holyoke Street—narrow thoroughfare jammed with fans, through whom club officials have to force a way to the entrance. Upstairs, in red-curtained reception room, Carson is to hold seminar with thirty hand-picked undergraduates who are studying the performing arts. This select bunch of initiates sits in circle of red armchairs. Carson takes his place among them and awaits interrogation. Standard of questions, dismal for allegedly high-powered assembly, seldom rises above gossip level; e.g.:

Q: As a regular viewer, may I ask why you have switched from wearing a Windsor knot to a four-in-hand?

CARSON: Well, I guess that's about all we have time for. (*Questioner presses for reply.*) Just between ourselves, it's a defense mechanism.

Q: Did Jack Paar have someone like Ed McMahon to work with?

CARSON: No. A psychiatrist worked with Jack Paar. The last time I saw Paar was in Philadelphia. He was sitting on a curb and he had a swizzle stick embedded in his hand. I removed it.

Q: I've noticed that people don't always laugh at your monologue. Why is that?

CARSON: Well, we don't actually *structure* it to go

down the toilet. But we work from the morning papers and sometimes the audience isn't yet aware of what's happened in the news.

Q: How do you really feel about Jimmy Carter?

CARSON: The Carter Administration is perfect comedy material. And I think he rented the family. I don't believe Lillian is his mother. I don't believe Billy is his brother. They're all from Central Casting.

Q: Do you normally watch the show when you get home?

CARSON: No. I'd get worn out from seeing it all over again. If we're breaking in a new character, I'll watch.

Q (*first of any substance*): Has the "Tonight Show" done anything more important than just brighten up the end of the day?

CARSON: I'd say it was quite important to let people hear the opinions of people like Paul Ehrlich, Carl Sagan, Gore Vidal, Margaret . . . (*Vide, supra, passim.*) We've also taken an interest in local politics. One year, there were eleven candidates for mayor of Burbank, and we had to give them all equal time. That was pretty public-spirited. But what's important? I think it's important to show ordinary people doing extraordinary things. Like we once had a Japanese guy from Cleveland who wanted to be a cop but he was too short, so his wife had been hanging him up every night by his heels. And it's important to help people live out their fantasies, like when I pitched to Mickey Mantle on the show, or when I played quarterback for the New York Jets. But a lot of the time TV is judged by the wrong standards. If Broadway comes up with two first-rate new plays in a season, the critics are delighted. That's a good season. But on TV they expect that every week. It's a very visible medium to jump on. And there's another thing that isn't generally realized. If you're selling hard goods —like soap or dog food—you simply can't afford to put on culture. Exxon, the Bank of America—organizations like that can afford to do it. But they aren't selling hard goods, and that's what the "Tonight Show" has to do.

[Applause for candor. This is the nearest approach to hard eloquence I have heard from Carson, and he sells it to great effect.]

Q: What is Charo really like?

This reduces Carson to silence, bringing the seminar to a close.

4:30 P.M.: Cocktail party for Carson at Club Casablanca, local haunt crowded to point just short of asphyxiation. Star and companions have changed into evening dress. Carson tells me how Prof. Finley sought to explain to him eternal simplicities of Aristotle's view of life, and adds, "He's out of touch with the real world." Subject for debate: By what criteria can Carson's world be said to be closer to reality than Aristotle's? Or, for that matter, than Professor Finley's? Carson group and nonacting Pudding dignitaries then proceed on foot to nearby bistro called Ferdinand's for early dinner. Eating quite exceptional soft-shell crabs, I sit next to Joanna C., who has flashing eyes and a quill-shaped Renaissance nose. Her mother's parents came from northern Italy; her father's family background is Sicilian. She introduced Carson to what is now his favorite Manhattan restaurant, an Italian place named Patsy's, and her immediate ambition is to coax him to visit Italy. Eying her husband (who must be well into his second gallon of coffee since breakfast), she tells me that the only time she has seen him cry was at the funeral of Jack Benny, who befriended and helped him from his earliest days in TV. She doesn't think he will still be on the "Tonight Show" when he's sixty (i.e., in 1985). "Of course, everybody wants him to act," she continues. "He was offered the Steve McQueen part in *The Thomas Crown Affair*, and Mel Brooks begged him to play the Gene Wilder part in *Blazing Saddles*. He read the script twice. Then he called Mel from Acapulco and said, 'I read it in L.A. and it wasn't funny, and it's even less funny in Mexico.'"

David Tebet, seated opposite, leans across the table and tells me what he does. His voice is a serrated baritone growl.

From what I gather, he is a combination of talent detector, ego masseur (of NBC stars), and thief (of other networks' stars). Has been quoted as saying that he judges performers by "a thing called gut reaction," and that he understands "their soft underbellies." To a thing called my surprise, he adds that these qualities of intestinal intuition help to keep stars reassured. According to an article in the *Wall Street Journal*, a two-thousand-year-old samurai sword hangs over the door of his New York office. Am not certain that this would have reassuring effect on me. It may, however, explain enigmatic remark of Bob Hope, who once referred to Tebet as "my Band-Aid." Razor-edged weapon is part of huge Tebet art collection (mainly Oriental but also including numerous prints and lithographs by Mucha, Klimt, Schiele, Munch, et al.), much of which adorns his NBC suite. Tebet claims this makes actors feel at home. But at whose home?

7 P.M.: Back to Pudding Club for pre-performance press conference. I count five movie and/or TV cameras, eight microphones, about thirty photographers, and several dozen reporters, all being jostled by roughly a hundred and fifty guests, gate-crashers, and ticket-holders diverted from route to auditorium by irresistible surge of Carson-watchers. Bar serves body-temperature champagne in plastic glasses; Carson requests slug of water.

Reporter asks what he thinks of Barbara Walters's million-dollar contract with ABC News.

He replies, "I think Harry Reasoner has a contract out for Barbara Walters."

Press grilling is routine stuff, except for:

Q: What would you like your epitaph to be?
CARSON (*after a pause for thought*): I'll be right back.

Laughter and applause for this line, the traditional cliché with which talk-show hosts segue into commercial break. Subsequent research reveals that Carson has used it before

in answer to same question. Fact increases my respect for his
acting ability. That pause for thought would have fooled
Lee Strasberg.

8 P.M.: Join expectant crowd in Pudding theatre, attractive
little blue auditorium with three hundred and sixty-three
seats. Standees line walls. In fat program I read tribute to
"that performer who has made the most outstanding contribution to the entertainment profession during the past years
—Johnny Carson." Article also states that in the fifties he
wrote for "The Red Skeleton Show"—ideal title, I reflect, for
Vincent Price Special—and concludes by summing up
Carson's gifts in a burst of baroque alliteration: "Outspoken
yet disciplined, he is a pool of profanity, a pit of profundity."
Audience by now buzzing with impatience to hear from pool
(or pit) in person.

Co-producer Palmer takes the stage and, reading from
notes, pays brief homage to "a performer whose wit, humor,
and showmanship rank him among America's greatest—ladies
and gentlemen, Mr. Johnny Carson!" Band plays "Tonight
Show" theme as Carson walks down the aisle and clambers
up to shake Palmer's hand. Standing ovation greets him. Co-
producer Sloane emerges from wings and solemnly presents
him with small golden pudding pot. Ovation persists—three
hundred and sixty-three seats are empty. When it and the
spectators have subsided, Carson holds up his hands for
silence and then makes speech precisely right for occasion.
(Without notes, of course, as befits man who, if program is
to be believed, has "liberated the airwaves from scripted
domination.") He begins by saying that it is gratifying to hear
so much applause without anyone's brandishing a sign marked
"Applause." He thanks the club for the honor bestowed on
him, even though (he adds) "I understand that this year
the short list for the award was me, Idi Amin, and Larry
Flynt." He expresses special gratitude for the hospitality extended to his wife and to him by Eliot House: "It's the first
time I've scored with a chick on campus since 1949." He has
never visited the university before. However, it has played a

small but significant role in his family history: "My Great-Uncle Orville was here at Harvard. Unfortunately, he was in a jar in the biology lab." Widening his focus, he throws in a couple of comments on the state of the nation. Apropos of the recent groundless panic over immunizing the population against a rumored epidemic of swine flu: "Our government has finally come up with a cure for which there is no known disease." And a nostalgic shot at a familiar target: "I hear that whenever anyone in the White House tells a lie, Nixon gets a royalty." End of address. Sustained cheers, through which Carson returns, blinking in a manner not wholly explicable by the glare of the spotlights, to his seat.

Cardinal Knowledge, the Pudding musical, at last gets under way. It's a farrago of melodramatic intrigue, with seventeenth-century setting and plethora of puns; e.g., characters called Barry de Hatchet and Viscount Hugh Behave. (How far can a farrago go?) Am pleased by high standard of performance, slightly dismayed by lack of obscenity in text. No need to dwell on show, except to praise Robert Peabody, mountainously flirtatious as Lady Della Tory, and Mark Szpak, president of Pudding Theatricals, who plays the heroine, Juana de Boise, with a raven-haired Latin vivacity that puts me in mind of the youthful Lea Padovani. Or the present Mrs. Carson.

10:15 P.M.: Intermission was yet over. Carson at bar, still on caffeine, besieged by mass of undergraduates, all of whom receive bright and civil answers to their questions. He has now been talking to strangers for thirteen hours (interrupted only by Act I of show) with no loss of buoyancy. "For the first time in my life," he remarks to me, "I know what it's like to be a politician."

Midnight has passed before the curtain falls and he makes his exit, to renewed acclamation. One gets the impression that the audience is applauding not just an admired performer but—why shun simplicities?—a decent and magnanimous man.

●   ●

Two thoughts in conclusion:

(1) If the most we ask of live television is entertainment within the limits set by commercial sponsorship, then Carson, week in, week out, is the very best we shall get. If, on the other hand, we ask to be challenged, disturbed, or provoked at the same time that we are entertained, Carson must inevitably disappoint us. But to blame him for that would be to accuse him of breaking a promise he never made.

(2) Though the written and rehearsed portions of what Carson does can be edited together into an extremely effective cabaret act, the skill that makes him unique—the ability to run a talk show as he does—is intrinsically, exclusively televisual. Singers, actors, and dancers all have multiple choices: they can exercise their talents in the theatre, on TV, or in the movies. But a talk-show host can only become a more successful talk-show host. There is no place in the other media for the gifts that distinguish him—most specifically, for the gift of reinventing himself, night after night, without rehearsal or repetition. Carson, in other words, is a grand master of the one show-business art that leads nowhere. He has painted himself not into a corner but onto the top of a mountain.

Long—or, at least, as long as the air at the summit continues to nourish and elate him—may he stay there.

[1978]

Frolics and detours
of a short little hebrew man
—MEL BROOKS

O N A WARM NIGHT in October, 1959, I was bidden to a party at Mamma Leone's, a restaurant on Forty-eighth Street that was (and is) one of the largest and most popular in Manhattan's theatre district. Random House had taken it over for the evening to celebrate the publication of *Act One*, the first volume of Moss Hart's autobiography, which in no way surprised its publishers by turning out to be a best-seller. A further excuse for festivity was the fact that the author's fifty-fifth birthday was to take place the following day. By any standards, the guest list—some three hundred strong—was fairly eye-catching. In addition to a favored bunch of critics and columnists, it included a representative selection of the show-business celebrities then active or resident in New York, among them Claudette Colbert, John Gielgud, Jose Ferrer, Margaret Leighton, Ed Sullivan, Alan Jay Lerner, Yves Montand, Simone Signoret, Ethel Merman, Alec Guinness, Truman Capote, Rosalind Russell, and Marlene Dietrich—at which point my memory gives out. A group of Moss Hart's admirers had put together a floor show in his honor, and this was already under way when I arrived. Betty Comden and Adolph Green were just finishing a routine that satirized some of the more disastrous ways in which *Act One* might be adapted for the screen. During the applause, I was burrowing through the resplendent mob, and like many of my fellow guests, I failed to catch the names of the next performers when they were introduced by the master of ceremonies, Phil Silvers.

Peering over the heads of a hundred or so standees, in front of whom the other spectators sat, squatted, or sprawled, I saw two men in business suits. One, tall and lean, was conducting an interview with the other, who was short and compact. Their faces were among the few in the room that were not instantly recognizable. Though I took no notes, I recall much of what they said, and the waves of laughter that broke over it, and the wonder with which I realized that every word of it was improvised. The tall man was suave but relentlessly probing, the stubby one urgent and eager in response, though capable of outrage when faced with questions he regarded as offensive. Here, having been shaken through the sieve of nineteen years, is what my memory retains:

Q.: I gather, sir, that you are a famous psychoanalyst?
A.: That is correct.
Q.: May I ask where you studied psychiatry?
A.: At the Vienna School of Good Luck.
Q.: Who analyzed you?
A.: I was analyzed by No. 1 himself.
Q.: You mean the great Sigmund Freud?
A.: In person. Took me during lunchtime, charged me a nickel.
Q.: What kind of man was he?
A.: Lovely little fellow. I shall never forget the hours we spent together, me lying on the couch, him sitting right there beside me, wearing a nice off-the-shoulder dress.

Q.: Is it true, sir, that Mr. Moss Hart is one of your patients?

A.: That is also correct.

[As everyone present knew, Moss Hart had been in analysis for many years, and made no secret of the benefits he had derived from it.]

Q.: Could you tell us, sir, what Mr. Hart talks about during your analytic sessions?

A.: He talks smut. He talks dirty, he talks filthy, he talks pure, unadulterated smut. It makes me want to puke.

Q.: How do you cope with this?

A.: I give him a good slap on the wrist. I wash his mouth out with soap. I tell him, "Don't talk dirty, don't say those things."

Q.: What are Mr. Hart's major problems? Does he have an Oedipus complex?

A.: What is that?

Q.: You're an analyst, sir, and you never heard of an Oedipus complex?

A.: Never in my life.

Q.: Well, sir, it's when a man has a passionate desire to make love to his own mother.

A. (*after a pause*): That's the dirtiest thing I ever heard. Where do you get that filth?

Q.: It comes from a famous play by Sophocles.

A.: Was he Jewish?

Q.: No, sir, he was Greek.

A.: With a Greek, who knows? But, with a Jew, you don't do a thing like that even to your wife, let alone your mother.

Q.: But, sir, according to Freud, *every* man has this intense sexual attachment to his—

A.: Wait a minute, wait a minute, whoa, hee-haw, just hold your horses right there. Moss Hart is a nice Jewish boy. Maybe on a Saturday night he takes the mother to the movies, maybe on the way home he gives her a little peck in the back of the cab, but going to bed with the mother—get out of here! What kind of smut is that?

Q.: During your sessions with Mr. Hart, does he ever become emotionally overwrought?

A.: Very frequently, and it's a degrading spectacle.

Q.: How do you handle these situations?

A.: I walk straight out of the room, I climb up a step-ladder, and I toss in aspirins through the transom.

When they stopped, after about a quarter of an hour, the cabaret ended, and that was just as well, for nobody could have followed them. A crowd of professional entertainers erupted in cheers. The idea of a puritanical analyst was a masterstroke of paradox, and the execution had matched the concept in brilliance. Moss Hart was heard to say that the act was the funniest fourteen minutes he could remember. The room buzzed with comment, yet hardly anyone seemed to know who the little maestro was. Diligent quizzing re-vealed that he was a thirty-three-year-old television writer, that he had spent most of the preceding ten years turning out sketches for Sid Caesar, and that his name was Mel Brooks. Facially, he had one attribute that is shared, for reasons I have never been able to fathom, by nearly all top-flight comedians; viz., a long upper lip. I later discovered that his interrogator was Mel Tolkin, another, and a senior, member of the renowned menagerie of authors whose scripts, as inter-preted by Caesar, Imogene Coca, and a talented supporting cast, had made "Your Show of Shows" a golden landmark in the wasteland of television comedy. Tolkin (a harassed-looking man, once compared by Brooks to "a stork that dropped a baby and broke it and is coming to explain to the parents") was standing in at the party for Carl Reiner, a gifted performer who had also been part of the Caesarean operation. Ever since they met, in 1950, Brooks and Reiner had been convulsing their friends with impromptu duologues. The Moss Hart jamboree was an important show-business event, and, the press being present in force, it would have marked their semi-public debut. Unfortunately, Reiner had a TV job in Los Angeles and could not make the date; hence his replacement by Tolkin, who had performed with Brooks

on several previous occasions, though never in front of such
a daunting audience. I knew nothing of this at the time;
Tolkin struck me as a first-rate straight man. All I knew as I
left Mamma Leone's that night was that his stubby, pseudo
Freudian partner was the most original comic improviser I
had ever seen.

We move forward to Hollywood in 1977. Carl Reiner, who
has just directed a boomingly successful comedy called *Oh,
God!*, recalls for me the events that led up to Brooks's appearance at the Hart party. "During the fifties," he says, "we
spent our days inventing characters for Caesar, but Mel was
really using Caesar as a vehicle. What he secretly wanted
was to perform himself. So in the evening we'd go to a party
and I'd pick a character for him to play. I never told him
what it was going to be, but I always tried for something
that would force him to go into panic, because a brilliant
mind in panic is a wonderful thing to see. For instance, I
might say, 'We have with us tonight the celebrated sculptor
Sir Jacob Epstone,' and he'd have to take it from there. Or
I'd make him a Jewish pirate, and he'd complain about how
he was being pushed out of the business because of the price
of sailcloth and the cost of crews nowadays. Another time,
I introduced him as Carl Sandburg, and he made up reams
of phony Sandburg poetry. There was no end to what he
could be—a U-boat commander, a deaf songwriter, an entire
convention of antique dealers.

"Once, I started a routine by saying 'Sir, you're the Israeli
wrestling champion of the world, yet you're extremely small.
How do you manage to defeat all those enormous opponents?'
'I give them a soul kiss,' he said, 'and they're so shocked they
collapse. Sometimes I hate doing it, like when it's a Greek
wrestler, because they have garlic breath.' I asked him
whether he was homosexual. 'No, I have a wife.' 'But what's
the difference between kissing her and kissing a wrestler?'
'My wife,' he said, 'is the only one I know who kisses from
the inside out.' That was pure Mel—a joke so wild it was

almost abstract. I used to enjoy trying to trap him. One night, when he was doing an Israeli heart surgeon, I said, 'Tell me, sir, who's that huge man standing in the corner?' 'Who knows? Who cares?' 'But surely, sir, you don't want a total stranger hanging around your operating theatre, bringing in germs?' 'Listen, in a hospital, a few germs more or less, what's the difference?' 'Even so,' I said, 'I'm still curious to know what that very large gentleman does.' 'Look,' he said. 'He's a big man, right? With a lot of muscle? You're small and Jewish, you don't mess around with big guys like that. Let him stand there if he wants to.' I still wouldn't let him off the hook. 'But what's that strange-looking machine beside him?' 'You mean the cyclotron?' 'No, the one next to that.' 'Oh,' he said, 'that is the Rokeach 14 machine. It makes Jewish soap powder. As you well know, we Jewish doctors are incredibly clean, and we try not to soil our patients during the macabre process of cutting them to pieces. We get through an awful lot of Rokeach 14.' Which is in fact a brand of kosher soap used by orthodox Jews." (Brooks later told me, apropos of Reiner's attempts to outwit him, "He was absolutely dazzling. I'd be going along pretty good, getting laughs, and he would suddenly people the room with alien characters bearing mysterious devices. What was I supposed to do? I had to come up with an explanation or die.")

"Another time," Reiner continues, "we created a family consisting of a Jewish mother, a black father, and a homosexual son. Mel was playing all three parts when I threw him a curve. 'Tell me,' I said, 'why is your son white-haired when you are not?' He answered as the mother. 'I told him always to stay inside the building,' he said, 'because it's full of Jews. One day, he went out and saw a whole bunch of Gentiles on the next block and his hair turned white overnight. It was his own fault. He should have stayed indoors.' Sometimes, if a party went on late, Mel would get punchy and forget the name of the character I'd given him. Once, I said, 'Here is Irving Schwartz, author of the best-selling novel *Up*.' We developed that for ten minutes or so, and then I said, 'Your book has a very unusual jacket. It's triangular in shape.' 'I'm glad you noticed that,' he said. 'It's a one-breasted seersucker jacket. The name is on the lapel—Irving Feinberg.' 'I think you've got that wrong, sir. Your name is Irving Schwartz.' 'Wait,' he said. 'Wait till I look at my driver's license.' He pulled out his wallet, looked at the license, and reacted with shock. 'Hey!' he said. 'My name is Mr. William Faversham.' 'Well, Mr. Faversham, could you tell us how you came to write a book under the name of Schwartz?' 'I think somebody stole my wallet.' But if Mel had a specialty, it was psychiatrists. He did dozens of them, maybe because he was in analysis himself between 1951 and 1957. When I made him a Greek psychiatrist, he said he was Dr. Corinne Corfu, the man who analyzed Socrates. And there was one amazing evening when he played eight different psychiatrists simultaneously, without getting any of them mixed up. He was never at a loss."

"Never" may be an overstatement. Mel Tolkin remembers a party at which Brooks, sans Reiner, delivered a soaringly funny monologue but could not find a satisfactory payoff line. He finally broke off in the middle of a sentence and walked out of the room. After the guests had waited for a while in expectant silence, Tolkin went out to look for him. He had gone home in self-disgust, leaving a scribbled note on a table. It read, "A Jew cries for help!"

"In the fifties," Reiner says, "Mel and I performed just for fun, among friends." Around 1953, Reiner bought a tape recorder on which to preserve some of their routines. One evening, after dinner at his home in Westchester, inspiration nudged him. He turned on the machine, picked up the microphone, strolled over to where Brooks was sitting, and said, "Ladies and gentlemen, we are fortunate to have with us tonight a man who was present at the crucifixion of Jesus Christ." The curve had been thrown. Brooks rose to the challenge and hit it out of the park, with repercussions to which we shall return: enough, for the moment, to note that this occasion marked the birth of a comic figure indestructible in every sense of the word; namely, the Two-Thousand-Year-Old Man. "The guy who gave us our entrée into the celebrity world was a well-known playwright named Joe Fields," Reiner goes on. "He heard us performing somewhere in the late fifties and invited us to eat at his apartment, along with people like Lerner and Loewe, Harold Rome, and Billy Rose. We became a sort of upper-bohemian cult. Then, in 1959, I appeared in a movie called *Happy Anniversary*, and Mel came to the wrap party for the cast and crew at a restaurant in the Village. Moss Hart was dining with his wife on the other side of the room. Mel recognized him. All of a sudden, he got up and walked across to Hart's table and said, very loudly, 'Hello. You don't know who I am. My name is Mel Brooks. Do you know who you are? Your name is Moss Hart. Do you know what you've written? You wrote *Once in a Lifetime* with George Kaufman, and *You Can't Take It with You* and *The Man Who Came to Dinner*. You wrote *Lady in the Dark* and you directed *My Fair Lady*.' And he ran right through the list of Hart's credits. 'You should be more arrogant!' he shouted. 'You have earned the right to be supercilious! *Why are you letting me talk to you?*' He went ranting on like that, and Hart looked petrified. It took him quite a time to realize that Mel wasn't just a nut case. But eventually he started laughing, and everything was fine. Later on, Mel and I did one of our bits. Hart couldn't help hearing it and that was how we got the invitation to Mamma Leone's."

In the autumn of 1959, Reiner's career was prospering, both on TV and in the cinema. As he put it to me, "I didn't need to sing for my supper anymore." Brooks's position was very different. Sid Caesar, for whom he had worked at a steeply rising salary for ten years, had been taken off the air, and Brooks was almost broke. "One day it's five thousand a week, the next day it's zilch," he said in a magazine interview long afterward, "I couldn't get a job anywhere! Comedy shows were out of style, and the next five years I averaged

eighty-five dollars a week. . . . It was a terrifying nose dive."
Recently, he told me, "At the time of that Random House
party, I was on the brink of disaster." Even during the high-
flying days with Caesar, he had been prone to recurrent fits
of depression. "There were fourteen or fifteen occasions when
I seriously thought of killing myself. I even had the pills."
One of his colleagues on "Your Show of Shows" recalls how
Brooks snapped out of a particularly black mood by grabbing
a straw hat and cane and ad-libbing a peppy, up-tempo
number that ended:

> Life may be rotten today, folks,
> But I take it all in stride,
> 'Cause tomorrow I'm on my way, folks—
> I'm committing suicide!

Mamma Leone's gave me my first sight of Brooks in performance. My last (to date) took place in the summer of
1977, when he was shooting his Hitchcockian comedy *High
Anxiety*. In the intervening eighteen years, and most drastically in the last three of them, his life had changed beyond
recognition. A trio of successive hits (*Blazing Saddles, Young
Frankenstein*, and *Silent Movie*) had made him a millionaire.
In December, 1976, the exhibitors of America had placed
him fifth on their annual list of the twenty-five stars who
exert the greatest box-office appeal—a fantastic achievement
for a middle-aged man whose only starring appearance up to
that time had been in a picture, *Silent Movie*, that did not
even require him to speak. His friend Burt Reynolds, rated
sixth that year, grew accustomed to picking up the phone and
hearing a jubilant voice announce, "Hello, Six, this is Five
speaking." In the 1977 poll, Reynolds rose to fourth position, while Brooks slipped to seventh, but considering that
no new film by Brooks had been shown in the preceding year,
it was remarkable, as he pointed out to me, that he had
retained a place in the top ten. "And in 1978," he said, "I'm
sure I'll be No. 5 again."

•　　•

I draw on my journal for the following impressions of the Once and Future Five at work (and play) on *High Anxiety*, a quintuple-threat Brooks movie in which he functioned as producer, director, co-author, title-song composer, and star:

July 14, 1977: Arrive in Pasadena for the last day of shooting. By pure but pleasing coincidence, location is named Brookside Park. Temperature ninety degrees, atmosphere smog-laden. Only performers present are Brooks, leaping around in well-cut charcoal-gray suit with vest, and large flock of trained pigeons. As at Mamma Leone's, he is playing a psychiatrist. Sequence in rehearsal is parody of *The Birds*, stressing aspect of avian behavior primly ignored by Hitchcock: Pigeons pursue fleeing Brooks across park, subjecting him to bombardment of bird droppings. Spattered star seeks refuge in gardener's hut, slams door, sinks exhausted onto upturned garbage can. After momentary respite, lone white plop hits lapel, harbinger of redoubled aerial assault through hole in roof. Brooks's hundred-yard dash is covered by tracking camera, while gray-haired technicians atop motorized crane mounted on truck squirt bird excreta (simulated by mayonnaise and chopped spinach) from height of thirty feet. Barry Levinson, one of four collaborators on screenplay, observes to me, "We have enough equipment here to put a man on the moon, and it's all being used to put bird droppings on Brooks." After each of numerous trial runs and takes, pigeons obediently return to their cages, putty in the hands of their trainer—"the same bird wrangler," publicity man tells me, "who was employed by Hitchcock himself." Find manic energy of Brooks, now fifty-one years old, awesome: by the time shot is satisfactorily in can, he will have sprinted, in this depleting heat, at least a mile, without loss of breath, ebullience, or directorial objectivity, and without taking a moment's break.

Each take is simultaneously recorded on videotape and instantly played back on TV screen—a technique pioneered by Jerry Lewis—to be scrutinized by Brooks, along with his fellow-authors, Levinson, Rudy DeLuca, and Ron Clark, who make comments ranging from condign approval to barbed derision. Dispelling myth that he is megalomaniac, Brooks listens persuadably to their suggestions, many of which he carries out. The writers, receiving extra pay as consultants, have been with him throughout shooting, except for three weeks when they went on strike for more money. Brooks coaxed them back by giving up part of his own share of profits not only of *High Anxiety* but of *Silent Movie*, on which he worked with same three authors. Main purpose of their presence is not to rewrite—hardly a line has been changed or cut—but to offer pragmatic advice. In addition, they all play supporting roles in picture. Later, as also happened on *Silent Movie*, they will view first assembly of footage and help Brooks with process of reducing it to rough-cut form. "Having us around keeps Mel on his toes," Levinson explains to me. "He likes to have constant feedback, and he knows we won't flatter him." All of which deals telling blow to already obsolescent *auteur* theory, whereby film is seen as springing fully armed from mind of director. Good to find Brooks, who reveres writers, giving them place in sun: he has often said that he became a director primarily in self-defense, to "protect my vision"— i.e., the script as written. "There's been no interference from the front office," Levinson continues, as Brooks trudges back to his mark for yet another charge through cloudburst of salad dressing. "Nobody from Fox has even come to see us. Mel has free rein. Jerry Lewis once had that kind of liberty, but who has it now? Only Mel and, I guess, Woody Allen."

Am reminded of remark made to me by Allen a few days earlier: "In America, people who do comedy are traditionally left alone. The studios feel we're on a wavelength that's alien to them. They believe we have access to some secret formula that they don't. With drama, it's different. Everybody thinks he's an expert."

Writers and camera crew gather round tree-shaded monitor to watch replay of latest take. Smothered in synthetic ordure, star bustles over to join them:

BROOKS: I stare at life through fields of mayonnaise.

(*Wipes eyes with towel.*) Was it for this that I went into movies? Did I say to my mother, "I'm going to be a big star, momma, and have birds shit on me"? I knew that in show business *people* shit on you—but *birds*! Some of this stuff is not mayonnaise, you know. Those are real pigeons up there.

The take (last of twenty) is generally approved, and Brooks orders it printed. Welcoming me to location, he expresses pleasure at hearing British accent, adding, "I love the Old World. I love the courteous sound of the engines of English cabs. I also love France and good wine and good food and good homosexual production designers. I believe all production designers should have a brush stroke, a scintilla, of homosexuality, because they have to hang out with smart people." (Brooks once declared, in an interview with *Playboy*, that he loved Europe so much that he always carried a photograph of it in his wallet. "Of course," he went on, "Europe was a lot younger then. It's really not a very good picture. Europe looks much better in person." He lamented the fact that his beloved continent was forever fighting: "I'll be so happy when it finally settles down and gets married.")

Brooks's version of shower scene from *Psycho*, shot several days before, now appears on monitor. An unlikely stand-in for Janet Leigh, Brooks is seen in bathrobe approaching fatal tub. Cut to closeup of feet as he daintily sheds sandals, around which robe falls to floor. Next comes rear view of Brooks, naked from head to hips, stepping into bath. Star watches himself entranced.

BROOKS (*passionately*): When people see this, I want them to say, "He may be just a small Jew, but I love him. A short little Hebrew man, but I'd follow him to the ends of the earth." I want every fag in L.A. to see it and say, "Willya *look* at that *back*?"

Before lunch break, he takes opportunity to deliver speech of thanks to assembled crew, whose reactions show that they have relished working with him.

Recall another apposite quote from Woody Allen, who

said to me in tones of stunned unbelief, "I hear there's a sense of enjoyment on Mel's set. I hear the people on his movies love the experience so much that they wish it could go on forever. On my movies, they're *thrilled* when it's over."

"As you all know," Brooks begins, "you'll never get an Academy Award with me, because I make comedies." This is a recurrent gripe. Brooks feels that film comedy has never received, either from industry or from audience, respect it deserves, and he is fond of pointing out that Chaplin got his 1971 Academy Award "just for surviving," not for *The Gold Rush* or *City Lights*.

BROOKS (*continuing*): I want to say from my heart that you're the best crew I ever found. Of course, I didn't look that hard. But you have been the most fun, and the costliest. I wish to express my sincere hope that the next job you get is—*work*.

Over lunch, consumed at long trestle tables under trees, he recounts—between and sometimes during mouthfuls—how he visited Hitchcock to get his blessings on *High Anxiety*.

BROOKS: He's a very emotional man. I told him that where other people take saunas to relax, I run *The Lady Vanishes*, for the sheer pleasure of it. He had tears in his eyes. I think he understood that I wasn't going to make fun of him. If the picture is a sendup, it's also an act of homage to a great artist. I'm glad I met him, because I love him. I love a lot of people that I want to meet so I can tell them about it before they get too old. Fred Astaire, for instance. And Chaplin. I've got to go to Switzerland and tell him—just a simple "Thank you," you know? [Chaplin died five months later, before this pilgrimage could be made.]

More Brooksian table talk, in response to student writing dissertation on his work:

STUDENT: What's the best way to become a director?

BROOKS: The royal road to direction used to be through the editing room. Today my advice would be: write a few successful screenplays. Anybody can direct. There are only eleven good writers. In all of Hollywood. I can name you many, many screenwriters who have gone on to become directors. In any movie, they are the prime movers.

STUDENT: Have you any ambition to make a straight dramatic film?

BROOKS (*vehemently*): No! Why should I waste my good time making a straight dramatic film? Sydney Pollack can do that. The people who can't make you laugh can do that. Suppose I became the Jean Renoir of America. What the hell would be left for the other guys to do? I would take all their jobs away. It would be very unfair of me.

STUDENT: In other words, "Shoemaker, stick to your last"?

BROOKS: Yes. And in Hollywood you're only as good as your last last.

STUDENT: But don't you want to surprise your audience?

BROOKS: Sure. Every time. I gave them *Blazing Saddles*, a Jewish Western with a black hero, and that was a megahit. Then I gave them a delicate and private film, *Young Franken-stein*, and that was a hit. Then I made *Silent Movie*, which I thought was a brave and experimental departure. It turned out to be another Mel Brooks hit. *High Anxiety* is the ulti-mate Mel Brooks movie. It has lunatic class.

STUDENT: But what if you had a serious dramatic idea that really appealed to you? Would you—

BROOKS: Listen, there are one hundred and thirty-one viable directors of drama in this country. There are only two viable directors of comedy. Because in comedy you have to do every-thing the people who make drama do—create plot and char-acter and motive and so forth—and *then*, on top of *that*, be funny.

UNIDENTIFIED BEARDED MAN: Have you ever thought of being funny onstage?

BROOKS: No, because I might become this white-belted, white-shoed, maroon-mohair-jacketed type who goes to Vegas and sprays Jew-jokes all over the audience. A few years of that and I might end up going to England, like George Raft or Dane Clark, wearing trench coats in B movies.

Debate ensues about differences (in style and personality) between Brooks and the other "viable director of comedy," Woody Allen. Both are New York Jewish, both wrote for Sid Caesar, both are hypochondriacs, much influenced by time spent in analysis. There is general agreement at table on obvious distinction—that Brooks is extrovert and Allen introvert.

BARRY LEVINSON: They're total opposites. Mel is a peasant type. His films deal with basic wants and greeds, like power and money. Woody's films are about inadequacies—especially sexual inadequacy—and frailty and vulnerability. Also, like Chaplin, Woody is his own vehicle. His movies are like episodes from an autobiography. You couldn't say that about Mel.

HOWARD ROTHBERG (*slim, dark-haired young man who has been Brooks's personal manager since 1975*): The big difference is that Mel's appeal is more universal. *Blazing Saddles* grossed thirty-five million domestically and *Silent Movie* is already up to twenty million. Woody, on the other hand, appeals to a cult. I love his pictures, but they have a box-office ceiling. They don't go through the roof.

BROOKS (*who has been wolfing cannelloni, followed by ice cream*): No matter how much *High Anxiety* grosses, it won't give me one more iota of freedom. I have the freedom right now to do anything I want. My contract is with the public—to entertain them, not just to make money out of them. I went into show business to make a noise, to *pronounce myself*. I want to go on making the loudest noise to the most people. If I can't do that, I'm not going to make a quiet, exquisite noise for a cabal of cognoscenti.

This is Brooks the blusterer speaking, the unabashed attention-craver who started out as a teenage timpanist and is still metaphorically beating his drum. Can testify that drummer has alter ego, frequently silenced by the din: Brooks the secret connoisseur, worshipper of good writing, and expert on the Russian classics, with special reference to Gogol, Turgenev, Dostoevski, and Tolstoy. Is it possible that—to adapt famous aphorism by Cyril Connolly—inside every Mel Brooks a Woody Allen is wildly signalling to be let out?

STUDENT: I think your films are somehow more benevolent and affirmative than Woody Allen's.

BROOKS: Let's say I'm beneficent. I produce beneficial things. A psychiatrist once told me he thought my psyche was basically very healthy, because it led to *product*. He said I was like a great creature that gave beef or milk. I'm munificent. I definitely feel kingly. Same kind of Jew as Napoleon.

STUDENT: Napoleon was Jewish?

BROOKS: Could have been. He was short enough. Also, he was very nervous and couldn't keep his hands steady. That's why he always kept them under his lapels. I put him in one of my records. [Fans will remember how the Two-Thousand-Year-Old Man took a summer cottage on Elba, where he met the exiled Emperor on the beach—"a shrimp, used to go down by the water and cry"—without at first realizing who he was: "The guy was in a bathing suit, how did I know? There was no place to put his hands."] Anyway, there's something disgustingly egotistical about me. I never truly felt inferior. I never developed small defenses. I never ran scared. Even in comedy, you don't want your hero to be a coward. You want him to go forth and give combat, which is what I do in *High Anxiety*. Now, Woody makes Fellini-ish, Truffaut-ish films. He starts out with the idea of making art. He feels that his art is his life. And more power to him. The difference is that if someone wants to call my movies art or crap, I don't mind.

Detect, once more, sound of obsessive drumbeating; last sentence, in particular, seems intended to convince drummer himself as much as anyone else. Conversation breaks off as Brooks returns to work. Hear him in distance inviting youthful assistant to take over direction of brief scene in gardener's hut, already rehearsed, where star is deluged anew with bird droppings—"a job," he graciously declares to the grinning apprentice, "fully commensurate with your latent talents."

Finishing my coffee, I mull over recent conversation with Gene Wilder, who has been directed thrice by Brooks (in *The Producers*, *Blazing Saddles*, and *Young Frankenstein*) and once by Allen (in *Everything You Always Wanted to Know about Sex but Were Afraid to Ask*). According to Wilder: "Working with Woody is what it must be like to work with Ingmar Bergman. It's all very hushed. You and I were talking quietly now, but if we were on Woody's set someone would already have told us to keep our voices down. He said three things to me while we were shooting—'You know where to get tea and coffee?' and 'You know where to get lunch?' and 'Shall I see you tomorrow?' Oh, and there was one other thing: 'If you don't like any of these lines, change them.' Mel would never say that. The way Woody makes a movie, it's as if he was lighting ten thousand safety matches to illuminate a city. Each one of them is a little epiphany, topical, ethnic, or political. What Mel wants to do is set off atom bombs of laughter. Woody will take a bow and arrow or a hunting rifle and aim it at small, precise targets. Mel grabs a shotgun, loads it with fifty pellets, and points it in the general direction of one enormous target. Out of fifty, he'll score at least six or seven huge bull's-eyes, and those are what people always remember about his films. He can synthesize what audiences all over the world are feeling, and suddenly, at the right moment, blurt it out. He'll take a universal and crystallize it. Sometimes he's vulgar and unbalanced, but when those seven shots hit that target, I know that little maniac is a genius. A loud kind of Jewish genius—maybe that's as close as you can get to defining him."

This reminds me of something written in 1974 by the critic Andrew Sarris:

> Allen's filmmaking is more cerebral, and Brooks's more intuitive. In a strange way, Brooks is more likable

than Allen. Thus, even when Allen tries to do the right
thing, he seems very narrowly self-centred, whereas even
when Mel Brooks surrenders to the most cynical calculations—as he does so often in *Blazing Saddles*—he still
spills over with emotional generosity. . . . What Allen
lacks is the reckless abandon and careless rapture of
Brooks.

Reflect that this positive judgment is not necessarily incompatible with negative opinion I have lately heard from
former colleague of Brooks; viz., "Woody has become a
professional, whereas Mel is still a brilliant amateur. Amateurs
are people putting on parties with multimillion-dollar
budgets."

Return to set, where, after nearly twelve weeks' shooting,
current party is over. Brooks has brought in picture—
budgeted at four million dollars—four days ahead of schedule.
Though in buoyant mood, he expresses horror at rocketing
cost of filmmaking: "One actor and a few birds, but I'll bet
you this has been a twenty-thousand-dollar day." (Studio
accounting department afterward confirms that he would
have won his bet.) I take my leave. Brooks clicks heels and
bows, saying, "Your obedient Jew." He misses no opportunity
to brandish his Jewishness, which he uses less as a weapon
than as a shield. Remember (he seems to be pleading) that I
must be liked, because it is nowadays forbidden to dislike a
Jew.

Manager Rothberg accompanies me to parking lot, explain-
ing how much success of movie means to Brooks. I suggest
that surely he can afford to make a flop. "Financially, he
can," Rothberg says. "Psychologically, he can't."

August 31, 1977: "My beloved, you are guinea pigs." It is
a balmy evening seven weeks later, and Brooks is introducing
first showing of rough-cut to audience of two hundred (including workers on picture, their friends and relations, and
minor studio employees such as waiters, cleaners, and parking
attendants) who have crowded into private theatre at Fox.
He continues, "There are children present. Some of them

may be mine, so I'm not going to do the filthy speech that is customary on these occasions. For the nonce, by which I mean no offense, this movie is called *High Anxiety*, a phrase that I hope will enter common parlance and become part of the argot of Americana. But what you will see tonight has no music, no sound effects, and no titles. You won't even see our swirling artwork. You will, however, see a lot of crayon lines, which I will explain for the benefit of the editor. They indicate something called opticals. This picture has one hundred and six dissolves, of which you will see *not one*. There are some other very fancy opticals that I am having processed in Cairo right now. There is also one crayon mark that should be on a men's room wall, but we couldn't get it out in time. As you know, it's incumbent on us all to be killed in a Hitchcock movie, and you will see several people being very tastefully slaughtered. I regret to tell you that in casting four crucial roles we ran out of money, so the people who *wrote* the picture are *in* it. Finally, let me say that I wish you well, but I wish myself better."

Screening gets warm response, punctuated by applause. Brooks scampers down front and thanks audience for their attention, their laughter, and their profound awareness that "there are eighteen million Arabs surrounding two hundred and six Jews, and—no, wait, that's from some other speech, at some hospital somewhere." He then requests detailed and candid criticism: Where did movie drag? Which gags failed? Was plot clear? He listens raptly to all answers, asks other spectators for corroboration or dissent, makes careful notes of points on which action should be taken. And goes back to three and a half more months of furious work, polishing the film for a December premiere, in order to qualify for the Academy Award, which, as he repeatedly, belligerently, fate-placatingly asserts, no comedy can ever win.

The man we know as Mel Brooks was born in a Brooklyn tenement on June 28, 1926. To the question "What were you born?" when it was posed by David Susskind on a TV panel show in 1960, he replied, "George M. Cohan." (Later in the program, he admitted that he really had two diametrically opposed selves, that there were two different sides to "the strange amalgam, the marvellous pastiche that is me." Under Susskind's remorseless interrogation, he confessed, "The first side of me is Sir Anthony Eden. . . . And the other is Fred Astaire.") In reality, what he was born was Melvin Kaminsky, the youngest of four boys, whose parents were Eastern European immigrants. His father, Maximilian Kaminsky, came from Danzig, and his mother, née Kate Brookman, from Kiev. According to Brooks, one reason for the success of his collaboration with people like Carl Reiner and Mel Tolkin was that they all shared "the same background, the second-generation Russian-Ukrainian-Jewish intellectual heritage." He told Susskind that his mother left Kiev in early childhood, never having learned Russian, and that her English was still fairly impenetrable, mainly because the voice of authority, which she took as her model on arrival in New York, invariably belonged to an Irish cop. The result, Brooks said, was that "she speaks no known language, and speaks it with an Irish accent."

His father, a process server, died suddenly of a kidney disease at the age of thirty-four, when Brooks was two and a half years old. The shock left him with a sense of loss that persisted into adult life. For example, he recognizes that his relationship with Sid Caesar was that of a child clamoring for the attention and approval of a father. When Brooks went into analysis, in 1951, his purpose, he recently told me, was "to learn how to be a father instead of a son." (His six years on the couch, two to four sessions per week, undoubtedly hastened the emergence of Brooks the father figure, patriarchal ruler of movie sets. "He's sometimes my mother hen, and sometimes even my brother," Gene Wilder says, "but most of the time he's my father." On a wall of Wilder's office at Fox, there is a photograph of the two men, inscribed "To my son Gene, with love, Daddy Mel.") Kate Kaminsky, widowed and penniless, with four boys to support, took a job in the garment district, putting in a ten-hour day and bringing home extra work in the evening. A miniature dynamo, less than five feet in height, she also found time and energy to keep her children fed, their clothes washed and mended, and their apartment in spotless trim. The roach or bedbug that entered her domain had signed its own death warrant. She exemplified what Brooks said to Susskind of Jewish mothers in general: "Until they die themselves, they *clean* and *kill*." He went on to sum up his feelings about this indomitable woman by declaiming, "If I could, I would go skinny-dipping with my mother." (Still vigorous in her eighty-third year, she nowadays lives in Florida.) Irving and Leonard, the eldest two sons, were sent out to work when they were twelve and, on a family income that averaged about thirty-five dollars a week, ends were precariously made to meet. Mrs. Kaminsky was obsessed with the idea of preserving what Brooks describes as a "certain threshold of dignity," and for this reason she always refused to go on relief. It must be remembered that her husband died shortly before the Wall Street crash and that Brooks spent his childhood in the roughest years of the Depression. To be Jewish, Brooklyn-born, fatherless, impoverished, and below average stature—no more classic recipe could be imagined for an American comedian. Or, one might suppose, for an American suicide.

Not long ago, discussing Brooks with a prosperous Jewish movie producer, I remarked that he had once been prone to suicidal impulses. "Nonsense," the producer said, "that's self-dramatization. Jews don't kill themselves. Look at their history. They're too busy fighting to survive."

When I reported this conversation to Brooks, he said, "You were talking to a rich Jew. Poor people kill themselves, and a lot of poor people are Jews. One evening, when I was a kid, a woman jumped off the top of a building next door to where I lived. She was Jewish. And there were plenty of other Jewish suicides during the Depression." The image of that death is burned into Brooks's memory. He was playing with friends on a nearby street. Hearing screams and police sirens, he ran to see what had happened. A corpse, covered by a sheet so that only the feet were visible, was being loaded into an ambulance, and he was sure he recognized the shoes as a pair belonging to his mother. His own apartment was empty. Unknown to him, Mrs. Kaminsky was working over-time in Manhattan. The hours that passed before she re-turned were the worst he ever lived through.

Some revealing sidelights on Brooks's relationship with his parents are thrown by the recorded routine in which he plays a two-hour-old baby, precociously endowed with the faculty of speech. Interviewed by Carl Reiner, he declares that he already knows his mother, though he hasn't yet "seen the outside."

> REINER: Do you hope she's good-looking?
> BROOKS: I don't care what she looks like. I'm not going to date her. I'm her child. But I know she's good. Because you can tell a person by what they are inside. . . . And I was there, I was inside, and I looked around. She's great. . . . I remember when I was a tadpole, a little fetus there, swimming around.
> REINER: You remember having a tail?
> BROOKS: Sure. Oh, that was the best part. I loved the tail.
> REINER: Were you unhappy when it disappeared?
> BROOKS: When I lost my tail, I got a nose. . . . The nose is much more important, because—you can't blow your tail, know what I mean?

He has a simple theory to account for the attacks of queasiness that women suffer during the early months of pregnancy:

> BROOKS: I think the moment they realize that there's a living creature in them, they puke.
> REINER: But why?
> BROOKS: Wouldn't you be nauseous if there was some-

body running around inside of you? . . . It's a frightening thing.

His knowledge of world celebrities is extremely limited. Reiner reels off a list of names including Queen Elizabeth, Winston Churchill, Fidel Castro, and Pandit Nehru, none of whom means anything to him. Then:

REINER: Have you heard of Cary Grant?
BROOKS: Oh, sure. Everybody knows Cary Grant.

Pressed by Reiner, he explains that while he was still in the womb his mother went to a lot of Cary Grant pictures, whereas she never took him to any Pandit Nehru pictures. "But I'm sure," he generously adds, "that he's a *hell* of an actor."

At one point, he leaps to the conclusion that he is a girl ("That's *adorable!*"), but Reiner gently disabuses him. "That's all right," he says, putting a bold face on it. "I'll play ball and get drunk and things. I'll be fine." He tentatively asks whether Burt Lancaster is a girl. Reiner gives him a negative answer, which seems to relieve him. "That's good," he says, reconciled at last to masculinity. "I'll be like him." It has been established earlier that Baby Brooks's linguistic skill is a freakish and short-lived gift, likely to be withdrawn at any moment. As long as the theme is his mother, he is eagerly articulate. Significantly, the withdrawal symptoms begin to appear in the following passage, when Reiner introduces a new subject.

REINER: I'd like to know what you feel about your father.
BROOKS: I feel that Dad is the kind of guy that will gah-gah-san.
REINER: Will what? I didn't get that.
BROOKS: I feel that my father will always be the kind of a guy that will take me to ballgames, and we'll be buddies, and we'll sy-ny-ny, ny-foy.

REINER: I don't understand you.

BROOKS: I think that my father and I will probably
get along well together, since we're both boys. We'll
probably run around and play ball and *nah-nah-hah,
nah-nah-hah.*

REINER: I do believe he's losing his intelligence.

And the track ends with Brooks regressing into wailing,
bawling, frantic inarticulacy. It is quite an unnerving sound.
Listening to it, I recall something that an old friend of
Brooks, the novelist Joseph Heller, once said to me: "There's
a side of Mel that will never be fulfilled, no matter how hard
he drives himself, and it all goes back to his father's death."

At P.S. 19, Brooks was bright but unstudious—the kind of
disruptive, obstreperous child that teachers slap down on
principle, wearily aware that he will bounce right back up. "I
wasn't an avid reader," he says. "I was always an avid
talker and doer. Reading books seemed too conservative for
me to bother with." He quickly established himself as the
clown of the classroom. One of his favorite movies was
Frankenstein (the 1931, James Whale version), and he discovered at the age of eight that he could reduce his closest
chum, a boy called Gene Cogen, to uncontrollable hysterics
by singing "Puttin' On the Ritz" in the manner of Boris
Karloff. "We had *folie à deux,*" Brooks told me. "It got so
bad that Cogen couldn't hear that song near a window,
because he might roll out and fall to his death. I would start
to sing and he would collapse. He would have to be dragged
to the principal's room by his feet, with his head banging
on the steps, still laughing." Thus the infant Brooks achieved
what every comic traditionally strives for—a knockdown,
drag-out exit. (He stored up this triumph for future use:
Peter Boyle performs the same routine in *Young Frankenstein.*) Despite, or perhaps because of, the damage to his
head, young Cogen remained a fan of Brooks, and said to
him one day, "You're going to be famous when you grow

up. I know that because nobody else uses words like 'urchin' in English composition."

On the streets, where Irish, Italian, and Polish gangs roamed only a few blocks away, Brooks was funny in self-defense. He later said to a *Playboy* interviewer, "If your enemy is laughing, how can he bludgeon you to death?" Whenever it was possible, he and his pals would travel in the company of a well-built Gentile. Even today, it is an article of faith with Brooks that "every small Jew should have a tall goy for a friend, to walk with him and protect him against assault." Much of Brooks's humor, as we shall see, is inspired by fear: fear of injury, illness, sex, and failure; and also of unfriendly Gentiles, especially large ones, and most particularly if they are Germans or Cossacks. Fear, too, of predatory animals, though not, apparently, of sharks. My evidence for this is drawn from the Susskind program mentioned previously.

> SUSSKIND: Now let's talk about Jewish mothers.
>
> DAVID STEINBERG (*another of the panellists*): Forget about Jewish mothers, let's talk about sharks.
>
> BROOKS (*instantly assuming a lecturer's voice, plummy and pedantic*): A shark could never harm you. The shark is a benign creature of the sea. Of course, if you thrash about in the water or if you wear shiny bracelets, the shark will be attracted to you. On occasion, the shark has followed people out of the water and has gone to their blanket and eaten their beach ball. One time, the shark followed my brother Irving home on the Brighton local, and, upon being admitted to the apartment house, the shark entered his apartment—Apartment 4-B—and ate his entire family and a brand-new hat. Apart from that, the shark is a pussycat.

All the apprehensions that surface in Brooks's comedy have the same eventual source: a fear—or, to put it more positively, a hatred—of death. The noise he makes it literally death-defying. I append some Brooksian reflections on mortality, culled from various conversations over the past year.

BROOKS: The whole business of death is too formal nowadays. Bing Crosby just succumbed to the great spectre at the age of seventy-three, but the way it's covered by radio and television and newspapers it is no longer a calamity. It is worded in correct obituary paragraphs and it becomes a normal and ordinary event. The good shock value is taken out of it. The moments of horrible grief over somebody's death are handled for us so that we don't experience them, and then they stay with us too long because we didn't grieve properly. The media formalize the tragedy, put a quick film of Saran Wrap over it, so that we don't feel, "My God, one of us has suddenly ceased to be," so that millions of people don't ask, "Where did Bing Crosby go?" Well, where *did* he go? Don't just tell me he died. I want to know where he went. And I want to grieve a little bit.

MYSELF: Are you scared of dying?

BROOKS: Not right now, not just this moment, because I'm feeling good, I'm not in a lot of pain. But I always intend to be afraid of it. To pay proper respect and homage to it. When I was nine, my friend Arnold said to me that we were both going to die. I said, "You're obviously not right, you can't be right. We're not going to die, because why were we born? It wouldn't make any sense." He said, "What about your grandfather? He died. And what about fish?" I said my grandfather was *very* old, *exceptionally* old, and fish had nothing to do with us. I thought I sounded very clever. All the same, that was the first time I knew I was going to die.

Again:

MYSELF: Do you believe in life after death?

BROOKS: No, I don't. I think that's silly. And there's no Judgment Day, either. There isn't a day when we all kiss the little fishes and shake hands and walk together into God's green heaven. So what are we doing here? My guess is that we are part of an evolving process that has no knowable purpose. What's happened is that we were given too many brains, and our brains have screwed up our biological evolution. If we didn't think so much, we'd know what it was all about. When one leaf on a tree begins to turn yellow, it doesn't turn to the other leaves and say, "Jesus Christ, all you guys are green and I'm turning yellow! What the hell is this?" They just turn yellow, and then red, and then brown, and then they leave the tree, and it's all proper. But we say, "Look at this gray hair! Look at this wrinkle! And, my God, I'm so tired after I walk up fourteen steps!" We defer far too much to our brains, our logic, our powers of rational thought. That's why we're so vain, so egotistical, so full of complaining. Leaves never complain.

MYSELF: You're saying that we ought to go along with the processes of nature. But science tells us that we live on a dying planet, where everything—leaves and people alike—is ultimately doomed to extinction. If that's correct, surely the best way to obey the laws of nature would be to kill ourselves now and have done with it?

BROOKS: But we don't have to, because we're going to die anyway. And, because of that, let's have a merry journey, and shout about how light is good and dark is not. What we should do is not *future* ourselves so much. We should *now* ourselves more. "*Now* thyself" is more important than "*Know* thyself." Reason is what tells us to ignore the present and live in the future. So all we do is make plans. We think that somewhere there are going to be green pastures. It's crazy. Heaven is nothing but a grand, monumental instance of future. Listen, *now* is good. *Now* is wonderful. (*Catching himself on the brink of sounding pretentious, he retreats to the safety of self-mockery, and adopts the tone of a humorless pseudo intellectual.*) By this, of course, I do not mean to intimate that I espouse a totally Sartrean position.

MYSELF: But you're in the movie business. You have to plan ahead.

BROOKS: I only look ahead commercially. I never look ahead spiritually.

On his records with Reiner, there was no advance planning;

Brooks lived entirely in the moment, wholly committed to *now*. For this reason (which we'll examine later), they may well represent his most personal comic achievements.

A final exchange with Brooks on eschatology:

MYSELF: When you're playing the Two-Thousand-Year-Old Man, Reiner asks whether you and your fellow cave dwellers believed in a superior being. You answer, "Yes. A guy Phil." You used to offer up prayers to him, like "O Philip, please don't take our eyes out." Then, one day, he was struck dead by lightning. Reiner asks how you felt about that, and you say, "We looked up. We said, 'There's something bigger than Phil.' " Is there?

BROOKS: Yes. There *is* something bigger than Phil, and I'm afraid of it. That's where my standards of morality come from —fear. And not only fear of God. I know how strong *I* am, how powerful *I* can be, how aggressive *I* can get. And I don't want a world where that kind of force can be turned against me. It frightens me. That's why we've all got to behave. That's the beginning of civil behavior. Fear of ourselves.

In 1939, the Kaminskys moved to Brighton Beach, where they shared a house a block and a half from the sea. "It was sort of rustic out there," Brooks recalls. "We actually got to see *trees*. I loved it." One of their neighbors was Buddy Rich, Artie Shaw's new drummer, who befriended Brooks and gave him an occasional free lesson in the art of percussion. The following summer, Brooks took a vacation job as a general helper at a hotel in the Catskills, washing dishes, keeping the tennis courts clean, and yelling things like "Mrs. Bloom, your time is up!" at people in rented rowboats. The food supplied to the staff still haunts his nightmares. Of one especially feculent pie, he says, "It lay under my heart for three years. I called it Harold. I used to pat it every morning and ask it how it was—'Remember how you were when I ate you, you little devil?' " He worked out a simple comedy routine, which, as a reward for good conduct, he was occasionally allowed to perform. Clad in a black overcoat and derby hat, and toting

two suitcases, the fourteen-year-old Brooks would trudge out
onto the high diving board. Pausing at the edge, he would
suddenly scream "Business is terrible! I can't go on!" and
plunge into the pool.

After two years of seaside life, Mrs. Kaminsky brought
her family back to the old neighborhood; the reason, Brooks
says, was that "she missed the friendships of the ghetto." He
attended Eastern District High School, where he was either
an all-talking, all-singing version of Harpo Marx or a major
nuisance, depending on whether you were his classmate or
his teacher. Through his brother Lenny, he met Don Appell,
a Broadway actor who had appeared with Canada Lee in
Orson Welles's 1941 production of *Native Son*. Appell introduced him to the social director of a borscht-belt hotel in
Ellenville. Brooks made a strong impression and was hired,
for the summer season of 1942, as drummer and part-time
tummler. Two quotations may here be helpful. (1) Brooks
to *Playboy*: "Jews don't do comedy in winter. In summer, all
right." (2) Brooks to me: "A *tummler* can be defined as a
resident offstage entertainer at a Jewish mountain resort,
mostly after lunch." He found it hard to decide on a professional name. Melvin Kaminsky was too overtly Jewish for
a comedian. David Daniel Kaminsky, also of Brooklyn but
unrelated to Brooks, had faced much the same problem a
decade or so earlier, and had solved it by billing himself as
Danny Kaye. (Just why Jews in the performing arts were—
and, for the most part, still are—expected to Anglicize their
names is a question worthy of a separate study. To take three
cases at random, is it to simplify pronunciation, to enhance
euphony, or to disarm bigotry that Emanuel Goldenberg
becomes Edward G. Robinson, Benny Kubelsky becomes
Jack Benny, and Isadore Demsky becomes Kirk Douglas? The
whole rigmarole discredits the public that demands it.)
Brooks's first thought was to borrow his mother's maiden
name, but Melvin Brookman turned out to be a nonstarter,
because, he told me, "I couldn't get it all on my drum."
Chopping off a syllable, he settled for Melvin Brooks.

That summer, two events occurred that helped to lay down the course of his future career. In the band at the Avon Lodge, a neighboring Catskill pleasure dome, there was a pretty good saxophone player called Sid Caesar. Brooks met him in off-duty hours, howled at his mimetic gifts, and formed a friendship that was renewed, to the lasting gratitude of TV audiences, after the war. The other significant event took place back in Ellenville. It was a classic demonstration of the First Show-Biz Law of Psychokinetics, according to which major talent, if unfulfilled, acquires the power of temporarily disabling minor talent that comes within its sphere of influence and impedes its development. One morning, in obedience to this law, the regular stand-up comic fell mysteriously sick and had to be shipped back to New York. Brooks, inevitably, was asked to replace him. He went on that night and improvised, using real characters—the manager, staff, and clientele of the lodge—as his points of departure into fantasy. He also found time to prepare a short blackout spot, for which he co-opted a girl assistant. "It was entitled 'S. and M.,' thirty years before anyone had heard of S. and M.," he told me. "The girl and I walked out from the wings and met in the center of the stage. I said, 'I am a masochist.' She said, 'I am a sadist.' I said, 'Hit me,' and she hit me, very hard, right in the face. And I said, 'Wait a minute, wait a minute, hold it. I think I'm a sadist.' Blackout. That was the first sketch I ever wrote." Within a few days, he had composed his own theme song, the climax of which was a rousing plea for sympathy:

> I'm out of my mind,
> So won't you be kind
> And please love Melvin Brooks?

He was not an overnight smash, but he improved with every performance and held down the job for the rest of the season, in the course of which, incidentally, he celebrated his sixteenth birthday.

•   •

One night last winter, Brooks dined with me at my rented house in Santa Monica. Although I was the host, he insisted on providing the wine, which turned out to be Mouton-Rothschild 1961. (He makes the same stipulation wherever he eats. Even at the most expensive restaurants in Beverly Hills, Brooks will arrive with a neat leather case that holds two bottles from his own cellar. He does this partly because few wine lists offer items of comparable quality and partly because he sees no reason to pay exorbitant markups if he can avoid it. Thus he exploits his status while restricting his expenditure, since the restaurateurs would rather slim their profits than lose his patronage.) Over dinner, he told me a little-known story, the saga of Brooks at war, which I here reproduce in his own words:

"I came in at the end. I went overseas with the artillery, and we docked at Le Havre, France, in February, 1945. Then I was transferred into the 1104th Combat Engineer Group. We travelled in a big truck through the nation of France on our way to Belgium, and every time we passed through a little town, we'd see these signs—'Boulangerie,' 'Pâtisserie,' and 'Rue' this, and 'Rue' that, and rue the day you came here, young man. When we got to our hundred and eightieth French village, I screamed at the top of my lungs, 'The joke is over! English, *please!*' I couldn't believe that a whole country couldn't speak English. One-third of a nation, all right, but not a whole country. There was very little actual shooting in Belgium, but there was plenty of mortar and artillery fire, and it was very noisy, and I thought that I would not want to be in the war very long, because of the noise. The earth was very hard when I was there, and I could not dig a V-shaped foxhole, as I wanted to, and stay down in the bottom of the V for the rest of the war. All these hot fragments of shrapnel and stuff were flying around, and I did not want to die, so it was awful. I remember hiding under a desk in a kindergarten while there were air battles going on above us, and bombs rattling.

"I was a PFC. Once, I was out on patrol with seven other

men, and we found a case of German rifles near an old railway siding—beautiful sharpshooting rifles with bolt action. Sure enough, there were some cartridges right next to them. So we had a contest. There were these white insulation things up on the telephone poles, and any man who shot one down won a dollar from each of the others. I was pretty good at that, and I'd made about twenty-one dollars when suddenly we got a strange call on our jeep radio. It said that German werewolves—guerrillas operating behind our lines—had cut all communication between the 1104th and the Ninth Army by destroying the telephone wires. Holy shit, I realized it was us, so we barrelled right back to camp, and they said, 'Did you see anything?' and we said 'Not a thing.' Then I became very brave. I said, 'Give me some men, sir, and I'll go back. We gotta stop these werewolves.' So I was sent out again on patrol to hunt them down. We hung around the railway siding for about four hours and then came back. My colonel offered to make me a corporal on the spot, and I said, 'No, no, sir, I'm not worthy of it.' Because I knew that noncoms and officers got killed and that somehow privates could survive in This Thing Called War.

"Along the roadside, you'd see bodies wrapped up in mattress covers and stacked in a ditch, and those would be Americans, that could be me. And I sang all the time; I made up funny songs; I never wanted to think about it. Some guy would say, 'We're gonna be killed, we'll never get out of this war,' and I'd say, 'Nobody dies—it's all made up.' Because otherwise we'd all get hysterical, and that kind of hysteria— it's not like sinking, it's like slowly taking on water, and that's the panic. Death is the enemy of everyone, and, even though you hate Nazis, death is more of an enemy than a German soldier.

"At the end, it was very sad, because the Germans were sending old men and little boys to fight against us. I was very good about that. I'd say, 'No shooting, throw down your guns and talk to them in Yiddish and German.' Of course, when we ran into pockets of trained German soldiers, genuine S.S. *Flammenwerfer* Nazis who wanted to die rather than surrender, I'd hide, because they'd kill you as soon as look at you. But these groups of little boys and old men wanted nothing but just to go to their mothers or their toilets. From around April 25 onward was the worst two weeks of my life. Then it was over, and it was V-E Day. And on V-E Day I hid again, because the Americans all got drunk and fired off every round of ammunition they had, and a lot of people were killed in the festivities. I knew if I went out on the street I'd get shot to death. I was in a village near Wiesbaden, and the May wine was still green. It can make you very drunk, so I found a wine cellar and opened a hundred bottles of it and poured it all over me. I stayed there for twenty-four hours, until the shooting had stopped."

"And then you went back to the States?" I asked.

"No," Brooks said. "You see, I was the barracks character, and they didn't want to lose me. My major said to me, 'Melvin, why not stay with us and travel around providing the boys with entertainment?' I said 'Great!' So he made me a corporal and gave me an old Mercedes, a real beauty. Then I told him I'd need a chauffeur, and he said, 'I can't let you have a military man.' I said, 'Could you spare a few pfennigs for a German civilian driver?' He said 'Fine,' so I found a German fiddle player named Helga, who became my chauffeuse. My official title was Noncom in Charge of Special Services, and I did shows for enlisted men and officers' clubs. Sometimes for a whole division, with tens of thousands of people out front. I told big, lousy jokes. Every time Bob Hope came by, I would write down all his jokes and use them. Nothing frightened me. I sang like Al Jolson. Everybody could do the low Jolson, but I did the high Jolson that nobody else could do—things like 'I love you as I loved you when you were *sweeeet sixteeeen.*' People said they appreciated that. My chauffeuse played the fiddle for them and together we fiddled in the back seat of the Mercedes.

"I used to go to Frankfurt with my special pass and obtain certain rare cognacs and stick them in my car. I shoved them

into every orifice that would take them. There wasn't a
nineteen-year-old soldier who got drunker than I did. Helga
played Brahms's 'Lullaby' beautifully. I'd say, 'Pull over to
the curb and play Brahms's "Lullaby." ' That dream world
lasted for four months. Then they told me my Occupation
duties were over and I could go back to civilian life. And I
said, 'No, no—let me die in the back of the Mercedes with
Helga.' But they sent me home anyway."

Professionally speaking, what he returned to was almost
three years of not very much. During his absence, things had
been moving fast for his friend Caesar. While serving in the
Coast Guard, Caesar had appeared in a recruiting revue
called *Tars and Spars*; its director was Max Liebman, a sharp-
eyed impresario who already numbered Imogene Coca and
Danny (Kaminsky) Kaye among his discoveries. Dominated
by Caesar's comedy routines, *Tars and Spars* opened in
Florida and then went on a national tour, after which
Columbia made a movie version that retained nothing of the
original except the title and Caesar. His notices when the
film was released, in 1946, launched him on a thriving career
in nightclubs and vaudeville houses. Nobody, however,
seemed inclined to discover Brooks. To demonstrate the
versatility of his face, he hired a photographer to snap him
in four contrasting moods—Brooks beaming, Brooks scowl-
ing, Brooks pensive, and Brooks aghast—and had the results
printed on one page, copies of which he sent to every agent
in town. He once arrived without an appointment at the
headquarters of the eminent producer Kermit Bloomgarden.
"There were dozens of actors waiting to see him, some of
them quite famous," Brooks told me. "I walked up to his
secretary and said, 'Paul Muni is here. I have to go in three
minutes.' She got on the intercom, and within ten seconds
Bloomgarden came running out of his office. He looked at
me and said, 'This boy is not Paul Muni.' I said, 'Muni's
name is Harold Gottwald. I am the *real* Paul Muni.' [Whose
real real name, incidentally was Muni Weisenfreund.] Then

Bloomgarden grabbed me by the collar and said, 'You've got a lot of moxie. I'm going to remember you.' But he didn't give me an audition."

Under the pressure of need or fear, Brooks was capable of any audacity. One night during this period, he went out to New Jersey to see the comedian Ronny Graham, who was a friend of his, performing in cabaret. After the show, Graham gave him a lift back to New York. To continue in Brooks's words: "We stopped off on the way to have a sandwich at a diner. It was about 3 A.M. and the place was full of enormous truck drivers. Ronny was still wearing his stage makeup and some pretty avant-garde clothes, and these big, hairy men all swivelled round and started to stare at us. Some of them even stood up. While we were eating, every-thing went very quiet. I was terrified. Suddenly, I turned on Ronny like a cobra and said, 'I want my ring back.' He said, 'What?' I said, 'You *spoke* to that *man*. Back at the club. Don't think I didn't see you speaking to him, because I did. *I want my ring back*. And I'll tell you something else—*you'll never have my tongue again!*' And we both went into this berserk faggot row. Finally, I picked up my cup of coffee and threw it in his face. Then I flounced out to the car with Ronny right behind me, wiping his eyes and screaming. Some of the truck drivers followed us out to the parking lot. They just stood there, dumbstruck, with their hands on their hips, as we drove off, kissing and making up. I waved at them out of the window."

In the autumn of 1947, Caesar invited Brooks to come and see him at the Roxy, where he was starring in the stage show that accompanied the long-running movie *Forever Amber*. Afterward, in his dressing room, Caesar mentioned that Max Liebman was planning a revue for presentation on television. "What is that?" Brooks claims to have asked, and to have received the reply "It's a thing that takes pictures of you and sends them into people's living rooms."

"Don't do it," Brooks begged him, straight-faced, "It's trafficking in graven images, and there are strict Jewish laws

against that. You better stay away from that stuff or you'll
never get your image back. The very least that can happen
is that you'll be sterilized by the cameras."

A superstitious man, Caesar was thoroughly unnerved by
Brooks's little joke. A few months later, however, when
Brooks was directing a shoestring production at Red Bank,
New Jersey, Caesar called him with the news that he had
decided to risk infertility. He had signed with NBC to appear
in "The Admiral Broadway Revue," a sixty-minute program,
produced by Liebman, that would make its debut in January,
1949. Caesar proposed a deal whereby he personally would
pay Brooks a weekly stipend of fifty dollars to supply him
with special material. Brooks jumped at the offer.

"The Admiral Broadway Revue," which ran for nineteen
sparkling weeks, was an acorn that soon grew into an oak.
With many of the same participants—e.g., Caesar and
Imogene Coca as performers, Mel Tolkin and Lucille Kallen
as principal writers, and Liebman as producer—it reappeared
in February, 1950, now expanded into a full-blown, high-
budget, prime-time, ninety-minute Saturday-night event, entitled "Your Show of Shows." Brooks refused to renew his
private arrangement with Caesar; as he put it, "I don't want
to be your boy." Instead, Liebman hired him, at a hundred
and fifty a week. His first contribution to the new series was
the famous sketch in which Caesar played a jungle boy who
is discovered, clad in a lion skin, roaming the streets of
New York.

> INTERVIEWER: Sir, how do you survive in New York
> City? . . . What do you eat?
> CAESAR: Pigeon.
> INTERVIEWER: Don't the pigeons object?
> CAESAR: Only for a minute.
> INTERVIEWER (*bringing up a recurrent Brooksian
> obsession*): What are you afraid of more than anything?
> CAESAR: Buick.
> INTERVIEWER: You're afraid of a Buick?

CAESAR: Yes. Buick can win in death struggle. Must sneak up on parked Buick, punch grille hard. Buick die.

Within a couple of months, Brooks's salary had risen to two hundred dollars, from which it steadily ascended to the peak of five thousand.

Many detailed accounts exist of the writing team that worked on "Your Show of Shows." Not since the Algonquin Round Table has a group of American wits been more extensively chronicled. In addition to Tolkin, Kallen, and Brooks, it eventually included Joseph Stein (who wrote the book of *Fiddler on the Roof*), Larry Gelbart, and Neil Simon, with Michael Stewart (author-to-be of *Hello, Dolly!*) acting as typist, a post in which he was later replaced by "a little red-headed rat"—to cite Brooks's affectionate phrase—named Woody Allen. Carl Reiner and Howard Morris, from the supporting cast, threw in ideas; and Caesar, with Liebman at his side, presided over the collective delirium, a madhouse of competing egos in which nobody could outshout Brooks. According to Miss Kallen, "Mel imitated everything from a rabbinical student to Moby Dick thrashing about on the floor with six harpoons sticking in his back."

Tolkin told me, "He used to bare his teeth like a rodent if you crossed him. Half of Mel's creativity comes out of fear and anger. He doesn't perform, he screams." (By the end of 1950, Tolkin and Caesar were already in psycho-analysis, and it is not surprising that in the following year Brooks also took to the couch. His therapist had been analyzed by Theodore Reik, who had been a protégé of Sigmund Freud. Brooks felt that what he learned, though it might not be straight from the horse's mouth, was at least feedbox noise from the same stable.)

Addressing the American Film Institute in 1977, Brooks said, "We wrote things that made *us* laugh, not what we thought the audience would dig. . . .What really collapsed us, grabbed our bellies, knocked us down on the floor and made us spit and laugh so that we couldn't breathe—*that* was what went into the script. Except for the dirty portions, which we couldn't do on live television."

A character in which Brooks specialized, and in which his distinctive comic style first began to assert itself, was the German Professor, played by Caesar. He appeared under many names—such as Kurt von Stuffer, the dietitian, or Siegfried von Sedativ, the authority on sleep—always pontificating with the same majestic fraudulence in the same bedraggled and ill-fitting frock coat. His ignorance, exposed by Carl Reiner's questions, was boundless in its scope and variety. How, for instance, do aircraft fly? As Dr. Rudolf von Rudder, aeronautical expert, he spelled out the answer in layman's language: "It's a simple theory. Matter is lighter than air. You see, the motors, they pull the plane forward and they cause a draft, and then it taxis faster down the field and the motors go faster and the whole plane vibrates, and then, when there's enough of a draft and a vacuum created, the plane rises off the runway into the air. From then on, it's a miracle. I don't know what keeps it up."

After a complex buildup, the laugh comes not from a witty, climactic payoff but from a sudden plunge into bathos. We hear exactly what we would expect to hear from this obvious half-wit. Cf. the reply of Dr. Heinrich von Heartburn when Reiner asked him for his advice on keeping one's marriage alive: "Make it interesting. . . . I showed a friend of mine once how to keep his marriage exciting. . . . One day he'd come home from work, his wife would open the door, he's a French soldier. . . . The next day he's a policeman, he comes in, he starts to run around with the handcuffs and the badges, and the next day he don't come through the door, he jumps through the window, he's a clown. He somersaults all over the living room and throws his wife all around the place. [Pause.] She left him. He was a maniac."

A final glimpse of the Professor (for which, as for the preceding quotes from the original scripts, I draw on the lengthy extracts reprinted in Ted Sennett's book *Your Show*

of Shows): in the guise of a mountaineering pundit, he is
mourning the loss of a colleague, Hans Goodfellow, who gave
his life trying to prove that it was possible to climb mountains
on roller skates. What should a climber do, Reiner inquires,
if his rope breaks?

> CAESAR: Well, as soon as you see the rope breaking,
> scream and keep screaming all the way down. . . . This
> way they'll know where to find you.
> REINER: But, Professor, isn't there anything else you
> can do?
> CAESAR: Well, there's the other method. As soon as
> the rope breaks, you spread your arms and begin to fly.
> REINER: But humans can't fly.
> CAESAR: How do you know? You might be the first
> one. Anyway, you can always go back to screaming.
> REINER: Was Hans Goodfellow a flier or a screamer?
> CAESAR: He was a flying screamer, and a crasher, too.

In this exchange, and dozens like it, Brooks was breaking
fresh ground, exploring territory that he was eventually to
make his own. He was inventing the interview as a new form
of comic art.

The last edition of "Your Show of Shows" went out in
1954, by which time Brooks was married to Florence Baum,
a dancer in Broadway musicals. They had three children—in
order of appearance, Stefanie, Nicholas, and Edward. The
youngest is now studying music in Manhattan, while both
of the older ones are taking courses in film at New York
University. Brooks refers to them as "these nice friends I've
grown." Their parents were divorced in 1962. "We had
married too young," Brooks said, more than a decade later.
"I expected I would marry my mother, and she expected she
would marry her father." Minus Coca, Caesar returned to the
small screen in 1954, starring in a show of his own called
"Caesar's Hour." He was also minus Brooks, who, determined
to go his own way, had rejected the offer of a top writing job
on the new program. Before long, however, Brooks regretted

his decision to quit the nest. His own way was leading him
nowhere but into debt, and after the show's first season,
unable to resist the money, he rejoined his old boss, under
whose paternal shadow he stayed until 1959. Which brings
us back to Mamma Leone's.

Although Brooks left a lasting impression on everyone who
saw him at the Moss Hart jamboree, it did nothing to help
his career. He was a brilliant party turn, but what had after-
dinner improvisation to do with professional comedy? In
1960, with his marriage crumbling and no source of income,
he went job-hunting to Hollywood, where Carl Reiner was
already working. Hearing that they were both in town, the
producer Joe Fields threw a party in their honor, on the tacit
understanding that they would provide the entertainment.
Before an audience of celebrities that included Steve Allen
and George Burns, they got up and did the Two-Thousand-
Year-Old Man. When the applause had died down, Burns
said, "Listen, you better put that on a record, because if you
don't, I'll steal it." Allen, who shared Burns's enthusiasm,
had highly placed friends in the recording business. He made
a call to one of them the following morning.

"A few days later," Reiner told me, "Mel and I walked
into a studio at World Pacific Records and ad-libbed for over
two hours." The edited result was an LP that came out in
the spring of 1961 and sold over a million copies. "That was
a turning point for Mel," Reiner continued. "It gave him an
identity as a performer for the first time." Moreover, it gave
him a comic persona that at once embodied and exorcised
his own deepest anxieties; for the main point about this
jaunty survivor—more than twice as old as Methuselah and
still going strong—is that he has conquered death. By playing a character who was immortal, Brooks may have staked
his principal claim to immortality as a comedian.

Gene Wilder summed up for me his mental image of
Brooks: "I see him standing bare-chested on top of a mountain, shouting 'Look at me!' and 'Don't let me die!' Those

are the two things that rule his life." They recur throughout
his records with Reiner, of which, to date, there are four.
Following the runaway success of the original LP, further
revelations by the garrulous oldster of his close encounters
with "the great and the near-great" of the past two millennia
were issued in the fall of 1961, with sequels in 1962, 1963,
and 1973. In these classic interviews, Brooks triumphs not
only over death, but over another of his besetting phobias,
that of the lifelong seeker after father substitutes who fears
he will never make a convincing father himself; for what is
the Two-Thousand-Year-Old Man if not the most prolific
parent on earth? He tells us that he has been married "several
hundred times" and that when he looks back on his wives
"a thousand violins explode in my mind."

> REINER: How many children do you have?
> BROOKS (*with stoical self-pity*): I have over forty-two
> thousand children, and not one comes to visit me.

But, at least, he misses their company, which is more
than can be said for Warren Bland, the Gentile advertising
executive who is one of the many other characters Brooks
plays on these remarkable discs. Bland lives in the city of
Connecticut, Connecticut, "a very exclusive community,"
where they don't allow children. They *have* children, of
course, but "we send them to Hartford . . . to Jewish and
Italian families, people who like children." From time to
time, Bland goes on, "I might just mosey over to Hartford,
say 'Hi, gang!' you know, then speed right back to Connecticut, Connecticut."

As Bland, Brooks's accent is quintessential WASP. As
the bimillenarian, it is not Jewish but—Brooks is insistent on
this—*American*-Jewish. "Within a couple of decades, there
won't be any more accents like that," he said to me. "They're
being ironed out by history, because there are no more
Jewish immigrants. It's the sound I was brought up on, and
it's dying." Beneath the jokes, these recordings are a
threnody. Even on the surface, there are odd moments of

unexpected melancholy, as when the patriarch reflects, "We mock the thing we are to be. We make fun of the old, and then we become them." Although he has foxed the grim reaper, it has often been by inches. He has led a life dominated by peril and hostility, in which practically every human activity springs from one motive.

> BROOKS: Everything we do is based on fear.
> REINER: Even love?
> BROOKS: Mainly love.
> REINER: How can love stem from fear?
> BROOKS: What do you need a woman for? . . . In my time, to see if an animal is behind you. You can't see alone, you don't have eyes in the back of your head. . . . The first marriages were: "Will you take a look behind me?" "OK, how long do you want?" "Forever." "We're married."
> REINER: I see. And you walked back to back for the rest of your life?
> BROOKS: Yes. You looked at her once in a while—
> REINER: When you knew you were safe?
> BROOKS: When you were on high ground.

All of which corroborates the spiritual doctrine that perfect love casteth out fear. (And, I might add, compares very favorably with the behavior of a well-known English writer who fled London during the wartime blitz, pausing only to explain to his girlfriend, "Perfect fear casteth out love.") Again, consider the following exchange:

> REINER: What was the means of transportation then?
> BROOKS: Mainly fear. . . . You would see an animal that would growl, you would go two miles in a minute. Fear would be the main propulsion.

As for the origins of human speech.

> BROOKS: We spoke Rock, basic Rock. . . . Two hundred years before Hebrew, there was the Rock language. Or Rock talk.

REINER: Could you give us an example of that?
BROOKS: Yes. "Hey, don't throw that rock at me!
What you doing with that rock? Put down that rock!"

In other words—or, rather, in no other words—the need to communicate arose from the threat of imminent assault. Similarly, the custom of shaking hands "stemmed from fear." In order to check whether the other fellow was carrying a rock or a dagger, "you grabbed his hand—'Hi there, Charlie!' 'How you doing, Bertram?'—and you held that hand, then you looked and you opened it up and you shook it a little." The primal art of dance evolved because it was an even more comprehensive means of self-protection. By dancing with your antagonist, you immobilize *both* his hands and "you keep the feet busy, so he can't kick you." Song, too, had its roots in terror. If you were in real danger, a high-pitched rhythmical yelling was the only way to make anyone pay attention. The message had to be simple and ear-catching, as witness the opening lines of the first lyric ever sung:

A lion is eating my foot off,
Will somebody call a cop?

Shortly afterward came national anthems, with which each group of cave dwellers tried to frighten its neighbors; e.g.:

Let them all go to hell
Except Cave Seventy-six.

The old man has immunized himself against death by obeying a number of rules—some pragmatic, some purely superstitious—which he is eager to share with us. Every morning, for instance, he sinks to his knees and prays "fiercely" for twenty-two minutes "that the ceiling shouldn't fall on me, and my heart should not attack me." Among his other precepts for longevity: avoid fried food; consume nectarines in bulk ("Even a rotten one is good. . . . I'd rather

eat a rotten nectarine than a fine plum"); never run for a
bus; and "stay out of a Ferrari or any small Italian car."
He has also preserved his pep by using drugs derived from
"certain barks of certain trees that made you jump in the
air and sing 'Sweet Sue.' "

His fear of illness, though intense, is more than matched
by his fear of hospitals, which are run today, he believes, on
principles that have not changed since his troglodytic youth.

REINER: What are these principles?
BROOKS: The principle of people walking past you
when you are screaming, and not caring. The same
wonderful indifference to the sick and the dying.

Over the centuries, some of this indifference has rubbed
off onto his own philosophy. It emerges most vividly when
Reiner challenges him to define the difference between
comedy and tragedy. His reply, brutally concise, is an
aphorism as memorable as any I have heard on this ancient
subject: "Tragedy is if I cut my finger. . . . Comedy is if you
walk into an open sewer and die."

He drops names like a drunken waiter dropping plates: few
great reputations pass through his hands unchipped. Robin
Hood "stole from everybody and kept everything"; Shakespeare, though personally "a pussycat," was a terrible writer
("He had the worst penmanship I ever saw"); Sigmund
Freud was nothing more than a good basketball player; and,
as for Michelangelo's painting, "I thought it stunk," because
it showed naked people flying around, and "you can't hang
a naked in your living room." Perhaps his most startling disclosure is that he cohabited with Joan of Arc. He volubly
describes the ups and downs of their relationship, after which
Reiner intervenes.

REINER: How did you feel about her being burned at
the stake?
BROOKS (with instant, understated finality): Terrible.

For me—and, I have discovered, for Brooks himself—this is the high point of the whole extravagant saga.

> Laughter becomes extreme only if it be consecutive. There must be no pauses for recovery. . . . The jester must be able to grapple his theme and hang on to it, twisting it this way and that, and making it yield magically all manner of strange and precious things, one after another, without pause. *He must have invention keeping pace with utterance.* He must be inexhaustible. Only so can he exhaust us.

The words are Max Beerbohm's, the italics mine. The Two-Thousand-Year-Old Man fulfills Beerbohm's demands to the letter. With this verdict Brooks, who is not noted for bashfulness, would probably agree. "Everybody knows," he has said of his work on these records, "that *that* is terrific stuff." It extracts a unique comic euphoria from a fundamentally pessimistic view of life. I've dwelt on it not only as a milestone in Brooks's past (and in the history of comedy) but as a signpost to which, in the future, he is likely to return for guidance.

Early in the nineteen-sixties, Brooks began to acquire a cult following. To the relatively small number of people who buy nonmusical LPs he became, in his own words, "a royal personage, an emperor of comedy." In other respects, he remembers the years between 1959 and 1965 as "that terrible period when I couldn't get anything off the ground." In 1961, Jerry Lewis had an idea for a screenplay, *The Ladies' Man,* and hired Brooks to work on it. To Brooks's furious chagrin, Lewis took the script and had it entirely rewritten, so that few of Brooks's lines survived. (Show business offers few pleasures keener than that of paying tribute to a former foe who happens to be in eclipse. Brooks's present opinion of Lewis is that "he was an exciting, dynamic creature, and I learned a lot from him." He cannot, however, resist adding,

"High-key comics like that always burn themselves out. Lewis could do thirty-one different takes [i.e., physical reactions], and when you'd seen them all, that was it. Low-key, laid-back comics like Jack Benny are the ones that last." Moreover, Lewis stooped to sentimentality—something utterly foreign to Brooks. Gene Wilder told me, "There's not much white sugar in Mel's veins. He would never ask an audience for sympathy.") For some time, Brooks had been working on a novel; he now revamped it as a play, called *Springtime for Hitler*. No producer would touch it. *All American*, a Broadway musical with a book by Brooks, was among the more resounding flops of 1962. In the same year, during which his divorce became final, he turned out another screenplay, entitled *Marriage Is a Dirty Rotten Fraud*. Nobody bought it. Meanwhile, most of his colleagues on the Caesar shows were prospering—a fact that neither escaped his attention nor soothed his frustration.

After separating from his wife in 1960, Brooks had spent a bleak and insolvent period in an unfurnished fourth-floor walkup on Perry Street, for which he paid seventy-eight dollars a month. He then moved in with a friend called Speed Vogel, who had an apartment on Central Park West and a studio on West Twenty-eighth Street, where he made what Brooks describes as "direct metal sculpture." Vogel had left his wife shortly before Brooks arrived. The two men cooked for themselves, carried their clothes to the laundromat, rose at conflicting hours (Brooks late, Vogel early), and bickered over practically every aspect of housekeeping—a setup uncannily prophetic of Neil Simon's *The Odd Couple*.

One Tuesday in the summer of 1962, Vogel gave a party at West Twenty-eighth Street. Among his guests were Zero Mostel, who had a studio in the same building; Joseph Heller, whose first novel, *Catch-22*, had appeared the previous year; and Ngoot Lee, a painter and calligrapher of Chinese parentage. These three, together with Vogel and Brooks, enjoyed one another's company so much that they decided to commemorate the occasion by reassembling every Tuesday

for food and talk. Meetings were held at cheap Chinese
restaurants selected by Ngoot Lee, who knew where the best
chefs worked, and kept track of their movements from job to
job. The nucleus, itself a fairly motley crew, grew steadily
motleyer as it swelled in numbers. Brooks introduced a
diamond dealer named Julie Green, who could do eccentric
impersonations of movie stars. Heller contributed a fellow-
novelist, George Mandel, who had a steel plate in his head
as a result of injuries suffered in the Battle of the Bulge.
"One night," Heller recalls, "Mandel told us in detail how
he had been wounded. There was a long pause, and then Mel
did something typical. He said, very slowly, 'I'm sure glad
that happened to you, and not to me.' He wasn't being cruel,
he was being honest. He just blurted out what we were all
thinking but didn't dare to say." Mandel, in turn, brought
in Mario Puzo, later to become famous as the author of *The
Godfather*. These were the charter members of the fraternity.
They called themselves the Group of the Oblong Table or,
in more pretentious moments, the Chinese Gourmet Club.
What bound them together, apart from revelry in conversation, is best epitomized in a statement volunteered to me by
Heller. "I'd rather have a bad meal out than a good meal at
home," he said. "When you're out, it's a party. Also, I like
a big mediocre meal more than a small good one."

   The membership list has been closed for many years. Approved outsiders, like Carl Reiner and Joseph Stein, are
invited to the Oblong Table from time to time, but merely
as "honored guests." The club has strict rules, some of which
I learned from Reiner: "You are not allowed to eat two
mouthfuls of fish, meat, or chicken without an intermediate
mouthful of rice. Otherwise, you would be consuming only
the expensive food. The check and tip, and the parking fees,
if any, are equally divided among the members. It is com-
pulsory, if you are in New York, are not working nights, and
are in reasonable health, to be present at every meeting." He
continued, "The members are very polite. Once, I had a seat
facing the kitchen door and I looked through and saw a rat

strolling across the floor. They immediately offered me a chair facing the other way." Anxious to retain his status of "honored guest," Reiner begged me to quote Heller and Brooks on the subject at greater length than I quoted him.

Brooks recently told an interviewer that the talk at the Oblong Table mainly deals with such weighty subjects as "whether there is a God, what is a Jew, and do homosexuals really do it." Reiner has other recollections. "From the sessions I've attended," he said to me, "I would put that group up against the Algonquin Round Table and bet that, line for line, they were funnier. The speed of the wit is breathtaking. It just flies back and forth." Brooks's comment on this: "I'm sure we're funnier than the Algonquin crowd, but we're not as bright."

Hershy Kay, the composer and Broadway arranger, had a bitter experience that confirmed what Reiner said about the club's rigorous eating procedure. According to Brooks: "Hershy Kay came once as a guest and took the nicest bits of the lobster and the choicest parts of the chicken, including the wings, which I like. He did not touch his rice. He had to go, and he went." There may, however, have been another reason for Kay's rejection. My source here is Heller, who said, "Bear in mind that I am the only tall member of the group. At the next meeting after the Hershy Kay incident, Mel made a little speech. 'Let's face it,' he said. 'Except for Joe, all of us are quite short. Some of us are very short. *Hershy is too short.*'"

Brooks, incidentally, has grave reservations about Heller's own table manners. "From the very start," he declares, "we accepted Joe on Speed Vogel's word that he would behave, and Speed lied to us, because he did not behave. He took the best pieces of everything and laughed in our faces. One Tuesday, we ordered a tureen of special soup full of delicious things, and Joe grabbed it, scooped all the good stuff into his own bowl, and then said, 'Here, let me serve this.' We each got a spoonful of nothing."

Far from denying this story, Heller openly confesses, "I am a greedy man. I'll eat anything. I even use a fork instead of chopsticks, so I can eat faster. I'm known in the club as the plague of locusts." Presumably, his physical bulk protects him against reprisals.

Puzo, the only non-Jewish member other than Ngoot Lee, is tolerated because of his limited appetite. "Being Italian, Puzo is no threat to us," Brooks says. "He doesn't really like exotic dishes. He prefers noodles and rice—things that remind him of home. He is provincial, and that saves us from the rape of our best food." A stickler for party discipline as well as a dedicated glutton, Brooks never misses a club meeting when he is in Manhattan. If business suddenly compels him to fly in from the Coast on a Tuesday evening, his first act on arrival at JFK is to ring every eligible restaurant in China-town until he finds the chosen venue. Thither he dashes, straight from the airport; and before saying a word, he heaps a plate with whatever is left.

Despite their differences over matters of etiquette, Heller has a high respect for Brooks. He freely admitted to me that he used a lot of Brooks's lines in his second novel, *Something Happened*, and that in his next book, *Good as Gold*, "the hero is a small Jewish guy, and there's a great deal of Mel in that." In the early seventies, Heller was teaching writing at City College of New York. He had long been aware that Brooks was vulnerable to practical jokes. One evening, Heller casually lied about his salary, saying that it was sixty-eight thousand dollars a year—more than double the truth. A couple of days later, Heller's accountant, who also worked for Brooks, called him up and said, "For God's sake, Joe, what the hell have you done? First thing this morning, Mel was up here screaming, 'Why am I in the entertainment business? Why aren't I teaching and earning seventy thousand a year like Joe Heller?' He was out of his mind!" Having told me this story, Heller went on, "Mel has always had plenty of resentment and aggression that he can sublimate into creativity. He's usually at his best when he's envying people more successful than he is. Now that there's hardly anyone more successful, what will he do?"

I cited a mot attributed to Gore Vidal: "It is not enough to succeed. Others must fail."

"I thought that was La Rochefoucauld," Heller said. "But anyway it doesn't apply to Mel. He likes to see his rivals fail, but not his friends. Provided, of course, that *he's* succeeding."

I asked whether, in Heller's opinion, fame had changed Brooks.

"Not a bit. He's just as nasty, hostile, acquisitive, and envious today as he ever was. Please be sure to quote me on that," Heller said warmly. He went on, "You have to distinguish between Mel the entertainer and Mel the private person. He puts on this manic public performance, but it's an act, it's something sought for and worked on. When he's being himself, he'll talk quietly for hours and then make a remark that's unforgettably funny because it comes out of a real situation. You might say that he's at his funniest when he's being most serious. He has a tremendous reverence for novelists and for literature in general, because it involves something more than gag writing. In his serious moments, I don't think he regards movies as an art. For Mel, the real art is literature."

Brooks staunchly challenges this view: "When Joe says things like that, he's just electioneering for the novel, because that's what he writes. I think *La Grande Illusion* is as good as *Anna Karenina*, and *Les Enfants du Paradis* is in the same class as *La Chartreuse de Parme*. If we're talking about art at the most exquisite level, Joe may conceivably have a point. But I'm a populist. I want color, I want visual images, I want the sound of the human voice."

In February, 1961, Brooks attended a rehearsal of a Perry Como TV special in which Anne Bancroft, then starring on Broadway in *The Miracle Worker*, was making a guest appearance. Brashly introducing himself, Brooks started to

woo her on the spot. They were married in 1964 and are still
together, now accompanied by a six-year-old son—"Mel in
miniature," according to Miss Bancroft—named Maximilian.
"On our second date," Brooks told me, "I asked her, 'Where
do you keep your awards?' She'd already won two Tonys. She
said she gave them to her mother. I said, 'Funny, so do I'—
although the only thing I'd won up to then was a Writers
Guild Award for 'Your Show of Shows.' Then I asked her,
'Where does your mother keep them?' She said, 'On top of
the TV set.' My heart stopped, and I said, 'So does mine.'
My mother now has two Oscars and an Emmy. But Annie
has something like thirty major awards—Oscars, Emmys,
Tonys, Cannes Festival, about everything an actress can win."
Miss Bancroft, whose parents were the children of immigrants, was christened Anna Maria Louisa Italiano, and it
took Brooks a long time to reveal to his mother that he intended to marry an Italian girl. If we believe (as we can't)
the account he gave David Susskind on TV, his mother's
reaction when he finally broke the news and announced that
he was bringing his lasagna-loving fiancée over to meet her
was simply to say, "That's fine. I'll be in the kitchen; my
head'll be in the oven."

In the early sixties, Miss Bancroft was continuously working, either on Broadway or in movies. Brooks had many
evenings to kill, and she suspects that this may explain why
he founded the Chinese Gourmet Club. "But in any case,
Mel really loves men, he has a terrific sense of male
camaraderie," she said to me recently. "Have you noticed
how all his films before *High Anxiety* end up with two men
together? His attitude toward women can be very primitive.
When we have big rows, he yells, 'No more monogamy with
women for me! Next time, it'll be with a man!' He actually
threatens me with Dom DeLuise! Once—and only once—I
managed to find out where the club was meeting, and I
crashed the dinner. As soon as I came in the restaurant, it
was as if a blanket had descended on the gathering. Dead
silence. Faces falling. I turned around and left, without

eating." She smiled and shrugged. "All the same," she said, "whenever he comes home at night the whole place lights up. He's like an incandescent schoolboy. There are no dull moments."

One evening in the spring of 1962, Brooks was sitting in a Manhattan movie theatre watching a dazzling abstract cartoon by the Canadian animator Norman MacLaren. "Three rows behind me," he recalls, "there was an old immigrant man mumbling to himself. He was very unhappy because he was waiting for a story line and he wasn't getting one." Brooks listened hard, and the result of his eavesdropping was that, for the first time, a film based on a Brooks idea actually got made. "I asked my pal Ernie Pintoff to do the visuals for a MacLaren-type cartoon," he says. "I told him, 'Don't let me see the images in advance. Just give me a mike and let them assault me.' And that's what he did. There was no script. I sat in a viewing theatre looking at what Ernie showed me, and I mumbled whatever I felt that old guy would have mumbled, trying to find a plot in this maze of abstractions. We cut it down to three and a half minutes and called it *The Critic*. It opened at the Sutton in New York, later to become renowned as the home of Mel Brooks hits. It was a smash then and has been ever since." In 1964, it won Academy Awards for both Brooks and Pintoff. A fact to remember: the film's comic impact was entirely dependent on something nonvisual—Brooks's mesmeric power of vocal improvisation.

Alan Schwartz, an urbane, silver-haired native of Brooklyn who has been Brooks's legal adviser and friend since 1962, said to me not long ago, "By Mel's standards, an improviser isn't class. He wanted to be classy. Writing is classy. A screenplay is classy." Schwartz's other clients include Peter Shaffer, Tom Stoppard, and Joseph Heller. "Mel is as intelligent as any of them," he says. "He must have a fantastic IQ. But sometimes, if he's with playwrights or novelists, he feels he has to prove that he's a serious literary person. When he met

Shaffer, for instance, he kept saying things like 'pari passu' and 'ipso facto.' "

Brooks's return to the affluence of network TV came in 1965, when he collaborated with Buck Henry on "Get Smart," a series of half-hour episodes from the career of Maxwell Smart, a dangerously incompetent secret agent. ABC, which financed the pilot script, found the central character too charmless and the satiric twists too bizarre. NBC took over the project (which nowadays looks tame enough), and it became a long-running success, relieving Brooks of such urgent financial worries as alimony and child support. It also left behind it a heritage of bad blood between Brooks and his co-author. Buck Henry, who wrote the screenplay of *The Graduate* a couple of years later, resented the billing he received on "Get Smart"—"By Mel Brooks with Buck Henry"—and there were rumors that, once the series was launched, Brooks's main contribution was to arrive at an advanced stage of rehearsals, propose a few radical and impracticable changes, and then disappear. Rebutting the charge of self-aggrandizement, Brooks says that his agent wanted to exclude Henry's name altogether and that it was he who demanded that both names should appear. "Buck envied me because of the hit I'd made with the Two-Thousand-Year-Old Man," Brooks asserts. "I'd galloped like a greedy child, and got ahead and taken off. I had a reputation for being a crazy Jew animal, whereas Buck thought of himself as an intellectual. Well, I was an intellectual, too. I knew that Dante's last name was Alighieri, but I didn't flaunt it. What Buck couldn't bear was the idea of this wacko Jew being billed over him. The truth is that he reads magazines, but he's not an intellectual, he's a pedant."

Time has not softened Henry's reciprocal animosity toward Brooks. "I'll bet you," he said to me in 1977, "that his name appears five times on the credits of *High Anxiety*."

Informed of this, Brooks replied, "Tell him from me he's wrong. The correct number is six."

The Producers, shot in New York in 1967, was the first

Brooks script to reach the movie screen. It also marked his
debut as a director—a job he undertook out of no sense of
vocation but simply to protect his work against the well-
meaning vandalism of rewrite experts. The script had gone
through a strangely protracted gestation period. Brooks had
originally conceived it, more than ten years earlier, as a novel.
He had never thought of himself as a writer until 1950, when
he saw his name on the credits of "Your Show of Shows." "I
got scared," he told me, "and I figured I'd better find out
what these bastards do. I went to the library, and read all the
books I could carry—Conrad, Fielding, Dostoevski, Gogol,
Tolstoy. I decided that Tolstoy was the most gifted writer
who ever lived. It's like he stuck a pen in his heart and it
didn't even go through his mind on its way to the page. He
may not even have been talented. And I said to myself,
'My God, I'm not a writer, I'm a *talker*.' I wished they'd
change my billing on the show so that it said 'Funny Talking
by Mel Brooks.' Then I wouldn't feel so intimidated." Before
long, however, he stifled his fears and embarked on a novel.
"One little word at a time, but, by God, I was going to do it."

The title was *Springtime for Hitler*, and the hero was a
nervous young accountant called Leopold Bloom. "I stole the
name from *Ulysses*," Brooks said to me. "I don't know what
it meant to James Joyce, but to me Leo Bloom always meant
a vulnerable Jew with curly hair. In the course of any narrative, the major characters have to metamorphose. They have
to go through an experience that forces them to learn something and change. So Leo was going to change, he was going
to bloom. He would start out as a little man who salutes
whatever society teaches him to salute. Hats are worn. Yes,
sir, I will wear a hat. Ties are worn. Definitely, sir. No dirty
language is spoken in this world. *Absolument, Monsieur*. But
in Leo Bloom's heart there was a much more complicated
and protean creature—the guy he'd never dare to be, because
he ain't gonna take them chances. He was going to play it
straight and trudge right to his grave, until he ran into
Max Bialystock, the Zero Mostel character. Bialystock is a

Broadway producer who's so broke he's wearing a cardboard belt. He sleeps with little old ladies on their way to the cemetery. They stop off to have quick affairs on the leather couch in his office, which charm them so much that they write out checks for any fictitious show he claims to be promoting. Compared with Bloom, Bialystock is the Id. Bite, kiss, take, grab, lavish, urinate—whatever you can do that's physical, he will do. When Bloom first meets him, he's appalled. But then they get embroiled in each other's lives, and they catalyze each other. Bialystock has a profound effect on Bloom—so much so that this innocent young guy comes up with the idea of making a fortune by producing a surefire flop and selling twenty-five thousand percent of the profits in advance to little old ladies. On the other hand, Bloom evokes the first sparks of decency and humanity in Bialystock. It was a nice give-and-take. But after a while all they did was talk to each other. So I said, 'Oh, shit, it's turning into a play,' and I rewrote it, with a big neo-Nazi musical number right in the middle."

At this point (1963), Anne Bancroft was appearing on Broadway in the title role of Brecht's *Mother Courage*. Gene Wilder played the Chaplain, her cynical hanger-on and occasional bedfellow. He is now Brooks's closest friend and most impassioned fan. "Whenever Mel says 'Let's go,'" he told me recently, "I drop anything I'm doing and follow him." They met backstage during the run of the Brecht play. "Anne introduced me to this little borscht-belt comic she was going with," Wilder recalls. "I knew his name from the Caesar shows, which I'd been brought up on. I used to do Caesar impersonations at junior high, and it turned out that all my favorite bits had been written by Mel. Now he started to give me advice on Brechtian acting. The Chaplain has these long ironic speeches and lyrics on war and injustice, and I didn't know how to handle them, with my Actors Studio and Uta Hagen training. Mel said to me, 'Don't try to work them out in terms of psychology and motivation. He's stopped his play to pamphleteer. Step out of

character and treat them like song-and-dance routines.' I
didn't agree with him then, but I do now. Without knowing
it, he was talking pure Brechtian technique. One day, we
went out to Fire Island, and he said, 'I've written a play with
a terrific part for you.' He read me the first twenty minutes
and I was knocked out. Brooks told me, 'You *are* that character, and if it's ever done on stage or screen you're going
to play it! But that's an easy promise, because I've never
written a play or a screenplay and you've never had a starring role in a movie, so let's just dream together and eat
warm pretzels and drink beer and think about reaching
the stars. Even so, he made me swear not to take any other
job without checking with him. Not long afterward, "I was
offered a part in the Broadway production of *One Flew
Over the Cuckoo's Nest*. I told Mel, and he made me write
a month's release clause into my contract, which I did. Then
three years passed, during which—nothing. He didn't even
call me. Finally, I'm back on Broadway, in Murray Schisgal's
play *Luv*. After a matinée, there's a knock on my dressing-
room door, and it's Mel. 'You didn't think I forgot, did you?'
he says. Then he explains that *Springtime for Hitler* has
become a movie and that I'm going to play Leopold Bloom.
I took the script home and read it, and at 3 A.M. I called
him and said, 'It's magnificent! When do we start?' I didn't
ask about my salary, and I don't think I ever did."

What had happened in the lengthy interim was that
Brooks had found the action of his play spreading all over
New York, spilling out onto sidewalks and rooftops, leaping
from place to place with a spatial flexibility for which film
seemed the obvious form. Helped by an inventive secretary
with the arresting name of Alfa-Betty Olsen, he refashioned
it as a movie. Several agents had "run with it"—to lapse into
Hollywood patois—and got nowhere. It then fell into the
hands of Sidney Glazier, a fund-raiser and contact man who
had won an Academy Award for producing *The Eleanor
Roosevelt Story*. Brooks describes Glazier, whom he met on
Fire Island, as "a crazy man, he drank and he bellowed, he

faced the ocean and roared like a sea lion." Glazier ordered
Brooks not to read the script to him but simply to tell him
the story. "About halfway through," Brooks continues,
"Sidney was drinking coffee and he laughed so much it went
up his nose. He collapsed on the floor, spitting and snorting
and coughing. As he rolled around, he stuck up his arm, and
when I reached out for it he grabbed my hand and said,
'We're going to make this movie. It's the funniest thing I
ever heard.' And he knew what an impossible deal I was
demanding: My first condition was that I had to direct the
picture." Glazier budgeted the production at a million dollars,
supplied half of it through his own company, and ran with
the script around all the major studios. No dice. He eventually
appealed to the independent producer Joseph E. Levine, who
had just raised what he claimed to be the last cent at his
disposal to finance an extremely risky project called *The
Graduate*. Like every other moneyman who had seen the
script, Levine said that no Jewish exhibitor would put
Springtime for Hitler on his marquee. Brooks, for his part,
rejected the suggestion that it should be retitled *Springtime
for Mussolini*. By now, however, he was reluctantly prepared
to settle for something as neutral as *The Producers*. There
was one major point in Levine's favor: he genuinely liked what
Brooks had written. Against this was the fact that he could
not see his way to hiring the author as director.

Desperate to resolve these matters, Glazier brought the
two men together over lunch. "I ate very nicely," Brooks
says. "Nothing dropped out of my mouth. I didn't eat bread
and butter, because I didn't know whether you should cut
bread or break it. Meanwhile, Joe Levine ate like an animal.
Just on top of some trout, he said, 'What would you do if
I said yes? Could you direct it? What do you say, kid? Tell
me from your heart. Don't lie to me; it may be the end for
me.' He was impressed with me because I was cute and funny,
so I said 'Yes, I can do it.' And he said 'OK,' and we shook
hands." (Long after the film was made, Levine admitted to
Brooks, "I was wrong. We should have called it *Springtime*

for Hitler." Brooks told me, "Actually, they did call it *Springtime for Hitler* in Sweden. And when *The Twelve Chairs* came out, they called it *Springtime for the Twelve Chairs. Blazing Saddles* was *Springtime for the Black Sheriff,* and *Young Frankenstein* was *Springtime for Frankenstein.* I'm big stuff in Sweden. Everything is springtime there.")

Ten years from conception to handshake, and still not an actor signed: such is the life-devouring pace at which the movie business conducts its affairs. A deal with Gene Wilder was quickly concluded, but Zero Mostel, whom Brooks had always wanted for the role of Bialystock, read the script with mounting horror. "What is this?" he bellowed to Brooks. "A Jewish producer going to bed with old women on the brink of the grave? I can't play such a part. I'm a Jewish person." Enlisting the support of Mostel's wife, Brooks finally managed to change his mind, but their working relationship, once shooting (and shouting) began, was not easy. Between takes, Mostel would be found lying in his dressing room like a beached whale, moaning, "That man is going to kill me! He keeps saying, 'Do it again.' "

According to Brooks: "He was wonderful and he was a great friend, and he was a great pain in the ass. It was like working in the middle of a thunderstorm. Bolts of Zero— blinding flashes of Zero—were all around you. When he wasn't *on,* he was very dear, very pensive, very accessible. We had family feuds. He had a sense of the grandeur of an artist. He had what I like in an actor—power, stature, and enormous bravery. I knew that if I could reach the end of the solar system of his talent, if I could just prod him into some outburst of insane anger, I could wake up the sleeping emotional depths of that extraordinary man. And I did, and, although he protested bitterly, he was fabulous."

The picture took eight weeks to shoot and eleven months to edit: Brooks was then learning his trade. Nowadays, he gets through the editing period in about four months. *The Producers* was brought in under budget, at nine hundred and forty-one thousand dollars. It opened in 1968 and, despite murderous notices, acquired a cult reputation that enabled it to creep into the black within four years. Brooks has little faith in critics, believing that they always catch up with him one movie too late. "I never got good reviews in my life and I never will," he declares. "They took one look at *The Producers* and said it stank. Then I gave them *The Twelve Chairs* and they said it lacked the great chaotic buoyancy of that majestic triumph *The Producers*. Then came *Blazing Saddles*, and they said that everything I'd learned about films had been forgotten in this disgusting mess."

Badly wounded by the reception of his maiden effort, Brooks was resoundingly compensated by the members of the Motion Picture Academy, who, showing an unusual disdain for the opinions of both the press and the general public, awarded him the Oscar for Best Original Screenplay of 1968. It was a bold and unexpected choice. In order to enjoy *The Producers*, you have to cultivate a taste for grotesque and deliberate overstatement. In the early scenes, Mostel and Wilder play together like figures out of a Jonsonian comedy of humors. Cupidity (Mostel) seduces Conformity (Wilder): in each, a single trait is exaggerated to the point of plethoric obsession, and beyond. These are cartoon creatures, whose dialogue seems to be written in capital letters, heavily italicized. To say that this makes it too "theatrical" is irrelevant, for as soon as we agree to abandon the convention of naturalism, anything goes, and the screen can be as unrealistic as the stage. (Who complains, after all, that the Marx Brothers' *Cocoanuts* is merely a photographed stage production?) The film's peak is the sequence, already a modern classic, in which a chorus of Storm Troopers, shot from above à la Busby Berkeley, sings "Springtime for Hitler"—a lilting melody composed by Brooks—while revolving in swastika formation. Afterward, everything runs downhill. The idea of playing the Führer as a southern red-neck high on flower power and LSD not only mixes up too many incompatible jokes but destroys the bed-

rock plausibility of plot without which even the looniest
farce collapses. Like most of Brooks's work for the cinema,
The Producers shows him at his best and at his worst.

Academy Award notwithstanding, there was no stampede
in the movie industry for Brooks's services. His fame is
now so widespread that we tend to forget (though he
does not) how recent its origins are. It was not until 1974,
with *Blazing Saddles*, that the days of wine and grosses
began. His second picture, *The Twelve Chairs*, opened in
1970, nearly three frustrating years after *The Producers*, and
crashed to immediate box-office failure. It was based on a
satirical Soviet novel of the nineteen-twenties, by Ilya Ilf and
Eugene Petrov. Like *The Producers*, it dealt with greed—
the prize in this case being a hoard of diamonds concealed
in one of a dozen chairs that are confiscated from a palace
during the revolution. Again, the characters are raging
obsessives, with the difference that here the model is Gogol
rather than Jonson. The atmosphere of rural Russia is
lovingly evoked, and Brooks himself, making his movie debut,
is superb in the minor role of a masochistic, vodka-sodden
caretaker with an insatiable yearning for the good old days
of servitude. Yet the film as a whole never comes to life; its
jokes seem shod with lead, and one watches glumly as, like
the wounded snake in Pope's poem, it drags its slow length
along. Perhaps excess of ambition was what betrayed it. Alan
Schwartz told me, "It was meant to be a great statement
about man's relationship to man, and how revolutions fail
to work because of human frailty. Mel wanted to be serious
and literary."

Two ironic footnotes should be added. (1) In 1945, an
updated travesty of the same novel, transplanted to New
York and entitled *It's in the Bag*, was shot in Hollywood.
Starring Fred Allen, it treats the source material as an
excuse for a parade of cameo appearances by well-known
names, among them (the roll is worth calling) Victor Moore,
Don Ameche, Jerry Colonna, William Bendix, Rudy Vallee,

Jack Benny, and Robert Benchley. Though rampantly disloyal to the original, it has many more laughs than the Brooks version, mired in reverence. Benchley, who plays a hotel ratcatcher, must surely have written his own best line. Frockcoated at his son's wedding, he draws the lad aside to calm his nerves with a last-minute word of advice. "In-laws' suits never fit," he says gravely. "Remember that, boy." (2) Nothing in *The Twelve Chairs* is as funny as the account of its making which Brooks gave in an interview with *Playboy*, published in February, 1975. Having explained that shooting took place in Yugoslavia, where he spent nine months, Brooks continued:

> It's a very long flight to Yugoslavia and you land in a field of full-grown corn. They figure it cushions the landing. . . . Now, at night, you can't do anything, because all of Belgrade is lit by a ten-watt bulb, and you can't go anywhere, because Tito has the car. It was a beauty, a green '38 Dodge. And the food in Yugoslavia is either very good or very bad. One day, we arrived on location late and starving and they served us fried chains. When we got to our hotel rooms, mosquitoes as big as George Foreman were waiting for us. They were sitting in armchairs with their legs crossed.

It is tempting to quote more. Brooks's performance throughout the twelve seventy-five-minute sessions he devoted to answering *Playboy*'s questions was a marathon display of his gift for chat in full flower. The printed result deserves a place in any anthology of modern American humor. The Master is back on home ground. Brooks is showing off his own invention—the interview as comic art —and doing so with a virtuosity that makes one wonder how any other form could ever put his talents to better use.

Fifty thousand dollars was Brooks's reward for writing, directing, coproducing, and acting in *The Twelve Chairs*.

It consumed three years of his life, and this means that, after taxes, he was subsisting on an annual sum of approximately eight thousand dollars. Since then—except on one eccentric and abortive occasion—he has shrunk from writing a film alone, preferring to test his ideas in the crucible of collaboration. In his words, "I didn't want to go back to the tables and risk another gambling session with my career." By resorting to teamwork, he has turned out the hits that have established his reputation; in pragmatic terms, he cannot be faulted. Even so, there are those—Alan Schwartz is one of them—who feel that the time may now have come for Brooks to trust his own intuitions and fly solo again. "Mel surrounds himself with other writers because the screenplay, to him, is the most important part of a movie," Schwartz told me. "But I'd like to see him doing his own stuff. He ought to give us pure, vintage Brooks, not Brooks riding on the backs of a lot of other people. There's a strange legal phrase that expresses what I mean. Suppose I'm working as a driver for a guy named Al. If I run someone over in the course of my duties, Al is responsible. But if I take the car to the beach and run someone over, that is called in law a 'frolic and detour,' and I'm responsible. I think Mel should go in for more frolics and detours."

In 1970, when *The Twelve Chairs* were pulled out from under him by critics and public alike, Brooks was forty-four years old and was still, by his own standards, a failure. ("To be the funniest has always been my aim"—statement to *Newsweek*, 1975.) Unable to resist another fling at the tables, he plunged into his last frolic and detour to date—a flirtation with culture which was so alien to his temperament that it seems, in retrospect, a gesture of self-destructive defiance. He saw and was impressed by an Off Broadway production of Goldsmith's comedy *She Stoops to Conquer*. The play struck him as "Mozartean," and he promptly adapted it for the screen. His plan was to shoot it in England, with Albert Finney as Tony Lumpkin. Not long before,

Finney had spent several weeks on a remote Pacific island with only one record, "The Two-Thousand-Year-Old Man," which he played every night. "When I met him in New York," Brooks recalls, "he was in awe of me, he couldn't believe I lived, he thought I was God." Finney listened to the divine proposition and reverently turned it down. Brooks took his screenplay on the familiar round of agents, producers, and studios without raising a flicker of interest, and got ready to face the fact that he was finished in show business.

David Begelman, recently fined for financial misdeeds committed while he was head of Columbia Pictures, here enters the story. Despite the cloud of scandal over Begelman's head, Brooks remains his impenitent admirer. "When he took over Columbia in 1973," Brooks says, "David Begelman turned it around and made it, by dint of his aggression and his perspicacity and his acumen, a wonderful, working, winning company. I love it the way I love Fox, where I work, because it is not Gulf & Western, it's not Transamerica, it's Columbia Pictures." Before Begelman moved to Columbia, he was vice-chairman of Creative Management Associates, perhaps the most powerful talent agency in the entertainment industry. One day in 1972, Brooks was aimlessly trudging the streets of New York. Begelman spotted him and approached him. According to Brooks, the following conversation took place:

> BEGELMAN: Where are you going?
> BROOKS: Nowhere. I am walking in circles.
> BEGELMAN: Why is the most talented man in the world walking in circles?
> BROOKS: Because the most talented man in the world is out of a job and is maybe not the most talented man in the world.
> BEGELMAN: Can I buy you lunch?
> BROOKS: Oh, I would be so happy if you would, because I haven't eaten in days.

(*They have lunch, after which Brooks is whisked off
to Begelman's sumptuous office, where "even the indirect
lighting is good."*)

BEGELMAN: The first thing you should do is sign with
me. You're nobody and I'm everybody. It's a good deal.

BROOKS: You're right. (*He signs.*)

Soon afterward, a friend in the script department of
Warner Brothers sent him a treatment by Andrew
Bergman of a Western comedy called *Tex X*. Would
Brooks like to rewrite it? Immobilized by self-mistrust,
Brooks passed the script on to Begelman for advice.
This led to another exquisitely lit confrontation.

BEGELMAN: I think this could be very funny. Do you
want to do it?

BROOKS: No.

BEGELMAN: All right, you don't want to do it. Fine.
You'll do it.

BROOKS: Why do I have to do it?

BEGELMAN: Because you owe a fortune in alimony,
because you are in debt, and because you have no
choice. You have to do it, and with all the talent you
possess.

BROOKS: OK. I'll do it. As long as I can have Andrew
Bergman to work with.

BEGELMAN: Swell. I'll make that one of the conditions.

BROOKS: And not only Bergman. (*His mind races to
recapture the security of the past.*) I want to do it the
way we did "Your Show of Shows." We'll get a black
writer, maybe Richard Pryor, and a comedy team like
Norman Steinberg and Alan Uger, and we'll lock ourselves up and write it together, fancy-free and crazy.

Through Begelman's mediation with Warners, this group
was rapidly assembled. He negotiated a contract whereby
Brooks received fifty thousand dollars for the screenplay (his
fellow authors split a smaller sum four ways) and a hundred
thousand more if the studio liked the result and asked Brooks
to direct it. Brooks regards *Blazing Saddles*—his new title for
Tex X—as "a landmark comedy," a historic blast of derision

at the heroic myths of the Old West. "I decided that this
would be a surrealist epic," he said to me. "It was time to
take two eyes, the way Picasso had done it, and put them
on one side of the nose, because the official movie portrait
of the West was simply a lie. For nine months, we worked
together like maniacs. We went all the way—especially
Richard Pryor, who was very brave and very far-out and very
catalytic. I figured my career was finished anyway, so I wrote
berserk, heartfelt stuff about white corruption and racism
and Bible-thumping bigotry. We used dirty language on the
screen for the first time, and to me the whole thing was like
a big psychoanalytic session. I just got everything out of me—
all my furor, my frenzy, my insanity, my love of life and
hatred of death."

Warners snapped up the completed script and hired Brooks
to direct his first Hollywood movie. There was one stipulation: the campfire sequence, in which the bean-fed cowpokes
audibly befoul the night air, must be cut. Brooks and his
colleagues stood firm: either the scene stayed or they quit.
Here, and elsewhere in the screenplay, they saw no reason
to disown what is called "healthy vulgarity" when it occurs
in Chaucer, but "childish smut" when it infiltrates the
cinema. Eventually the studio gave in, provided that Brooks
would consent, as an executive put it, "to for God's sake
hold the decibels down." Casting, however, was not without
problems. Brooks wanted Richard Pryor to play the black
protagonist, whom knavish State Procurer Harvey Korman
appoints as sheriff of a white chauvinist community in the
hope of destroying its faith in law and order. Warners rejected Pryor, whom they thought too undisciplined. Cleavon
Little (a suave performer with no flair for comedy) got the
job instead. Dan Dailey was engaged for the role of the
Waco Kid, the burnt-out alcoholic gun-fighter whom Little
enlists to support him. On the Friday before shooting began,
Dailey suffered an attack of qualms and cabled that he was
pulling out. With forty-eight hours to go, he was replaced by
Gig Young, but when Young arrived on the set it was obvi-

ous that he was in no shape to act. Personal problems, it seemed, were oppressing him, and at the end of a wasted day he was discreetly fired.

"It's a sign from God!" Brooks suddenly cried. "Get me Gene Wilder on the phone in New York!" Though Wilder knew the script and was eager to help, he was about to leave for England, where he was due to appear in *The Little Prince*, directed by Stanley Donen. "Nothing's impossible!" Brooks shouted at him. "Call Donen in London now and ask him to rearrange his schedule. If he can let you out for three weeks, or even two, it's enough."

A couple of hours later, Wilder called back with the news that Donen had generously agreed to reshuffle his plans and release Wilder for three and a half weeks. "I'll fly out tomorrow," Wilder said. Brooks met him at Los Angeles Airport and drove him straight to the costume department of Warners, where he was transformed within minutes into something out of *Stagecoach*. Next morning, roughly thirty-six hours after the idea had first come up, Gene Wilder, word perfect, was playing the Waco Kid. "I don't believe in fate," Wilder said to me recently, "but I'm tempted to when I think of my relationship with Mel. If I hadn't been miscast in *Mother Courage*, none of this would have happened. And if two actors hadn't dropped out of *Blazing Saddles* at the last moment, I would never have got the part."

When shooting (ten weeks) and editing (nine months) were over, Brooks and his producer, Michael Hertzberg, held an afternoon showing of their rough-cut for a dozen top executives at Warner Brothers. The occasion was about as festive—to borrow a phrase dear to Laurence Olivier—as a baby's open grave. The jury sat like so many statues on Easter Island and filed out at the end in frozen silence. Brooks was shattered, convinced that he had thrown away his last chance in movies. Hertzberg was more resilient. Grabbing a phone, he instructed his staff that he was going to run the picture again that evening, in a larger viewing theatre, and that he wanted it packed with at least two hundred people:

secretaries, janitors, cleaning women, waiters—anyone but studio brass. Let Brooks continue the story: "So 8 P.M. comes and two hundred and forty people are jammed into this room. Some of them have already heard the film is a stinker because of the afternoon disaster. So they're very quiet and polite. Frankie Laine sings the title song, with the whip cracks. Laughs begin—good laughs. We go to the railroad section. The cruel overseer says to the black workers, 'Let's have a good old nigger work song.' Everybody gets a little chilled. Then the black guys start to sing 'I get no kick from champagne. . . .' And that audience was like a Chagall painting. People left their chairs and floated upside down and the laughter never stopped. It was big from that moment to the last frame of the last reel."

Blazing Saddles opened in 1974 and went on to become one of the two top-grossing comedies in the history of the cinema, out-earned only by Robert Altman's *M*A*S*H*. It is a farce with the gloves off, a living proof of the adage that a feast can be every bit as good as enough. We are not invited to smile: we either laugh or cringe. The major gags are blatant to the point of outrage, as when a thug on foot, faced with a mounted adversary, fells his opponent's horse with a roundhouse right to the jaw. Brooks's method is the comedy of deliberate overkill. The annoyance of Hedley Lamarr (the Harvey Korman character) at being addressed as Hedy is funny the first time and tedious the third, but by the fifth or sixth it is funnier than ever; in a film full of unexpected twists, the expected twist can pay surprising dividends. Though the jokes run wild, the plot is tightly organized, and parts of the script are remarkably literary—e.g., this far from untypical exchange:

> Q.: Don't you see it's the last act of a desperate man?
> A.: I don't care if it's the first act of *Henry V*.

With *Blazing Saddles*, a low comedy in which many of the custard pies are camouflaged hand grenades, Brooks made his first conquest of Middle America. He told *Playboy* that it was "designed as an esoteric little picture," but the statement simply does not ring true; he had always wanted the big audience in addition to the art-house minority, and now he had both.

Young Frankenstein (1974) started life as a phrase doodled by Gene Wilder during an Easter vacation at West Hampton in 1973. He called Brooks and explained what he had in mind: one of Frankenstein's scions revisits the family castle in Transylvania and revives the monster his ancestor created. Brooks had no time to do more than express interest, since *Blazing Saddles* was already in preparation. A deal was set up with Columbia whereby Wilder would write a first draft and then, after *Blazing Saddles* was finished, work with Brooks on a revised version. Their collaboration was speedy and harmonious, Brooks supplying the broad comic emphases and Wilder the grace notes. Wilder restrained Brooks, who, in turn, liberated Wilder. "Mel has all kinds of faults," Wilder said to me. "Like his greed, his megalomania, his need to be the universal father and teacher, even to people far more experienced than he is. Why I'm close to him is not in spite of those faults but because of them. I need a leader, someone to tell me what to do. If he were more humble, modest, and considerate, he would probably have more friends, but I doubt whether he and I would be such good friends. He made me discover the *me* in Mel. He taught me never to be afraid of offending. It's when you worry about offending people that you get in trouble." (Compare something that Cocteau once said: "Whatever the public blames you for, cultivate it—it is yourself.")

Brooks and Wilder presented their final draft to Columbia before *Blazing Saddles* appeared. The estimated budget was two million two hundred thousand dollars. The studio wanted it reduced to a million and three-quarters. Happy to compromise, Brooks asked, "How about two million?" The answer was an unyielding no. "So we took the script to Fox, and made the picture there for two million eight," Wilder told me. "We were already shooting when *Blazing Saddles* came out and hit the jackpot." Wilder thinks—and is not alone in thinking—that this was the biggest mistake Columbia ever made. Since *Young Frankenstein,* which has so far grossed over thirty-four million dollars, Brooks has remained unshakably loyal to Fox. (In his office on the Fox lot, the wall overlooking his desk is dominated by a large portrait of Tolstoy, hanging alongside a blown-up label from a bottle of Château Latour 1929—"to remind me," Brooks says, "that there are more important things than grosses.") "On the set of *Blazing Saddles,* there was a lot of love in the air," Wilder continues. "But *Young Frankenstein* was the most pleasurable film I've ever done. I couldn't bear to leave Transylvania."

It would be fair to call *Young Frankenstein* the Mel Brooks movie that appeals to people who don't like Mel Brooks. "I like *things* in all his films," Woody Allen said to me cautiously, "but they're a little in-and-out for my taste. *Young Frankenstein* is the most consistent whole." The parts mesh instead of clashing. The pace throughout, audaciously stately for comedy, is modelled on that of James Whale's *Frankenstein*; and Gerald Hirschfeld's black-and-white photography exactly matches Whale's crepuscular visual style. The members of the supporting cast play together with a self-denying temperance unique in Brooks's work: I think particularly of Frau Blücher (Cloris Leachman), the fright-wigged housekeeper, at every mention of whose name we hear the distant whinnying of terrified horses; and of the Transylvanian police chief (Kenneth Mars), with an expatriate accent even less penetrable than the late Albert Bassermann's, and with a prosthetic arm that he uses as a battering ram when he leads the pitchfork-brandishing peasants against the gates of Schloss Frankenstein. In the title role, Gene Wilder—his eyes burning, his voice an exalted, slow-motion tenor—gives the finest performance yet seen in a Brooks picture. In the best sequence, fit to be set beside the "Springtime for Hitler" routine in *The Producers,* Wilder proudly appears before an assembly of grave Victorian scientists to introduce his new, improved monster, who clumps onto the stage and goes into a halting impression of Boris Karloff singing "Puttin' on the Ritz." The spectators instantly subject the zombie and his master to a bombardment of cabbages and broccoli, the underlying joke being that an audience of bearded savants should have come laden with vegetable missiles in the first place. It is not the gags, however, that give the film its motive force. We have seen that Brooks is driven by a fear, amounting to hatred, of mortality; and what is *Young Frankenstein* but the story of a man who succeeds in defeating death?

Brooks now began to savor the delights of power. "It's an achievement of a kind," he told me some time ago, "to know that I can walk into any studio—any one in town—and just say my name, and the president will fly out from behind his desk and open his door. It's terrific, it's a great feeling. My worst critic is my wife. She keeps me straight. She says, 'Are you pleasing that mythical public of yours again, or is this really funny and heartfelt?' " Brooks refers to the byproducts of success under the collective title of the Green Awning Syndrome. He explains what he means in an imaginary anecdote: "Mike Nichols has just made *The Graduate*, and it's a worldwide smash, and he goes to his producer, Joe Levine, and says, 'Now I want to do *The Green Awning.*' 'The what?' '*The Green Awning.*' 'What is that?' 'It's a movie about a green awning.' 'Does any famous star walk under the green awning?' 'No, all unknowns.' 'Are there any naked women near the green awning?' 'No, no naked women.' 'Are people talking and eating scrambled eggs under the green awning?' 'No. It's just a green awning. Panavision. It doesn't move.' 'How long would it be?' 'Two hours. Nothing but a green awning.' Levine sticks out his hand. 'All right, what the hell, we'll do it!' That's the Green Awning Syndrome."

Brooks knew that the syndrome had descended upon him when he proposed *Silent Movie* as his next picture for Fox: given his track record, the studio simply dared not turn it down, though Brooks admits that he helped Fox to be brave

by revealing that there would be cameo roles for Liza
Minnelli, Anne Bancroft, Paul Newman, James Caan, and
Burt Reynolds. The idea for a movie with no spoken words
(apart from a resonant "No!" to be uttered by the mime
Marcel Marceau) had come from Ron Clark, a laconic playwright and comedy writer. Clark suggested that he and
Brooks should collaborate on the script with Rudy DeLuca
and Barry Levinson, widely admired as the writers of "The
Carol Burnett Show"; and so it worked out. For more than
twelve months—very much on and off, to fit in with their
other assignments—the four men met in a room at Fox and
reduced one another to hysteria. Shooting began in January,
1976, and the film had its premiere before the end of the
year.

A string of sight gags linked by captions (the verbals in
many instances being funnier than the visuals), *Silent Movie*
consolidated Brooks's international fame. No dubbing was
required to make its more explosive set pieces as accessible in
Bora Bora as they were in South Bend. It spoke softly but
carried a big slapstick. Moreover, it established Brooks as a
movie star: Mel Funn, the ex-alcoholic director who saves his
old studio from conglomerate takeover with a silent movie
called *Silent Movie*, was the first leading role he had ever
played. The picture was his third comedy hit in three years,
and up to the beginning of 1978 it had brought in more than
twenty million dollars at the box office. Yet there are times
when one not only can but must argue with success. Even as
I smiled (which was more often than I laughed) at *Silent
Movie*, I knew I was watching an act of supreme perversity.
Here was a master of the improvised word devoting more
than a year of his life to something speechless and meticulously planned in advance. Do not suppose, by the way, that
Brooks is a director who works on impulse, prancing around
the set in ecstasies of Felliniesque free association. The final
script of *Silent Movie* was the film the public saw, except for
a brief but expensive sequence that Brooks described to me
afterward: "It was called 'Lobsters in New York,' and it starts

with a restaurant sign that reads 'Chez Lobster.' Inside, a huge lobster in maître d's tuxedo is greeting two very well-dressed lobsters in evening dress and leading them to a table. Already we thought this was hysterical. Then a waiter lobster in a white jacket shows them a menu that says 'Flown in Fresh from New York.' They get up and follow the waiter lobster to an enormous tank, where a lot of little human beings in bathing suits are swimming nervously around. The diner lobsters point to a tasty-looking middle-aged man. The waiter's claw reaches into the tank. It picks up the man, who is going bananas, and that was the end of the scene. We loved it; we thought it was sensational. Every time we saw it, there was not enough Kleenex to stuff into our mouths." Nobody else, however, so much as snickered—not even at the sneak previews—with the result that Brooks decided to jettison the whole sequence. Never before had he faced such a setback, and the memory of it still ruffles him. Seeing *Silent Movie* for the second time, I found myself recalling and endorsing something that Gene Wilder had said to me: "Mel has no physical skills, like Chaplin or Fields. His skills are vocal. Not verbal but vocal." And in *Silent Movie*, for all its popularity, rusting unused.

Excerpts from a dinner with Brooks at the Chambord Restaurant in Beverly Hills late in 1977. He is wearing a dark-blue coat, gray slacks, a light-blue shirt, and a striped blue tie; as usual, he has arrived with a leather case containing two bottles of absurdly expensive wine from his own cellar. Neither of them, alas, comes from the case of magnums of Haut Brion, 1961, which Alfred Hitchcock recently sent him as a gesture of gratitude for *High Anxiety*. In reminiscent mood, Brooks speaks: "Just before *Silent Movie* came out in 1976, I was approached by a staff writer from *Time* who asked me whether I'd like to be on the cover. Well, I expected to be described in *Time* as 'Mel Brooks, flinty, chunky Jew,' but nevertheless I said yes. I had no idea what an insane Pandora's box of heartache would be opened by this simple exchange. Reporters followed me around night

and day for weeks. They tortured my mother and my
children, all the time looking for negative things about me.
Everyone I ever knew was called and cross-examined. Everyone eagerly cooperated. Then, a couple of weeks before the
cover was due, I was told I'd been dumped and replaced by
Nadia Comaneci. So I asked, 'Isn't the election coming up
soon?' 'Don't worry,' they said. 'It's you next week for sure.'
Next week, Ford gets the cover. I called them up and said,
'I'm disgusted with myself. I feel used and humiliated, and I
may hang myself in my cell.' They said, 'Look, if you'll just
help us fill in one or two gaps, there's a good chance that
next week, perhaps . . .' Even then I hesitated, but I finally
said no."

I asked what seemed the obvious question.

After a pause, Brooks slowly replied, "If I could get a legal
guarantee that they wouldn't bother my immediate family,
and if that guarantee was signed by every member of the
Supreme Court, then the answer is yes, I *would* do it all
again for a *Time* cover."

High Anxiety, which featured the same star, director, and
writing team as *Silent Movie,* made its debut in the closing
weeks of 1977. Sniffed at by some of the critics (though not
by the public, which has swept it into the black with a box-
office take that so far amounts to about twenty million
dollars), it borrows elements from a number of Hitchcock
films—in particular, *Spellbound, Vertigo, Psycho, The Birds,*
and *North by North-West*—and, having given them all a
ferociously farcical twist, arranges them in a way that would
make narrative sense to an audience entirely ignorant of
Hitchcock. Brooks once told me that for him the Marx
Brothers were "the healthiest of all the comics," and it is not
fortuitous that the middle initial of Dr. Robert H. Thorndyke, the character he plays in *High Anxiety,* stands for
Harpo. The best half-dozen moments in the picture have the
antisocial outrageousness that was always the Brothers' trademark—moments when inhibitions evaporate and excesses long

dreamed of are allowed free play; e.g., Thorndyke's fulsome impersonation of Frank Sinatra in a hotel nightclub, and his first dinner as the newly appointed head of the Psycho-Neurotic Institute for the Very, Very Nervous. In the latter sequence an establishing shot shows us, by night, a mansion like Manderley in *Rebecca*. The script continues:

> *The lights are on in the elegantly appointed dining room.* CAMERA SLOWLY MOVES *toward the lighted window. It* MOVES *closer and closer, until it actually hits the window and crashes through. We* HEAR *the* SOUND *of the window panes breaking. Everybody at the dining table stops eating their fruit cup, their spoons poised in mid-air.*

When *High Anxiety* failed to receive a single nomination, either from the Academy or from the Writers Guild, Brooks was in despair. "He was as low as I've ever known him," his wife said to me.

Despite its virtues, *High Anxiety* fitted into a confining pattern. Brooks had now made four films in succession, all of them based on other kinds of films—the Western, the horror picture, the silent comedy, and the Hitchcock thriller. Nor was he alone in this dependence on incest—or, if you prefer, cannibalism. Barry Levinson remarked to me, "*Rocky* is a remake even though it's never been made before." In the *Times* on September 25, 1977, Roger Copeland dealt with the whole subject of movies about movies:

> Consider, for example, George Lucas's "Star Wars"—a film that makes so many references to earlier films and styles of film-making that it could just as easily, and perhaps more accurately, have been called "Genre Wars."

Among other pictures cited by Copeland were Martin Scorese's *New York, New York*, Brian De Palma's *Obsession*, Don Siegel's *The Shootist*, Marty Feldman's *The Last*

Remake of Beau Geste, and Herbert Ross's *Play It Again,
Sam* (written by Woody Allen), all of which drew their
inspiration from celluloid sources. Nor did he overlook the
career of Peter Bogdanovich, an extended act of homage to
the achievements of other directors. He concluded:

> There are dangers involved; the dangers of decadence,
> of art feeding so completely on itself that it becomes
> totally cut off from life as lived.

In 1965, in an introduction to Malcolm Lowry's novel
Under the Volcano, Stephen Spender wrote, "Someone
should write a thesis perhaps on the influence of the cinema
on the novel—I mean the *serious* novel." I should say that
there was a more urgent need for a study of the influence of
the cinema on the cinema—and I do not mean only the
serious cinema. It is self-evident that all the arts live off and
grow out of their own past. What is new about film is that
it is the first narrative art to be instantly accessible, twenty-
four hours a day, in virtually every living room. To immerse
oneself in drama, opera, or literature, it is necessary, from
time to time, to carry out certain errands, like going to a
theatre, an opera house, a record shop, a bookstore, or a
library; but to become saturated in cinema you do not even
have to go to the movies. They come to you. The lover of
stage acting will never know exactly how Sarah Siddons or
Edmund Kean performed, or what the theatre in Periclean
Athens was really like, but for the movie buff such problems
do not arise, since the art of his choice is on permanent
record, its whole history an open book, visible at the turn
of a switch. This explains why so many contemporary novels
and plays, as well as films, are swollen with references to,
quotations from, and parodies of old movies. A process of
artistic colonization is going on. Never before, I believe, has
one art form exercised such hegemony over the others; and
the decisive factor is not intrinsic superiority but sheer
availability.

The first generation of children nourished, via television, on films has only recently reached maturity, yet it's already clear how deeply—in their private behavior, not to mention their work as artists—the movies are imprinted on them. As the amount of exposed and edited film inexorably piles up, its ascendancy will increase, and we may have to cope with a culture entirely molded by cinematic habits and values. Edmund Wilson, I suspect, was hovering over this point as long ago as 1949, when, having seen a pastiche Hollywood musical called *Oh, You Beautiful Doll*, he indignantly wrote to a friend: "All these attempts to exploit the immediate past show the rapidity of the bankruptcy of the movies as purveyors of popular entertainment."

Brooks, discussing his future plans, sometimes sounds worryingly unaware of the perils involved in continued addiction to the Self-Regarding Cinema. In the past twelve months, I have heard him frothing with enthusiasm about such projects as (1) "a World War Two picture to end all World War Two pictures"; (2) a remake of the Lubitsch masterpiece *To Be or Not to Be*, starring Anne Bancroft and himself; and (3) "a Busby Berkeley-style musical where crazy people sing for no reason," which would be tantamount to self-plagiarism, since the perfect comment on Berkeley already exists in the "Springtime for Hitler" sequence from *The Producers*. Not long ago, he called up Gene Wilder and said, "When we work together again, we're going to have to bring up the big guns, and there are only two—love and death." Which is all very well except for the fact that *Love and Death* is the title of a film by Woody Allen.

Intermittently, however, Brooks will say something that bolsters one's faith in the curious inner compass that guides him. This, for instance: "I've tied myself to no end but the joy of observation. And I need to pass that on. I'm a celebrator. That's why I like the Russians. They'll look at a tree and cry out, 'Look at that tree!' They're full of original astonishments." And, still more reassuringly, this—a remark uttered in a context that had nothing to do with Brooks's

own career: "We are all basically antennae. If we let ourselves be bombarded by cultural events based on movies, we
won't get a taste of what's happening in the world."

Springtime, 1978: A sunny lunch in Los Angeles with
Anne Bancroft, who is, according to her husband, "a strange
combination of the serf and the intellectual." They live in
a one-story house (no pool) in Malibu. She tells me that
Brooks's newest obsession is to make a film called, *tout
court*, *The History of the World, Part One*. She likes the
idea, because it means, as she puts it, "that he can play any
period in which he feels happy." This, of course, was precisely what he did in the footloose days when he was recording "The Two-Thousand-Year-Old Man." The story of mankind would be an ideal frolic, a definitive detour; and Miss
Bancroft agrees with me that he ought to write it on his own.
"One evening, I came back late from a difficult rehearsal,"
she says. "Mel had been working at home all day. I was
feeling very sorry for myself, and I wailed, 'Acting is so
hard.' Mel picked up a blank sheet of paper and held it in
front of me. '*That's* what's hard,' he said. I've never com-
plained about acting again."

[1978]

The girl in the black helmet
—LOUISE BROOKS

N
ONE OF THIS would have happened if I had not
noticed, while lying late in bed on a hot Sunday morning
last year in Santa Monica and flipping through the TV
guide for the impending week, that one of the local public-
broacasting channels had decided to show, at 1 P.M. that
very January day, a film on which my fantasies had fed ever
since I first saw it, a quarter of a century before. Even for
Channel 28, it was an eccentric piece of programming. I
wondered how many of my Southern Californian neighbors
would be tempted to forgo their poolside champagne
brunches, their bicycle jaunts along Ocean Front Walk,
their health-food picnics in Topanga Canyon, or their surf-
board battles with the breakers of Malibu in order to watch
a silent picture, shot in Berlin just fifty years earlier, about
an artless young hedonist who, meaning no harm, rewards
her lovers—and eventually herself—with the prize of violent
death. Although the film is a tragedy, it is also a celebration
of the pleasure principle. Outside in the midday sunshine,

California was celebrating the same principle, with the shadows of mortality left out.

I got to my set in time to catch the credits. The director: G. W. Pabst, reigning maestro of German cinema in the late nineteen-twenties. The script: Adapted by Ladislaus Vajda from *Erdgeist* (*Earth Spirit*) and *Die Büchse der Pandora* (*Pandora's Box*), two scabrously erotic plays written in the eighteen-nineties by Frank Wedekind. For his movie, Pabst chose the title of the later work, though the screenplay differed markedly from Wedekind's original text: *Pandora's Box* belongs among the few films that have succeeded in improving on theatrical chefs-d'œuvre. For his heroine, Lulu, the dominant figure in both plays, Pabst outraged a whole generation of German actresses by choosing a twenty-one-year-old girl from Kansas whom he had never met, who was currently working for Paramount in Hollywood, and who spoke not a word of any language other than English. This was Louise Brooks. She made only twenty-four films, in a movie career that began in 1925 and ended, with enigmatic suddenness, in 1938. Two of them were masterpieces—*Pandora's Box* and its immediate successor, also directed by Pabst, *The Diary of a Lost Girl*. Most, however, were assembly-line studio products. Yet around her, with a luxuriance that proliferates every year, a literature has grown up. I append a few excerpts:

> Her youthful admirers see in her an actress who needed no directing, but could move across the screen causing the work of art to be born by her mere presence.—*Lotte H. Eisner, French critic.*

> An actress of brilliance, a luminescent personality, and a beauty unparalleled in film history.—*Kevin Brownlow, British director and movie historian.*

> One of the most mysterious and potent figures in the history of the cinema . . . she was one of the first

performers to penetrate to the heart of screen acting.—
David Thomson, British critic.

Louise Brooks is the only woman who had the ability
to transfigure no matter what film into a masterpiece.
. . . Louise is the perfect apparition, the dream woman,
the being without whom the cinema would be a poor
thing. She is much more than a myth, she is a magical
presence, a real phantom, the magnetism of the cinema.
—*Ado Kyrou, French critic.*

Those who have seen her can never forget her. She
is the modern actress *par excellence*. . . . As soon as she
takes the screen, fiction disappears along with art, and
one has the impression of being present at a documentary. The camera seems to have caught her by
surprise, without her knowledge. She is the intelligence
of the cinematic process, the perfect incarnation of that
which is photogenic; she embodies all that the cinema
rediscovered in its last years of silence: complete natural-
ness and complete simplicity. Her art is so pure that it
becomes invisible.—*Henri Langlois, director of the
Cinémathèque Française.*

On Channel 28, I stayed with the film to its end, which is
also Lulu's. Of the climactic sequence, so decorously understated, Louise Brooks once wrote in *Sight & Sound*, "It is
Christmas Eve and she is about to receive the gift which has
been her dream since childhood. Death by a sexual maniac."
When it was over, I switched channels and returned to the
real world of game shows and pet-food commercials, re-
lieved to find that the spell she cast was still as powerful as
ever. Brooks reminds me of the scene in *Citizen Kane* in
which Everett Sloane, as Orson Welles's aging business
manager, recalls a girl in a white dress whom he saw in his
youth when he was crossing over to Jersey on a ferry. They
never met or spoke. "I only saw her for one second," he says,
"and she didn't see me at all—but I'll bet a month hasn't
gone by since then that I haven't thought of that girl."

I had now, by courtesy of Channel 28, seen *Pandora's Box* for the third time. My second encounter with the film had taken place several years earlier, in France. Consulting my journal, I found the latter experience recorded with the baroque extravagance that seems to overcome all those who pay tribute to Brooks. I unflinchingly quote:

> Infatuation with L. Brooks reinforced by second viewing of "Pandora." She has run through my life like a magnetic thread—this shameless urchin tomboy, this unbroken, unbreakable porcelain filly. She is a prairie princess, equally at home in a waterfront bar and in the royal suite at Neuschwanstein; a creature of impulse, a creator of impulses, a temptress with no pretensions, capable of dissolving into a giggling fit at a peak of erotic ecstasy; amoral but totally selfless, with that sleek jet *cloche* of hair that rings such a peal of bells in my subconscious. In short, the only star actress I can imagine either being enslaved by or wanting to enslave; and a dark lady worthy of any poet's devotion:
>
> For I have sworn thee fair and thought thee bright,
> Who art as black as hell, as dark as night.

Some basic information about Rochester, New York: With two hundred and sixty-three thousand inhabitants, it is the sixth-largest city in the state, bestriding the Genesee River at its outlet into Lake Ontario. Here, in the eighteen-eighties, George Eastman completed the experiments that enabled him to manufacture the Kodak camera, which, in turn, enabled ordinary people to capture monochrome images, posed or spontaneous, of the world around them. He was in at the birth of movies, too. The flexible strips of film used in Thomas Edison's motion-picture machine were first produced by Eastman, in 1889. Rochester is plentifully dotted with monuments to the creator of the Kodak, among them a palatial Georgian house, with fifty rooms and a lofty neoclassical portico, that he built for himself in 1905. When he

died, in 1932, he left his mansion to the University of
Rochester, of whose president it became the official home.
Shortly after the Second World War, the Eastman house
took on a new identity. It opened its doors to the public,
and offered, to quote from its brochure, "the world's most
important collection of pictures, films, and apparatus showing the development of the art and technology of photography." In 1972 it was imposingly renamed the International Museum of Photography. Its library now contains
about five thousand movies, many of them unique copies,
and seven of them—a larger number than any other archive
can boast—featuring Louise Brooks. Hence I decide to pay
a visit to the city, where I check in at a motel in the late
spring of 1978. Thanks to the generous cooperation of Dr.
John B. Kuyper, the director of the museum's film department, I am to see its hoard of Brooks pictures—six of them
new to me—within the space of two days. Screenings will
be held in the Dryden Theatre, a handsome auditorium that
was added to the main building in 1950 as a gift from Eastman's niece and her husband, George Dryden.

On the eve of Day One, I mentally recap what I have
learned of Brooks's early years. Born in 1906 in Cherryvale,
Kansas, she was the second of four children sired by Leonard
Brooks, a hardworking lawyer of kindly disposition and
diminutive build, for whom she felt nothing approaching
love. She herself was never more than five feet two and a half
inches tall, but she raised her stature onscreen by wearing
heels as high as six inches. Her mother, née Myra Rude, was
the eldest member of a family of nine, and she warned Mr.
Brooks before their marriage that she had spent her entire
life thus far looking after kid brothers and sisters, that she
had no intention of repeating the experience with children
of her own, and that any progeny she might bear him would,
in effect, have to fend for themselves. The result, because
Myra Brooks was a woman of high spirits who took an infectious delight in the arts, was not a cold or neglectful upbringing. Insistent on liberty for herself, she passed on a love

of liberty to her offspring. Louise absorbed it greedily. Pirouetting appealed to her; encouraged by her mother, she took dancing lessons, and by the age of ten she was making paid appearances at Kiwanis and Rotary festivities. At fifteen, already a beauty *sui generis*, as surviving photographs show, with her hair, close-cropped at the nape to expose what Christopher Isherwood has called "that unique imperious neck of hers," cascading in ebony bangs down the high, intelligent forehead and descending on either side of her eyes in spit curls slicked forward at the cheekbones, like a pair of enamelled parentheses—at fifteen, she left high school and went to New York with her dance teacher. There she successfully auditioned for the Denishawn Dancers, which had been founded in 1915 by Ruth St. Denis and Ted Shawn, and was by far the most adventurous dance company in America. She started out as a student, but soon graduated to full membership of the troupe, with which she toured the country from 1922 to 1924. One of her fellow-dancers, Martha Graham, became a lifelong friend. "I learned to act while watching Martha Graham dance," she said later, "and I learned to move in film from watching Chaplin."

Suddenly, however, the discipline involved in working for Denishawn grew oppressive. Brooks was fired for lacking a sense of vocation, and the summer of 1924 found her back in New York, dancing in the chorus of George White's *Scandals*. After three months of this, a whim seized her, and she embarked without warning for London, where she performed the Charleston at the Café de Paris, near Piccadilly Circus. By New York standards, she thought Britain's Bright Young Things a moribund bunch, and when Evelyn Waugh wrote *Vile Bodies* about them, she said that only a genius could have made a masterpiece out of such glum material. Early in 1925, with no professional prospects, she sailed for Manhattan on borrowed money, only to be greeted by Florenz Ziegfeld with the offer of a job in a musical comedy called *Louie the 14th*, starring Leon Errol. She accepted, but the pattern of her subsequent behavior left no doubt that what she meant by liberty and independence was what others defined as irresponsibility and self-indulgence. Of the director of *Louie the 14th,* she afterward wrote, "He detested all of Ziegfeld's spoiled beauties, but most of all me, because on occasion, when I had other commitments, I would wire my nonappearance to the theatre." In May, 1925, she made her movie début, at the Paramount Astoria Studio, on Long Island, playing a bit part in *The Street of Forgotten Men,* of which no print is known to exist. She has written a vivid account of filmmaking in its Long Island days:

> The stages were freezing in the winter, steaming hot in the summer. The dressing rooms were windowless cubicles. We rode on the freight elevator, crushed by lights and electricians. But none of that mattered, because the writers, directors, and cast were free from all supervision. Jesse Lasky, Adolph Zukor, and Walter Wanger never left the Paramount office on Fifth Avenue, and the head of production never came on the set. There were writers and directors from Princeton and Yale. Motion pictures did not consume us. When work finished, we dressed in evening clothes, dined at the Colony or "21," and went to the theatre.
>
> The difference in Hollywood was that the studio was run by B. P. Schulberg, a coarse exploiter who propositioned every actress and policed every set. To love books was a big laugh. There was no theatre, no opera, no concerts—just those god-damned movies.

Despite Brooks's erratic conduct in *Louie the 14th,* Ziegfeld hired her to join Will Rogers and W. C. Fields in the 1925 edition of his *Follies.* It proved to be her last Broadway show. One of her many admirers that year was the atrabilious wit Herman Mankiewicz, then employed as second-string drama critic of the *Times.* Blithely playing truant from the *Follies,* she attended the opening of *No, No, Nanette* on Mankiewicz's arm. As the houselights faded, her escort, who was profoundly drunk, announced his intention of falling asleep, and asked Brooks to make notes on the show for use in his review. She obliged, and the *Times* next day echoed her opinion that *No, No, Nanette* was as "a highly meritorious paradigm of its kind." (Somewhat cryptically, she added that the score contained "more familiar quotations from itself . . . than even *Hamlet*.") Escapades like this did nothing to endear her to the other, more dedicated Ziegfeld showgirls, but an abiding intimacy grew up between her and W. C. Fields, in whose dressing room she was always graciously received. Later, in a passage that tells us as much about its author as about her subject, she wrote:

> He was an isolated person. As a young man he stretched out his hand to Beauty and Love and they thrust it away. Gradually he reduced reality to exclude all but his work, filling the gaps with alcohol whose dim eyes transformed the world into a distant view of harmless shadows. He was also a solitary person. Years of travelling alone around the world with his juggling act taught him the value of solitude and the release it gave his mind. . . . Most of his life will remain unknown. But the history of no life is a jest.

In September, 1925, the *Follies* left town on a national tour. Brooks stayed behind and sauntered through the role of a bathing beauty in a Paramount movie called *The American Venus*. Paramount and M-G-M were both pressing her to sign five-year contracts, and she looked for advice to Walter Wanger, one of the former company's top executives, with whom she was having an intermittent affair. "If, at this crucial moment in my career," she said long afterward, "Walter had given me some faith in my screen personality and my acting ability, he might have saved me from further mauling by the beasts who prowled Broadway and Hollywood." Instead, he urged her to take the Metro offer, arguing that if she chose Paramount everyone would assume that she got the job by sharing his bed and that her major attribute was not talent but sexual accessibility. Incensed by his line of reasoning, she defiantly signed with Paramount.

In the course of twelve months—during which Brooks's friend Humphrey Bogart, seven years her senior, was still laboring on Broadway, with four seasons to wait before the dawn of his film career—Brooks made six full-length pictures. The press began to pay court to her. *Photoplay*, whose reporter she received reclining in bed, said of her, "She is so very Manhattan. Very young. Exquisitely hard-boiled. Her black hair and black eyes are as brilliant as Chinese lacquer. Her skin is white as a camellia. Her legs are lyric." She worked with several of the bright young directors who gave Paramount its reputation for sophisticated comedy; e.g., Frank Tuttle, Malcolm St. Clair, and Edward Sutherland. Chronologically, the list of her credits ran as follows: *The American Venus* (for Tuttle, who taught her that the way to get laughs was to play perfectly straight; he directed Bebe Daniels in four movies and Clara Bow in six). *A Social Celebrity* (for St. Clair, who cast Brooks opposite the immaculately caddish Adolphe Menjou, of whose style she later remarked, "He never felt anything. He used to say, 'Now I do Lubitsch No. 1,' 'Now I do Lubitsch No. 2.' And that's exactly what he did. You felt nothing, working with him, and yet see him on the screen—he was a great actor"). *It's the Old Army Game* (for Sutherland, who had been Chaplin's directorial assistant on *A Woman of Paris*, and who made five pictures with W. C. Fields, of which this was the first; the third, *International House*, is regarded by many Fieldsian authorities as the Master's crowning achievement. Brooks married Sutherland, a hard-drinking playboy, in 1926 —an error that was rectified inside two years by divorce). *The Show-Off* (for St. Clair, adapted from the Broadway hit by George Kelly). *Just Another Blonde* (on loan to First National). And, finally, to round off the year's work, *Love 'Em and Leave 'Em* (for Tuttle), the first Brooks film of which the Eastman house has a copy. Here begin my notes on the sustained and solitary Brooks banquet that the museum laid before me.

Day One: Evelyn Brent is the nominal star of Love 'Em and Leave 'Em, a slick and graceful comedy about Manhattan shopgirls, but light-fingered Louise, as Brent's jazz-baby younger sister, steals the picture with bewitching insouciance. She is twenty, and her body is still plump, quite husky enough for work in the fields; but the face, framed in its black proscenium arch of hair, is already Lulu's in embryo, especially when she dons a white top hat to go to a costume ball (at which she dances a definitive Charleston). The plot calls for her to seduce her sister's boyfriend, a feckless window dresser, and she does so with that fusion of amorality and innocence which was to become her trademark. (During these scenes, I catch myself humming a tune from Pins and Needles: "I used to be on the daisy chain, but now I'm a chain-story daisy.") Garbo could give us innocence, and Dietrich amorality, on the grandest possible scale; only Brooks could play the simple, unabashed hedonist, whose appetite for pleasure is so radiant that even when it causes suffering to herself and others we cannot find it in ourselves to reproach her. Most actresses tend to pass moral judgments on the characters they play. Their performances issue tacit commands to the audience: "Love me," "Hate me," "Laugh at me," "Weep with me," and so forth. We get none of this from Brooks, whose presence before the camera merely declares, "Here I am. Make what you will of me." She does not care what we think of her. Indeed, she ignores us. We seem to be spying on unrehearsed reality, glimpsing what the great photographer Henri Cartier-Bresson later called "le moment qui se sauve." In the best of her silent films, Brooks —with no conscious intention of doing so—is reinventing the art of screen acting. I suspect that she was helped rather than hindered by the fact that she never took a formal acting lesson. "When I acted, I hadn't the slightest idea of what I was doing," she said once to Richard Leacock, the documentary-film maker. "I was simply playing myself, which is the hardest thing in the world to do—if you *know* that it's hard. I didn't, so it seemed easy. I had nothing to unlearn. When I first worked with Pabst, he was furious, because he approached people intellectually and you couldn't approach me intellectually, because there was nothing to approach." To watch Brooks is to recall Oscar Wilde's Lady Bracknell, who observes, "Ignorance is like a delicate, exotic fruit; touch it, and the bloom is gone."

Rereading the above paragraph, I pause at the sentence "She does not care what we think of her." Query: Was it precisely this quality, which contributed so much to her success on the screen, that enabled her, in later years, to throw that success so lightly away?

To return to Frank Tuttle's film: Tempted by a seedy and lecherous old horseplayer who lives in her rooming house, Brooks goes on a betting spree with funds raised by her fellow-shopgirls in aid of the Women's Welfare League. The aging gambler is played by Osgood Perkins (father of Tony), of whom Brooks said to Kevin Brownlow years afterward, "The best actor I ever worked with was Osgood Perkins. . . . You know what makes an actor great to work with? Timing. You don't have to feel anything. It's like dancing with a perfect dancing partner. Osgood Perkins would give you a line so that you would react perfectly. It was timing—because *emotion means nothing.*" (Emphasis mine.) This comment reveals what Brooks has learned about acting in the cinema: Emotion *per se*, however deeply felt, is not enough. It is what the actor shows—the contraband that he or she can smuggle past the camera—that matters to the audience. A variation of this dictum cropped up in the mouth of John Striebel's popular comic-strip heroine Dixie Dugan, who was based on Brooks and first appeared in 1926. Bent on getting a job in *The Zigfold Follies*, Dixie reflected, "All there is to this Follies racket is to *be cool and look hot.*" Incidentally, Brooks's comparison of Perkins with a dancing partner reminds me of a remark she once made about Fatty Arbuckle, who, under the assumed name of William Goodrich, apathetically directed her in a 1931 two-reeler called *Windy Riley Goes to Hollywood*: "He sat in his chair like a dead man. He had been very nice and sweetly dead ever since the scandal that ruined his career. . . . Oh, I thought he was magnificent in films. He was a wonderful dancer—a wonderful ballroom dancer in his heyday. It was like floating in the arms of a huge doughnut."

What images do I retain of Brooks in *Love 'Em and Leave 'Em*? Many comedic details; e.g., the scene in which she fakes tears of contrition by furtively dabbling her cheeks with water from a handily placed goldfish bowl, and our last view of her, with all her sins unpunished, merrily sweeping off in a Rolls-Royce with the owner of the department store. And, throughout, every closeup of that blameless, unblemished face.

In 1927, Brooks moved with Paramount to Hollywood and starred in four pictures—*Evening Clothes* (with Menjou), *Rolled Stockings*, *The City Gone Wild*, and *Now We're in the Air*, none of which are in the Eastman vaults. To commemorate that year, I have a publicity photo taken at a house she rented in Laurel Canyon: poised on tiptoe with arms outstretched, she stands on the diving board of her pool, wearing a one-piece black bathing suit with a tight white belt, looking like a combination of Odette and Odile in some modern-dress version of *Swan Lake*. Early in 1928, she was lent to Fox for a picture (happily preserved by the museum) that was to change her career—*A Girl in Every Port*, written and directed by Howard Hawks, who had made his first film only two years before. Along with Carole Lombard, Rita Hayworth, Jane Russell, and Lauren Bacall, Brooks thus claims a place among the actresses on David Thomson's list (in his *Biographical Dictionary of Film*) of performers who were "either discovered or brought to new life by Hawks." As in *Love 'Em and Leave 'Em*, she plays an amoral pleasure-lover, but this time the mood is much darker. Her victim is Victor McLaglen, a seagoing roughneck engaged in per-

petual sexual rivalry with his closest friend (Robert Armstrong); the embattled relationship between the two men
brings to mind the skirmishing of Flagg and Quirt in *What
Price Glory?*, which was filmed with McLaglen in 1926. In
A Girl in Every Port, McLaglen, on a binge in Marseilles,
sees a performance by an open-air circus whose star turn is
billed as "Mam'selle Godiva, Neptune's Bride and the Sweet-
heart of the Sea." The submarine coquette is, of course,
Brooks, looking svelter than of old, and clad in tights, span-
gled panties, tiara, and black velvet cloak. Her act consists
of diving off the top of a ladder into a shallow tank of water.
Instantly besotted, the bully McLaglen becomes the fawning
lapdog of this "dame of class." He proudly introduces her to
Armstrong, who, unwilling to wreck his buddy's illusions,
refrains from revealing that the lady's true character, as he
knows from a previous encounter with her, is that of a small-
time gold-digger. In a scene charged with the subtlest eroti-
cism, Brooks sits beside Armstrong on a sofa and coaxes
McLaglen to clean her shoes. He readily obeys. As he does
so, she begins softly, reminiscently, but purposefully, to
fondle Armstrong's thigh. To these caresses Armstrong does
not respond, but neither does he reject them. With one man
at her feet and another at her fingertips, she is like a cat
idly licking its lips over two bowls of cream. This must
surely have been sequence that convinced Pabst, when
the film was shown in Berlin, that he had found the actress
he wanted for *Pandora's Box*. By the end of the picture,
Brooks has turned the two friends into mortal enemies, reducing McLaglen to a state of murderous rage, mixed with
grief, that Emil Jannings could hardly have bettered. There
is no melodrama in her exercise of sexual power. No effort,
either: she is simply following her nature.

After her fling with Fox, Paramount cast its young star
(now aged twenty-one) in another downbeat triangle drama,
Beggars of Life, to be directed by another young director,
William Wellman. Like Hawks, he was thirty-two years old.
(The cinema is unique among the arts in that there was a

time in its history when almost all of its practitioners were
young. This was that time.) At first, the studio had trouble
tracing Brooks's whereabouts. Having just divorced Edward
Sutherland, she had fled to Washington with a new lover—
George Marshall, a millionaire laundry magnate, who later
became the owner of the Redskins football team. When she
was found, she promptly returned to the Coast, though her
zest for work was somewhat drained by a strong antipathy to
one of her co-stars—Richard Arlen, with whom she had appeared in *Rolled Stockings*—and by overt hostility from
Wellman, who regarded her as a dilettante. Despite these
malign auguries, *Beggars of Life*—available at Eastman house
—turned out to be one of her best films. Adapted from
a novel by Jim Tully, it foreshadows the Depression movies
of the thirties. Brooks plays the adopted daughter of a penniless old farmer who attempts, one sunny morning, to rape
her. Seizing a shotgun, she kills him. As she is about to
escape, the crime is discovered by a tramp (Arlen) who
knocks at the door in search of food. They run away together,
with Brooks wearing oversized masculine clothes, topped off
by a large peaked cap. (This was her first serious venture into
the rich territory of sexual ambiguity, so prosperously cultivated in later years by Garbo, Dietrich, et al.) Soon they fall
in with a gang of hoboes, whose leader—a ferocious but
teachable thug, beautifully played by Wallace Beery—forms
the third point of the triangle. He sees through Brooks's
disguise and proposes that since the police already know
about her male imposture, it would be safer to dress her as
a girl. He goes in search of female attire, but what he brings
back is marginally too young: a gingham dress, and a bonnet
tied under the chin, in which Brooks looks like a woman
masquerading as a child, a sort of adult Lolita. She stares at
us in her new gear, at once innocent and gravely perverse.
The rivalry for her affection comes to its height when Beery
pulls a gun and tells Arlen to hand her over. Brooks jumps
between them, protecting Arlen, and explains that she would
prefer death to life without him. We believe her; and so,

to his own befuddled amazement, does Beery. There is really
no need for the caption in which he says that he has often
heard about love but never until now known what it was. He
puts his gun away and lets them go.

Footnote: During the transvestite scenes, several dangerous
feats were performed for Brooks by a stunt man named
Harvey. One night, attracted by his flamboyant courage, she
slept with him. After breakfast next day, she strolled out onto
the porch of the hotel in the California village where the
location sequences were being shot. Harvey was there, accompanied by a group of hoboes in the cast. He rose and gripped
her by the arm. "Just a minute, Miss Brooks," he said loudly.
"I've got something to ask you. I guess you know my job
depends on my health." He then named a Paramount executive whom Brooks had never met, and continued, "Everybody
knows you're his girl and he has syphilis, and what I wanted
to know is: Do you have syphilis?" After a long and frozen
pause, he added, "Another reason I want to know is that my
girl is coming up at noon to drive me back to Hollywood."
Brooks somehow withdrew to her room without screaming.
Events like these may account for the lack of agonized regret
with which she prematurely ended her movie career. Several
years later, after she had turned down the part that Jean
Harlow eventually played in Wellman's *Public Enemy*, she
ran into the director in a New York bar. "You always hated
making pictures, Louise," he said sagely. She did not bother
to reply that it was not pictures she hated but Hollywood.

The Canary Murder Case (directed by Malcolm St. Clair
from a script based on S. S. Van Dine's detective story, with
William Powell as Philo Vance: not in the Eastman collection) was the third, and last, American movie that Brooks
made in 1928. By now, her face was beginning to be internationally known, and the rushes of this film indicated that
Paramount would soon have a major star on its hands. At the
time, the studio was preparing to take the plunge into talkies.
As Brooks afterward wrote in *Image* (a journal sponsored by
Eastman house), front offices all over Hollywood saw in this

radical change "a splendid opportunity . . . for breaking contracts, cutting salaries, and taming the stars." In the autumn of 1928, when her own contract called for a financial raise, B. P. Schulberg, the West Coast head of Paramount, summoned her to his office and said that the promised increase could not be granted in the new situation. *The Canary Murder Case* was being shot silent, but who knew whether Brooks could speak? (A fragile argument, since her voice was of bell-like clarity.) He presented her with a straight choice: either to continue at her present figure (seven hundred and fifty dollars a week) or to quit when the current picture was finished. To Schulberg's surprise, she chose to quit. Almost as an afterthought, he revealed when she was rising to leave that he had lately received from G. W. Pabst a bombardment of cabled requests for her services in *Pandora's Box*, all of which he had turned down.

Then forty-three years old, Pabst had shown an extraordinary flair for picking and molding actresses whose careers were upward bound; Asta Nielsen, Brigitte Helm, and Greta Garbo (in her third film, *The Joyless Street*, which was also her first outside Sweden) headed a remarkable list. Unknown to Schulberg, Brooks had already heard about the Pabst offer —and the weekly salary of a thousand dollars that went with it—from her lover, George Marshall, whose source was a gossipy director at M-G-M. She coolly told Schulberg to inform Pabst that she would soon be available. "At that very hour in Berlin," she wrote later in *Sight & Sound,* "Marlene Dietrich was waiting with Pabst in his office." This was two years before *The Blue Angel* made Dietrich a star. What she crucially lacked, Pabst felt, was the innocence he wanted for his Lulu. In his own words, "Dietrich was too old and too obvious—one sexy look and the picture would become a burlesque. But I gave her a deadline, and the contract was about to be signed when Paramount cabled saying I could have Louise Brooks." The day that shooting ended on *The Canary Murder Case,* Brooks raced out of Hollywood en route for Berlin, there to work for a man who was one of the four or five leading European directors but of whom a few weeks earlier she had never heard.

Pandora's Box, with which I had my fourth encounter at the Eastman house, could easily have emerged as a cautionary tale about a *grande cocotte* whose reward is the wages of sin. That seems to have been the impression left by Wedekind's two Lulu plays, which were made into a film in 1922 (not by Pabst) with Asta Nielsen in the lead. Summing up her predecessor's performance, Brooks said, "She played in the eye-rolling style of European silent acting. Lulu the man-eater devoured her sex victims . . . and then dropped dead in an acute attack of indigestion." The character obsessed many artists of the period. In 1928, Alban Berg began work on his twelve-tone opera *Lulu,* the heart of which—beneath the stark and stylized sound patterns—was blatantly theatrical, throbbing with romantic agony. Where the Pabst-Brooks version differs from the others is in its moral coolness. It assumes neither the existence of sin nor the necessity for retribution. It presents a series of events in which all the participants are seeking happiness, and it suggests that Lulu, whose notion of happiness is momentary fulfillment through sex, is not less admirable than those whose quest is for wealth or social advancement.

First sequence: Lulu in the Art Deco apartment in Berlin where she is kept by Peter Schön, a middle-aged newspaper proprietor. (In this role, the great Fritz Kortner, bulky but urbane, effortless in the exercise of power over everyone but his mistress, gives one of the cinema's most accurate and objective portraits of a capitalist potentate.) Dressed in a peignoir, Lulu is casually flirting with a man who has come to read the gas meter when the doorbell rings and Schigolch enters, a squat and shabby old man who was once Lulu's lover but is now down on his luck. She greets him with delight; as the disgruntled gas man departs, she swoops to rest on Schigolch's lap with the grace of a swan. The protective curve of her neck is unforgettable. Producing a mouth organ, Schigolch strikes up a tune, to which she performs a brief,

Dionysiac, and authentically improvised little dance. (Until this scene was rehearsed, Pabst had no idea that Brooks was a trained dancer.) Watching her, I recollect something that Schigolch says in the play, though not in the film: "The animal is the only genuine thing in man. . . . What you have experienced as an animal, no misfortune can ever wrest from you. It remains yours for life." From the window, he points out a burly young man on the sidewalk: this is a friend of his named Rodrigo, a professional athlete who would like to work with her on an adagio act.

Unheralded, Peter Schön lets himself into the apartment, and Lulu has just time to hide Schigolch on the balcony with a bottle of brandy. Schön has come to end his affair with Lulu, having decided to make a socially advantageous match with the daughter of a Cabinet Minister. In Lulu's reaction to the news there is no fury. She simply sits on a sofa and extends her arms toward him with something like reassurance. Unmoved at first, Schön eventually responds, and they begin to make love. The drunken Schigolch inadvertently rouses Lulu's pet dog to a barking fit, and this disturbance provokes the hasty exit of Schön. On the stairs, he passes the muscle man Rodrigo, whom Schigolch presents to Lulu. Rodrigo flexes his impressive biceps, on which she gleefully swings, like a schoolgirl gymnast.

A scene in Schön's mansion shows us his son Alwa (Francis Lederer in his pre-Hollywood days) busily composing songs for his new musical revue. Alwa is joined by the Countess Geschwitz (Alice Roberts), a tight-lipped lesbian who is designing the costumes. Lulu dashes in to announce her plans for a double act with Rodrigo, and it is immediately clear that both Alwa and the Countess have eyes for her. She strolls on into Peter Schön's study, where she picks up from the desk a photograph of his bride-to-be. Typically, she studies it with genuine interest; there's no narrowing of eyes or curling of lip. Peter Schön, who has entered the room behind her, snatches the picture from her hands and orders her to leave. Before doing so, she mischievously invents a rendezvous next

day with Alwa, whom she kisses, to the young man's embarrassed bewilderment, full on the mouth. With a toss of
the patent-leather hair and a glance, half-playful, half-
purposeful, at Alwa, she departs. Alwa asks his father why
he doesn't marry her. Rather too explosively to carry conviction, Peter replies that one doesn't marry women like that.
He proposes that Alwa give her a featured role in the revue,
and guarantees that his newspapers will make her a star.
Alwa is overjoyed; but when his father warns him at all costs
to beware of her, he quits the room in tongue-tied confusion.

So much for the exposition; the principal characters and
the main thrust of the action have been lucidly established.
Note that Lulu, for all her seductiveness, is essentially an exploited creature, not an exploiter; also that we are not (nor
shall we ever be) invited to feel sorry for her. I've already
referred to her birdlike movements and animal nature: let me
add that in the context of the plot as a whole she resembles
a glittering tropical fish in a tank full of predators. For the
remainder of this synopsis, I'll confine myself to the four
great set pieces on which the film's reputation rests.

(1) Intermission at the opening night of Alwa's revue:
Pabst catches the backstage panic of scene-shifting and
costume-changing with a kaleidoscopic brilliance that looks
forward to Orson Welles's handling, twelve years later, of the
operatic début of Susan Alexander Kane. Alwa and Geschwitz are there, revelling in what is obviously going to be a hit.
Peter Schön escorts Marie, his fiancée, through the pass
door to share the frenzy. Lulu, changing in the wings, catches
sight of him and smiles. Stricken with embarrassment, he
cuts her and leads Marie away. This treatment maddens Lulu,
and she refuses to go on with the show: "I'll dance for the
whole world, but not in front of that woman." She takes
refuge in the property room, whither Peter follows her. Leaning against the wall, she sobs, shaking her head mechanically
from side to side, and then flings herself onto a pile of
cushions, which she kicks and pummels. Despite her tantrum,
she is watching Schön's every move. When he lights a cigar-

ette to calm himself, she snaps "Smoking isn't allowed in here," and gives him a painful hack on the ankle. The mood of the scene swings from high histrionics through sly comedy to voluptuous intimacy. Soon Schön and Lulu are laughing, caressing, wholeheartedly making love. At this point, the door opens, framing Marie and Alwa. Unperturbed, Lulu rises in triumph, gathers up her costume, and sweeps past them to go onstage. Peter Schön's engagement is obviously over.

(2) The wedding reception: Lulu is in a snow-white bridal gown, suggesting less a victorious *cocotte* than a girl celebrating her first Communion. Peter's wealthy friends flock admiringly round her. She dances cheek to cheek with Geschwitz, who rabidly adores her. (The Belgian actress Alice Roberts, here playing what may be the first explicit lesbian in movie history, refused point-blank to look at Brooks with the requisite degree of lust. To solve the problem, Pabst stood in her line of vision, told her to regard him with passionate intensity, and photographed her in closeups, which he then intercut with shots of Brooks. Scenes like these presented no difficulty to Brooks herself. She used to say of Fritzi LaVerne, one of her best friends in the *Follies*, "She liked boys when she was sober and girls when she was drunk. I never heard a man or a woman pan her in bed, so she must have been very good." A shocked Catholic priest once asked her how she felt playing a sinner like Lulu. "Feel!" she said gaily. "I felt fine! It all seemed perfectly normal to me." She explained to him that, although she herself was not a lesbian, she had many chums of that persuasion in Ziegfeld's chorus line, and added, "I know two millionaire publishers, much like Schön in the film, who backed shows to keep themselves well supplied with Lulus.") The action moves to Peter's bedroom, where Schigolch and Rodrigo are drunkenly scattering roses over the nuptial coverlet. Lulu joins them, and something between a romp and an orgy seems imminent. It is halted by the entrance of the bridegroom. Appalled, he gropes for a gun in a nearby desk and chases the two men out of his house. The other guests, shocked and aghast, rapidly depart.

When Peter returns to the bedroom, he find Alwa with his
head in Lulu's lap, urging her to run away with him. The
elder Schön orders his son to leave. As soon as Alwa has left,
there follows, between Kortner and Brooks, a classic demonstration of screen acting as the art of visual ellipsis. With
the minimum of overt violence, a struggle for power is fought
out to the death. Schön advances on Lulu, presses the gun
into her hand, and begs her to commit suicide. As he grips
her fingers in his, swearing to shoot her like a dog if she lacks
the courage to do it herself, she seems almost hypnotized by
the desperation of his grief. You would think them locked in
an embrace until Lulu suddenly stiffens, a puff of smoke
rises between them, and Schön slumps to the floor. Alwa
bursts in and rushes to his father, from whose lips a fat
thread of blood slowly trickles. The father warns Alwa that
he will be the next victim. Gun in hand, Lulu stares at the
body, wide-eyed and transfixed. Brooks wrote afterward that
Pabst always used concrete phrases to trigger the emotional
response he wanted. In this case, the key image he gave her
was *"das Blut."* "Not the murder of my husband," she said,
"but the sight of the blood determined the expression on my
face." What we see is not *Vénus toute entière à sa proie
attachée* but a petrified child.

(3) Trial and flight: Lulu is sentenced to five years' imprisonment for manslaughter, but as the judge pronounces
the sentence, her friends, led by Geschwitz, set off a fire
alarm, and in the ensuing courtroom chaos she escapes. With
perfect fidelity to her own willful character, Lulu, in defiance
of movie cliché, comes straight back to Schön's house, where
she acts like a débutante relaxing after a ball—lighting a
cigarette, idly thumbing through a fashion magazine, trying
out a few dance steps, opening a wardrobe and stroking a new
fur coat, running a bath and immersing herself in it. Only
Brooks, perhaps could have carried off this solo sequence—
so unlike the behavior expected of criminals on the run—
with such ingrained conviction and such lyrical aplomb. Now
Alwa arrives and is astounded to find her at the scene of the

crime. The two decide to flee together to Paris. No sooner
have they caught the train, however, than they are recognized
by a titled pimp, who blackmails them into accompanying
him aboard a gambling ship. Geschwitz, Schigolch, and the
tediously beefy Rodrigo are also afloat, and for a while the
film lurches into melodrama—sub-Dostoevski with a touch
of ship's Chandler. Rodrigo threatens to expose Lulu unless
she sleeps with him; the Countess, gritting her teeth, dis-
tracts his attention by making love to him herself—an unlikely coupling—after which she disdainfully kills him.
Meanwhile, the pimp is arranging to sell Lulu to an Egyp-
tian brothelkeeper. Anxious to save her from this fate, Alwa
frenetically cheats at cards and is caught with a sleeve full
of aces. The police arrive just too late to prevent Alwa, Lulu,
and Schigolch from escaping in a rowboat. For the shipboard
episode, Pabst cajoled Brooks, much against her will, into
changing her coiffure. The spit curls disappeared; the black
bangs were parted, waved, and combed back to expose her
forehead. These cardinal errors of taste defaced the icon. It
was is if an Italian master had painted the Virgin and left
out the halo.

(4) London and catastrophe: The East End, icy and fog-
bound, on Christmas Eve. The Salvation Army is out in
force, playing carols and distributing food to the poor. A
sallow, mournfully handsome young man moves aimlessly
through the crowds. He gives cash for the needy to an attractive Army girl, and gets in return a candle and a sprig of
mistletoe. Posters on the walls warn the women of London
against going out unescorted at night: there is a mass
murderer at large. In a garret close by, its broken skylight
covered by a flapping rag, Lulu lives in squalor with Alwa and
Schigolch. The room is unfurnished except for a camp bed,
an armchair, and a kitchen table with an oil lamp, a few
pieces of chipped crockery, and a bread knife. Lulu's curls
and bangs have been restored, but her clothes are threadbare:
all three exiles are on the verge of starvation. Reduced by now
to prostitution, Lulu ventures down into the street, where

she accosts the young wanderer we have already met. He
follows her up the stairs but stops halfway, as if reluctant to
go farther. We see that he is holding behind his back a
switchblade knife, open. Lulu proffers her hand and leans en-
couragingly toward him. Her smile is lambent and beckoning.
Hesitantly, he explains that he has no money. With transparent candor, she replies that it doesn't matter: she likes
him. Unseen by Lulu, he releases his grip on the knife and
lets it fall into the stairwell. She leads him into the attic,
which Alwa and Schigolch have tactfully vacated. The scene
that follows is tender, even buoyant, but unsoftened by sentimentality. The cold climax, when it comes, is necessary and
inevitable. Ripper and victim relax like familiar lovers. He
leans back in the armchair and stretches out his hand; she
leaps onto his lap, landing with both knees bent, as weightless
as a chamois. Her beauty has never looked more ripe. While
they happily flirt, he allows her to pry into his pockets, from
which she extracts the gifts he received from the Salvation
Army. She lights the candle and places it ceremonially on the
table, with the mistletoe beside it. In a deep and peaceful
embrace, they survey the tableau. The Ripper then raises the
mistletoe over Lulu's head and requests the traditional kiss.
As she shuts her eyes and presents her lips, the candle flares
up. Its gleam reflected in the bread knife on the table holds
the Ripper's gaze. He can look at nothing but the shining
blade. Long seconds pass as he wrestles, motionless, with his
obsession. Finally, leaning forward to consummate the kiss,
he grasps the handle of the knife. In the culminating shot,
he is facing away from the camera. All we see of Lulu is her
right hand, open on his shoulder, pressing him toward her.
Suddenly, it clenches hard, then falls, limply dangling, behind
his back. We fade to darkness. Nowhere in the cinema has
the destruction of beauty been conveyed with more eloquent
restraint. As with the killing of Peter Schön, extreme violence
is implied, not shown. To paraphrase what Freddy Buache,
a Swiss critic, wrote many years later, Lulu's death is in no
sense God's judgment on a sinner; she has lived her life in

accordance with the high moral imperatives of liberty, and stands in no need of redemption.

After the murder, the Ripper emerges from the building and hurries off into the fog. It is here, in my view, that the film should end. Instead, Pabst moves on to the forlorn figure of Alwa, who stares up at the garret before turning away to follow the Salvation Army procession out of sight. A glib anticlimax indeed; but I'm not sure that I prefer the alternative proposed by Brooks, who has said, with characteristic forthrightness, "The movie should have ended with the knife in my vagina." It may be worth adding that Gustav Diessl, who played the Ripper, was the only man in the cast whom she found sexually appealing. "We just adored each other," she has said in an interview with Richard Leacock, "and I think the final scene was the happiest in the picture. Here he is with a knife he's going to stick up into my interior, and we'd be singing and laughing and doing the Charleston. You wouldn't have known it was a tragic ending. It was more like a Christmas party." At Brook's request, Pabst had hired a jazz pianist to play between takes, and during these syncopated interludes Brooks and Diessl would often disappear beneath the table to engage in intimate festivities of their own.

The Berlin critics, expecting Lulu to be portrayed as a monster of active depravity, had mixed feelings about Brooks. One reviewer wrote, "Louise Brooks cannot act. She does not suffer. *She does nothing.*" Wedekind himself, however, had said of his protagonist, "Lulu is not a real character but the personification of primitive sexuality, who inspires evil unawares. She plays a purely passive role." Brooks afterward stated her own opinion of what she had achieved. "I played *Pabst's* Lulu," she said, "and she isn't a destroyer of men, like Wedekind's. She's just the same kind of nitwit that I am. Like me, she'd have been an impossible wife, sitting in bed all day reading and drinking gin." Modern critics have elected Brooks's Lulu to a secure place in the movie pantheon. David Thomson describes it as "one of the major female performances in the cinema," to be measured beside such other pinnacles as "Dietrich in the von Sternberg films, Bacall with Hawks, Karina in *Pierrot le Fou*." It is true that in the same list Thomson included Kim Novak in *Vertigo*. It is also true that we are none of us perfect.

Day Two: My first view of the second Pabst-Brooks collaboration—*The Diary of a Lost Girl*, based on *Das Tagebuch einer Verlorenen*, a novel by Margarethe Boehme, and shot in the summer of 1929. After finishing *Pandora*, Brooks had returned to New York and resumed her affair with the millionaire George Marshall. He told her that a new movie company, called RKO and masterminded by Joseph P. Kennedy, was anxious to sign her up for five hundred dollars a week. She replied, "I hate California and I'm not going back." Then Paramount called, ordering her to report for duty on the Coast; it was turning *The Canary Murder Case* into a talkie and required her presence for retakes and dubbing. She refused to come. Under the impression that this was a haggling posture, the studio offered ever vaster sums of money. Brooks's determination remained undented. Goaded to fury, Paramount planted in the columns a petty but damaging little story to the effect that it had been compelled to replace Brooks because her voice was unusable in talkies.

At this point—April, 1929—she received a cable from Pabst. It said that he intended to co-produce a French film entitled *Prix de Beauté*, which René Clair would direct, and that they both wanted her for the lead—would she therefore cross the Atlantic as soon as possible? Such was her faith in Pabst that within two weeks she and Clair ("a very small, demure, rather fragile man" is how she afterward described him) were posing together for publicity shots in Paris. When the photographic session was over, Clair escorted her back to her hotel, where he dampened her enthusiasm by revealing that he proposed to pull out of the picture forthwith. He advised her to do the same; the production money, he said, simply wasn't there, and might never be. A few days later, he officially retired from the project. (Its place in his schedule was taken by *Sous les Toits de Paris*, which, together with its immediate successors—*Le Million* and À *Nous la Liberté* —established his international reputation.) With nothing to do, and a guaranteed salary of a thousand dollars a week to do it on, Brooks entrained for a spree in Antibes, accompanied by a swarm of rich admirers. When she got back to Paris, Pabst called her from Berlin. *Prix de Beauté*, he said, was postponed; instead, she would star under his direction in *Diary of a Lost Girl*, at precisely half her present salary. As submissive as ever to her tutor, she arrived in Berlin aboard the next train.

Lovingly photographed by Sepp Allgeier, Brooks in *Lost Girl* is less flamboyant but not less haunting than in *Pandora's Box*. The traffic in movie actors traditionally moved westward, from Europe to Hollywood, where their national characteristics were sedulously exploited. Brooks, who was among the few to make the eastbound trip, became in her films with Pabst completely Europeanized. To be more exact: in the context that Pabst prepared for her, Brooks's American brashness took on an awareness of transience and mortality. The theme of *Lost Girl* is the corruption of a minor—not by sexuality but by an authoritarian society that condemns sexuality. (Pabst must surely have read Wilhelm Reich, the Freudian Marxist, whose theories about the relationship between sexual and political repression were hotly debated in Berlin at the time.) It is the same society that condemns Lulu. In fact, *The Education of Lulu* would make an apt alternative title for *Lost Girl*, whose heroine emerges from her travails ideally equipped for the leading role in *Pandora's Box*. Her name is Thymiane Henning, and she is the sixteen-year-old daughter of a prosperous pharmacist. In the early sequences, Brooks plays her shy and faunlike, peering wide-eyed at a predatory world. She is seduced and impregnated by her father's libidinous young assistant. As soon as her condition is discovered, the double standard swings into

action. The assistant retains his job; but, to save the family
from dishonor, Thymiane's baby is farmed out to a wet nurse,
and she herself is consigned to a home for delinquent girls,
run by a bald and ghoulish superintendent and his sadistic
wife.

Life in the reformatory is strictly regimented: the inmates
exercise to the beat of a drum and eat to the tapping of a
metronome. At length, Thymiane escapes from this archetypal hellhole (precursor of many such institutions in subsequent movies; e.g., *Mädchen in Uniform*) and goes to reclaim
her baby, only to find that the child has died. Broke and
homeless, she meets a street vendor who guides her to an
address where food and shelter will be hers for the asking.
Predictably, it turns out to be a brothel; far less predictably,
even shockingly, Pabst presents it as a place where Thymiane
is not degraded but liberated. In the whorehouse, she
blossoms, becoming a *fille de joie* in the literal sense of the
phrase. Unlike almost any other actress in a similar situation,
Brooks neither resorts to pathos nor suggests that there is
anything immoral in the pleasure she derives from her new
profession. As in *Pandora*, she lives for the moment, with
radiant physical abandon. Present love, even for sale, hath
present laughter, and what's to come is not only unsure but
irrelevant. I agree with Freddy Buache when he says of
Brooks's performances with Pabst that they celebrated "the
victory of innocence and *amour-fou* over the debilitating
wisdom imposed on society by the Church, the Fatherland,
and the Family." One of her more outré clients can achieve
orgasm only by watching her beat a drum. This ironic echo
of life in the reform school is used by Pabst to imply that
sexual prohibition breeds sexual aberration. (Even more
ironically, the sequence has been censored out of most of
the existing prints of the movie.) Brooks is at her best—
a happy animal in skintight satin—in a party scene at a nightclub, where she offers herself as first prize in a raffle. "Pabst
wanted realism, so we all had to drink real drinks," she said

later. "I played the whole scene stewed on hot, sweet German champagne."

Hereabouts, unfortunately, the film begins to shed its effrontery and to pay lip service to conventional values. Thymiane catches sight of her father across the dance floor; instead of reacting with defiance—after all, he threw her out of his house—she looks stricken with guilt, like the outcast daughter of sentimental fiction. In her absence, Papa has married his housekeeper, by whom he has two children. When he dies, shortly after the nightclub confrontation, he leaves his considerable wealth to Thymiane. Nobly, she gives it all to his penniless widow, so that the latter's offspring "won't have to live the same kind of life as I have." Thereby redeemed, the former whore soon becomes the wife of an elderly aristocrat. Revisiting the reform school, of which she has now been appointed a trustee, she excoriates the staff for its self-righteous cruelties. "A little more kindness," her husband adds, "and no one in the world would ever be lost." Thus lamely, the movie ends.

"Pabst seemed to lose interest," Brooks told an interviewer some years afterward. "He more or less said, 'I'm tired of this picture,' and he gave it a soft ending." His first, and much tougher, intention had been to demonstrate that humanitarianism alone could never solve society's problems. He wanted Thymiane to show her contempt for her husband's liberal platitudes by setting herself up as the madam of a whorehouse. The German distributors, however, refused to countenance such a radical dénouement, and Pabst was forced to capitulate. The result is a flawed masterpiece, with a shining central performance that even the closing, compromised sequences cannot dim. Brooks has written that during the making of the film she spent all her off-duty hours with rich revellers of whom Pabst disapproved. On the last day of shooting, "he decided to let me have it." Her friends, he said, were preventing her from becoming a serious actress, and sooner or later they would discard her like an old toy. "Your

life is exactly like Lulu's, and you will end the same way,"
he warned her. The passage of time convinced her that Pabst
had a valid point. "Lulu's story," she told a journalist, "is as
near as you'll get to mine."

In August, 1929, she returned to Paris, where backing had
unexpectedly been found for *Prix de Beauté*, her last European movie and her first talkie—although, since she spoke no
French, her voice was dubbed. The director, briefly surfacing
from obscurity, was Augusto Genina, and René Clair received a credit for the original idea. Like so much of French
cinema in the thirties, *Prix de Beauté* is a *film noir*, with
wanly tinny music, about a shabby suburban crime of
passion. Brooks plays Lucienne, a typist who enters a newspaper beauty contest. It's the kind of role with which one
associates Simone Simon, though the rapture that Brooks
displays when she wins, twirling with glee as she shows off
her presents and trophies, goes well beyond the emotional
range accessible to Mlle. Simon. Lucienne-Brooks is triumphantly unliberated; she rejoices in being a beloved, fleshly
bauble, and she makes it clear to her husband, a compositor
employed by the prize-giving newspaper, that she wants a
grander, more snobbish reward for her victory than a visit
to a back-street fairground, which is all he has to offer. She
leaves him and accepts a part in a film. Consumed by
jealousy, he follows her one night to a projection theatre in
which a rough cut of her movie is being shown. He bursts
in and shoots her. As she dies, the French infatuation with
irony is fearsomely indulged: her image on the screen behind
her is singing the movie's theme song, "Ne Sois Pas Jaloux."
In *Prix de Beauté*, Brooks lends inimitable flair and distinction to a cliché; but it is a cliché nonetheless.

At this point, when Brooks was at the height of her beauty,
her career began a steep and bumpy decline. In 1930, she
went back to Hollywood, on the strength of a promised
contract with Columbia. Harry Cohn, the head of the studio,
summoned her to his office for a series of meetings, at each
of which he appeared naked from the waist up. Always a

plain speaker, he left her in no doubt that good parts would come her way if she responded to his advances. She rebuffed them, and the proffered contract was withdrawn. Elsewhere in Hollywood, she managed to get a job in a feeble two-reel comedy pseudonymously directed by the disgraced Fatty Arbuckle; her old friend Frank Tuttle gave her a supporting role in *It Pays to Advertise* (starring Carole Lombard); and she turned up fleetingly in a Michael Curtiz picture called *God's Gift to Women*. But the word was out that Brooks was difficult and uppity, too independent to suit the system. Admitting defeat, she returned to New York in the summer of 1931. Against her will, but under heavy pressure from George Marshall, her lover and would-be Svengali, she played a small part in *Louder Please*, a featherweight comedy by Norman Krasna that began its pre Broadway run in October. After the opening week in Jackson Heights, she was fired by the director, George Abbott. This was her farewell to the theatre; it took place on the eve of her twenty-fifth birthday.

For Brooks, as for millions of her compatriots, a long period of unemployment followed. In 1933, determined to break off her increasingly discordant relationship with Marshall, she married Deering Davis, a rich young Chicagoan, but walked out on him after six months of rapidly waning enthusiasm. With a Hungarian partner named Dario Borzani, she spent a year dancing in nightclubs, including the Persian Room of the Plaza, but the monotony of cabaret routine dismayed her, and she quit the act in August, 1935. That autumn, Pabst suddenly arrived in New York and invited her to play Helen of Troy in a film version of Goethe's *Faust*, with Greta Garbo as Gretchen. Her hopes giddily soared, only to be dashed when Garbo opted out and the project fell through. Once again, she revisited Hollywood, where Republic Studios wanted to test her for a role in a musical called *Dancing Feet*. She was rejected in favor of a blonde who couldn't dance. "That about did it for me," Brooks wrote later. "From then on it was straight downhill. And no dough to keep the wolves from the door." In 1936, Universal cast her as the ingénue

(Boots Boone) in *Empty Saddles,* a Buck Jones Western, which is the last Brooks movie in the Eastman collection. She looks perplexed, discouraged, and lacking in verve; and her coiffure, with the hair swept back from her forehead, reveals disquieting lines of worry. (Neither she nor Jones is helped by the fact that all the major sequences of an incredibly complex plot are shot at night.) The following year brought her a bit part at Paramount in something called *King of Gamblers,* after which, in her own words, "Harry Cohn gave me a personally conducted tour of hell with no return ticket." Still wounded by her refusal to sleep with him in 1930, Cohn promised her a screen test if she would submit to the humiliation of appearing in the corps de ballet of a Grace Moore musical entitled *When You're in Love.* To his surprise, Brooks accepted the offer—she was too broke to spurn it—and Cohn made sure that the demotion of an erstwhile star was publicized as widely as possible. Grudgingly, he gave her a perfunctory screen test, which he dismissed in two words: "It stunk." In the summer of 1938, Republic hired Brooks to appear with John Wayne (then a minor figure) in *Overland Stage Raiders.* After this low-budget oater, she made no more pictures.

In her entire professional career, Brooks had earned according to her own calculations, exactly $124,600—$104,500 from films, $10,100 from theatre, and $10,000 from all other sources. Not a gargantuan sum, one would think, spread over sixteen years; yet Brooks said to a friend, "I was astonished that it came to so much. But then I never paid any attention to money." In 1940, she left Hollywood for the last time.

The Eastman house stands in an affluent residential district of Rochester, on an avenue of comparably stately mansions, with broad, tree-shaded lawns. When my second day of séances with Brooks came to an end, I zipped up my notes in a briefcase, thanked the curator and his staff for their help, and departed in a taxi. The driver took me to an apartment building only a few blocks away, where I paid him off. I rode up in the elevator to the third floor and pressed a doorbell a few paces along the corridor. After a long pause, there was a loud snapping of locks. The door slowly opened to reveal a petite woman of fragile build, wearing a woollen bed jacket over a pink nightgown, and holding herself defiantly upright by means of a sturdy metal cane with four rubber-tipped prongs. She had salt-and-pepper hair combed back into a ponytail that hung down well below her shoulders, and she was barefoot. One could imagine this gaunt and elderly child as James Tyrone's wife in *Long Day's Journey into Night*; or, noting the touch of authority and *panache* in her bearing, as the capricious heroine of Jean Giraudoux's *The Madwoman of Chaillot*. I stated my name, adding that I had an appointment. She nodded and beckoned me in. I greeted her with a respectful embrace. This was my first physical contact with Louise Brooks.

She was seventy-one years old, and until a few months earlier I had thought she was dead. Four decades had passed since her last picture, and it seemed improbable that she had survived such a long period of retirement. Moreover, I did not then know how young she had been at the time of her flowering. Spurred by the TV screening of *Pandora's Box* in January, 1978, I had made some inquiries, and soon discovered that she was living in Rochester, virtually bedridden with degenerative osteoarthritis of the hip, and that since 1956 she had written twenty vivid and perceptive articles, mainly for specialist film magazines, on such of her colleagues and contemporaries as Garbo, Dietrich, Keaton, Chaplin, Bogart, Fields, Lillian Gish, ZaSu Pitts, and (naturally) Pabst. Armed with this information, I wrote her a belated fan letter, to which she promptly replied. We then struck up a correspondence, conducted on her side in a bold and expressive prose style, which matched her handwriting. Rapport was cemented by telephone calls, which resulted in my visit to Rochester and the date I was now keeping.

She has not left her apartment since 1960, except for a few trips to the dentist and one to a doctor. (She mistrusts the

medical profession, and this consultation, which took place
in 1976, was her first in thirty-two years.) "You're doing a
terrible thing to me," she said as she ushered me in. "I've
been killing myself off for twenty years, and you're going to
bring me back to life." She lives in two rooms—modest, spotless, and austerely furnished. From the larger, I remember
Venetian blinds, a green sofa, a TV set, a Formica-topped
table, a tiny kitchenette alcove, and flesh-pink walls sparsely
hung with paintings redolent of the twenties. The other room
was too small to hold more than a bed (single), a built-in
cupboard bursting with press clippings and other souvenirs,
a chest of drawers surmounted by a crucifix and a statue of
the Virgin, and a stool piled high with books, including
works by Proust, Schopenhauer, Ruskin, Ortega y Gasset,
Samuel Johnson, Edmund Wilson, and many living authors
of serious note. "I'm probably one of the best-read idiots in
the world," my hostess said as she haltingly showed me round
her domain. Although she eats little—she turns the scale at
about eighty-eight pounds—she had prepared for us a perfectly mountainous omelette. Nerves, however, had robbed
us of our appetites, and we barely disturbed its mighty
silhouette. I produced from my briefcase a bottle of expensive
red Burgundy which I had brought as a gift. (Brooks, who
used to drink quite heftily, nowadays touches alcohol only
on special occasions.) Since she cannot sit upright for long
without discomfort, we retired with the wine to her bedroom,
where she reclined, sipped, and talked, gesturing fluently, her
fingers supple and unclenched. I pulled a chair up to the
bedside and listened.

Her voice has the range of a dozen birdcalls, from the cry
of a peacock to the fluting of a dove. Her articulation, at
whatever speed, is impeccable, and her laughter soars like a
kite. I cannot understand why, even if she had not been a
beauty, Hollywood failed to realize what a treasure it
possessed in the *sound* of Louise Brooks. Like most people
who speak memorably, she is highly responsive to vocal

nuances in others. She told Kevin Brownlow, the British film historian, that her favorite actress ("the person I would be if I could be anyone") was Margaret Sullavan, mainly because of her voice, which Brooks described as "exquisite and far away, almost like an echo," and, again, as "strange, fey, mysterious—like a voice singing in the snow." My conversations with the Ravishing Hermit of Rochester were spread over several days; for the sake of convenience, I have here compressed them into one session.

She began, at my urging, by skimming through the story of her life since she last faced the Hollywood cameras: "Why did I give up the movies? I could give you seven hundred reasons, all of them true. After I made that picture with John Wayne in 1938, I stayed out on the Coast for two years, but the only people who wanted to see me were men who wanted to sleep with me. Then Walter Wanger warned me that if I hung around any longer I'd become a call girl. So I fled to Wichita, Kansas, where my family had moved in 1919. But that turned out to be another kind of hell. The citizens of Wichita either resented me for having been a success or despised me for being a failure. And I wasn't exactly enchanted with them. I opened a dance studio for young people, who loved me, because I dramatized everything so much, but it didn't make any money. In 1943, I drifted back to New York and worked for six months in radio soaps. Then I quit, for another hundred reasons, including Wounded Pride of Former Star. [Peal of laughter. Here, as throughout our chat, Brooks betrayed not the slightest trace of self pity.] During '44 and '45, I got a couple of jobs in publicity agencies, collecting items for Winchell's column. I was fired from both of them, and I had to move from the decent little hotel where I'd been living to a grubby hole on First Avenue at Fifty-ninth Street. That was when I began to flirt with fancies related to little bottles filled with yellow sleeping pills. However, I changed my mind, and in July, 1946, the proud, snooty Louise Brooks started work as a salesgirl at Saks Fifth

Avenue. They paid me forty dollars a week. I had this silly idea of proving myself 'an honest woman,' but the only effect it had was to disgust all my famous New York friends, who cut me off forever. From then on, I was regarded as a questionable East Side dame. After two years at Saks, I resigned. To earn a little money, I sat down and wrote the usual autobiography. I called it *Naked on My Goat*, which is a quote from Goethe's *Faust*. In the *Walpurgisnacht* scene, a young witch is bragging about her looks to an old one. 'I sit here naked on my goat,' she says, 'and show my fine young body.' But the old one advises her to wait awhile: 'Though young and tender now, you'll rot, we know, you'll rot.' Then, when I read what I'd written, I threw the whole thing down the incinerator."

Brooks insists that her motive for this act of destruction was *pudeur*. In 1977, she wrote an article headed "Why I Will Never Write My Memoirs," in which she summed herself up as a prototypical midwesterner, "born in the Bible Belt of Anglo-Saxon farmers, who prayed in the parlor and practiced incest in the barn." Although her sexual education had been conducted by the élite of Paris, London, Berlin, and New York, her pleasure was, she wrote, "restricted by the inbred shackles of sin and guilt." Her conclusion was as follows:

> In writing the history of a life I believe absolutely that the reader cannot understand the character and deeds of the subject unless he is given a basic understanding of that person's sexual loves and hates and conflicts. It is the only way the reader can make sense out of innumerable apparently senseless actions. . . . We flatter ourselves when we assume that we have restored the sexual integrity which was expurgated by the Victorians. It is true that many exposés are written to shock, to excite, to make money. But in serious books characters remain as baffling, as unknowable as ever. . . . I too am unwilling to write the sexual truth that would make my life worth reading. I cannot unbuckle the Bible Belt.

Accepting a drop more wine, she continued the tale of her wilderness years. "Between 1948 and 1953, I suppose you could call me a kept woman," she said. "Three decent rich men looked after me. But then I was *always* a kept woman. Even when I was making a thousand dollars a week, I would always be paid for by George Marshall or someone like that. But I never had anything to show for it—no cash, no trinkets, nothing. I didn't even *like* jewelry—can you imagine? Pabst once called me a born whore, but if he was right I was a failure, with no pile of money and no comfortable mansion. I just wasn't equipped to spoil millionaires in a practical, farsighted way. I could live in the present, but otherwise everything has always been a hundred percent wrong about me. Anyway, the three decent men took care of me. One of them owned a sheet-metal manufacturing company, and the result of that affair is that I am now the owner of the only handmade aluminum wastebasket in the world. He designed it, and it's in the living room, my solitary trophy. Then a time came, early in 1953, when my three men independently decided that they wanted to marry me. I had to escape, because I wasn't in love with them. As a matter of fact, I've never been in love. And if I *had* loved a man, could I have been faithful to him? Could he have trusted me beyond a closed door? I doubt it. It was clever of Pabst to know even before he met me that I possessed the tramp essence of Lulu."

Brooks hesitated for a moment and then went on in the same tones, lightly self-mocking, "Maybe I should have been a writer's moll. Because when we were talking on the phone, a few Sundays ago, some secret compartment inside me burst, and I was suddenly overpowered by the feeling of love—a sensation I'd never experienced with any other man. Are you a variation of Jack the Ripper, who finally brings me love that I'm prevented from accepting—not by the knife but by old age? You're a perfect scoundrel, turning up like this and wrecking my golden years! [I was too stunned to offer any comment on this, but not too stunned to note, with a

distinct glow of pride, that Brooks was completely sober].
Anyhow, to get back to my three suitors, I decided that the
only way to avoid marriage was to become a Catholic, so
that I could tell them that in the eyes of the Church I was
still married to Eddie Sutherland. I went to the rectory of
a Catholic church on the East Side and everything was fine
until my sweet, pure religious instructor fell in love with me.
I was the first woman he'd ever known who acted like one
and treated him like a man. The other priests were furious.
They sent him off to California and replaced him with a stern
young missionary. After a while, however, even *he* began to
hint that it would be a good idea if he dropped by my apartment in the evenings to give me special instruction. But I
resisted temptation, and in September, 1953, I was baptized
a Catholic."

Having paused to light a cigarette, which provoked a mild
coughing spasm, Brooks resumed her story. "I almost forgot
a strange incident that happened in 1952. Out of the blue, I
got a letter from a woman who had been a Cherryvale
neighbor of ours. She enclosed some snapshots. One of them
showed a nice-looking gray-haired man of about fifty holding
the hand of a little girl—me. On the back she'd written,
'This is Mr. Feathers, an old bachelor who loved kids. He
was always taking you to the picture show and buying you
toys and candy.' That picture brought back something I'd
blacked out of my mind for—what?—thirty-seven years.
When I was nine years old, Mr. Feathers molested me
sexually. Which forged another link between me and Lulu:
when *she* had *her* first lover, she was very young, and
Schigolch, the man in question, was middle-aged. I've often
wondered what effect Mr. Feathers had on my life. He must
have had a great deal to do with forming my attitude toward
sexual pleasure. For me, nice, soft, easy men were never
enough—there had to be an element of domination—and
I'm sure that's all tied up with Mr. Feathers. The pleasure
of kissing and being kissed comes from somewhere entirely
different, psychologically as well as physically. Incidentally,

I told my mother about Mr. Feathers, and—would you believe it? [Peal of laughter.] She blamed *me!* She said I must have led him on. It's always the same, isn't it?" And Brooks ran on in this vein, discussing her sex life openly and jauntily, unbuckling one more notch of the Bible Belt with every sentence she uttered.

The year 1954 was Brooks's nadir. "I was too proud to be a call girl. There was no point in throwing myself into the East River, because I could swim; and I couldn't afford the alternative, which was sleeping pills." In 1955, just perceptibly, things began to look up, and life became once more a tolerable option. Henri Langlois, the exuberant ruler of the Cinémathèque Française, organized in Paris a huge exhibition entitled "Sixty Years of Cinema." Dominating the entrance hall of the Musée d'Art Moderne were two gigantic blowups, one of the French actress Falconetti in Carl Dreyer's 1928 classic, *La Passion de Jeanne d'Arc,* and the other of Brooks in *Pandora's Box.* When a critic demanded why he had preferred this nonentity to authentic stars like Garbo and Dietrich, Langlois exploded, "There is no Garbo! There is no Dietrich! There is only Louise Brooks!" In the same year, a group of her friends from the twenties clubbed together to provide a small annuity that would keep her from outright destitution; and she was visited in her Manhattan retreat by James Card, then the curator of film at Eastman House. He had long admired her movies, and he persuaded her to come to Rochester, where so much of her best work was preserved. It was at his suggestion that, in 1956, she settled there.

"Rochester seemed as good a place as any," she told me. "It was cheaper than New York, and I didn't run the risk of meeting people from my past. Up to that time, I had never seen any of my films. And I still haven't—not right through, that is. Jimmy Card screened some of them for me, but that was during my drinking period. I would watch through glazed eyes for about five minutes and sleep through the rest. I haven't even seen *Pandora.* I've been present on two occasions when it was being run, but I was drunk both times. By that I mean I was *navigating* but not *seeing*." When she watched other people's movies, however, she felt no need for alcoholic sedation. As a working actress, she had never taken films seriously; under Card's tuition, she recognized that the cinema was a valid form of art, and began to develop her own theories about it. In 1956, drawing on her powers of near-total recall, she wrote a study of Pabst for *Image*. This was the first of a sheaf of articles, sharp-eyed and idiosyncratic, that she has contributed over the years to such magazines as *Sight & Sound* (London), *Objectif* (Montreal), *Film Culture* (New York), and *Positif* (Paris).

The Brooks cult burgeoned in 1957, when Henri Langlois crossed the Atlantic to meet her. A year later, he presented "Hommage à Louise Brooks"—a festival of her movies that filled the Cinémathèque. The star herself flew to Paris, all expenses paid, and was greeted with wild acclaim at a reception after the Cinémathèque's showing of *Pandora's Box*. (Among those present was Jean-Luc Godard, who paid his own tribute to Brooks in 1962, when he directed *Vivre Sa Vie*, the heroine of which—a prostitute—was played by Anna Karina in an exact replica of the Brooks hairdo. Godard described the character as a "young and pretty Parisian shopgirl who gives her body but retains her soul.") In January, 1960, Brooks went to New York and attended a screening of *Prix de Beauté* in the Kaufman Concert Hall of the 92nd Street Y, where she made a hilarious little speech that delighted the packed audience. The next day, she returned to Rochester, from which she has never since emerged.

Interviewers and fans occasionally call on her, but for the most part, as she put it to me, "I have lived in virtual isolation, with an audience consisting of the milkman and a cleaning woman." She continued, "Once a week, I would drink a pint of gin, become what Dickens called 'gincoherent,' go to sleep, and drowse for four days. That left three days to read, write a bit, and see the odd visitor. No priests, by the way—I said goodbye to the Church in 1964. Now and then, there would be a letter to answer. In 1965, for

instance, an Italian artist named Guido Crepax started a very
sexy and tremendously popular comic strip about a girl called
Valentina, who looked exactly like me as Lulu. In fact, she
identified herself with me. Crepax wrote to thank me for the
inspiration and said he regarded me as a twentieth-century
myth. I appreciated the tribute and told him that at last I
felt I could disintegrate happily in bed with my books, gin,
cigarettes, coffee, bread, cheese, and apricot jam. During the
sixties, arthritis started to get a grip, and in 1972 I had to buy
a medical cane in order to move around. Then, five years
ago, the disease really walloped me. My pioneer blood did
not pulse through my veins, rousing me to fight it. I collapsed. I took a terrible fall and nearly smashed my hip. That
was the end of the booze or any other kind of escape for me.
I knew I was in for a bad time, with nothing to face but the
absolute meaninglessness of my life. All I've done since then
is try to hold the pieces together. And to keep my little
squirrel-cage brain distracted."

As an emblematic figure of the twenties, epitomizing the
flappers, jazz babies, and dancing daughters of the boom
years, Brooks has few rivals, living or dead. Moreover, she is
unique among such figures in that her career took her to all
the places—New York, London, Hollywood, Paris, and
Berlin—where the action was at its height, where experiments in pleasure were conducted with the same zeal (and
often by the same people) as experiments in the arts. From
her bedroom cupboard Brooks produced an avalanche of
manila envelopes, each bulging with mementoes of her
halcyon decade. This solitary autodidact, her perceptions
deepened by years of immersion in books, looked back for
my benefit on the green, gregarious girl she once was, and
found much to amuse her. For every photograph she supplied a spoken caption. As she reminisced, I often thought
of those Max Beerbohm cartoons that depict the Old Self
conversing with the Young Self.

"Here I am in 1922, when I first hit New York, and the
label of 'beautiful but dumb' was slapped on me forever.

Most beautiful-but-dumb girls think they are smart, and get away with it, because other people, on the whole, aren't much smarter. You can see modern equivalents of those girls on any TV talk show. But there's also a very small group of beautiful women who *know* they're dumb, and this makes them defenseless and vulnerable. They become the Big Joke. I didn't know Marilyn Monroe, but I'm sure that her agonizing awareness of her own stupidity was one of the things that killed her. I became the Big Joke, first on Broadway and then in Hollywood. . . . That's Herman Mankiewicz—an ideal talk-show guest, don't you think, born before his time? In 1925, Herman was trying to educate me, and he invented the Louise Brooks Literary Society. A girl named Dorothy Knapp and I were Ziegfeld's two prize beauties. We had a big dressing room on the fifth floor of the New Amsterdam Building, and people like Walter Wanger, Michael Arlen, and Gilbert Miller would meet there, ostensibly to hear my reviews of books that Herman gave me to read. What they actually came for was to watch Dorothy doing a striptease and having a love affair with herself in front of a full-length mirror. I get some consolation from the fact that, as an idiot, I have provided delight in my time to a very select group of intellectuals. . . . That must be Joseph Schenck. Acting on behalf of his brother Nick, who controlled M-G-M, Joe offered me a contract in 1925 at three hundred a week. Instead, I went to Paramount for two hundred and fifty. Maybe I should have signed with M-G-M and joined what I called the Joe Schenck Mink Club. You could recognize the members at '21' because they never removed their mink coats at lunch. . . . Here's Fritzi LaVerne, smothered in osprey feathers. I roomed with her briefly when we were in the Follies together, and she seduced more Follies girls than Ziegfeld and William Randolph Hearst combined. That's how I got the reputation of being a lesbian. I had nothing against it in principle, and for years I thought it was fun to encourage the idea. I used to hold hands with Fritzi in public. She had a little Bulgarian boyfriend who was just our height, and we

would get into his suits and camp all over New York. Even
when I moved out to Yahoo City, California, I could never
stop by a lesbian household without being asked to strip and
join the happy group baring their operation scars in the sun.
But although I went through a couple of mild sexual audi-
tions with women, I very soon found that I only loved men's
bodies. What maddens me is that because of the lesbian
scenes with Alice Roberts in *Pandora* I shall probably go
down in film history as one of the gloomy dikes. A friend of
mine once said to me, 'Louise Brooks, you're not a lesbian,
you're a pansy.' Would you care to decipher that? By the
way, are you getting tired of hearing my name? I'm thinking
of changing it. I noticed that there were five people called
Brooks in last week's *Variety* How about June Caprice? Or
Louise Lovely?"

I shook my head.

Brooks continued riffling through her collection. "This, of
course, is Martha Graham, whose genius I absorbed to the
bone during the years we danced together on tour. She had
rages, you know, that struck like lightning out of nowhere.
One evening when we were waiting to go onstage—I was
sixteen—she grabbed me, shook me ferociously, and shouted,
'Why do you ruin your feet by wearing those tight shoes?'
Another time, she was sitting sweetly at the makeup shelf
pinning flowers in her hair when she suddenly seized a bottle
of body makeup and exploded it against the mirror. She
looked at the shattered remains for a spell, then moved her
makeup along to an unbroken mirror and went on quietly
pinning flowers in her hair Reminds me of the night when
Buster Keaton drove me in his roadster out to Culver City,
where he had a bungalow on the back lot of M-G-M. The
walls of the living room were covered with great glass book-
cases. Buster, who wasn't drunk, opened the door, turned on
the lights, and picked up a baseball bat. Then, walking calmly
round the room, he smashed every pane of glass in every
bookcase. Such frustration in that little body! . . . Here,
inevitably, are Scott and Zelda. I met them in January, 1927,

at the Ambassador Hotel in L.A. They were sitting close
together on a sofa, like a comedy team, and the first thing
that struck me was how *small* they were. I had come to see
the genius writer, but what dominated the room was the
blazing intelligence of Zelda's profile. It shocked me. It was
the profile of a witch. Incidentally, I've been reading Scott's
letters, and I've spotted a curious thing about them. In the
early days, before Hemingway was famous, Scott always
spelled his name wrong, with two "m"s. And when did he
start to spell it right? At the precise moment when Hemingway became a bigger star than he was. . . . This is a pool
party at somebody's house in Malibu. I know I knock the
studio system, but if you were to ask me what it was like to
live in Hollywood in the twenties I'd have to say that we were
all—oh!—marvellously degenerate and happy. We were a
world of our own, and outsiders didn't intrude. People tell
you that the reason a lot of actors left Hollywood when
sound came in was that their voices were wrong for talkies.
That's the official story. The truth is that the coming of
sound meant the end of the all-night parties. With talkies,
you couldn't stay out till sunrise anymore. You had to rush
back from the studios and start learning your lines, ready for
the next day's shooting at 8 A.M. That was when the studio
machine really took over. It controlled you, mind and body,
from the moment you were yanked out of bed at dawn until
the publicity department put you back to bed at night."

Brooks paused, silently contemplating revels that ended
half a century ago, and then went on. "Talking about bed,
here's Tallulah—although I always guessed that she wasn't as
keen on bed as everyone thought. And my record for guessing
things like that was pretty good. I watched her packing her
douche-bag one night for a meeting with a plutocratic boyfriend of hers at the Elysée Hotel. She forgot to wear the
emerald ring he'd given her a few days before, but she didn't
forget the script of the play she wanted him to produce for
her. Her preparations weren't scheming or whorish. Just

businesslike. . . . This is a bunch of the guests at Mr. Hearst's
ranch, sometime in 1928. The girl with the dark hair and the
big smile is Pepi Lederer, one of my dearest friends. She was
Marion Davies' niece and the sister of Charlie Lederer, the
screenwriter, and she was only seventeen when that picture
was taken. My first husband, Eddie Sutherland, used to say
that for people who didn't worship opulence, weren't crazy
about meeting celebrities, and didn't need money or advancement from Mr. Hearst, San Simeon was a deadly-dull place.
I suppose he was right. But when Pepi was there it was
always fun. She created a world of excitement and inspiration wherever she went. And I never entered that great dining hall without a shiver of delight. There were medieval
banners from Siena floating overhead, and a vast Gothic fireplace, and a long refectory table seating forty. Marion and
Mr. Hearst sat with the important guests at the middle of
the table. Down at the bottom, Pepi ruled over a group—
including me—that she called the Younger Degenerates, and
that's where the laughter was. Although Mr. Hearst disapproved of booze, Pepi had made friends with one of the
waiters, and we got all the champagne we wanted. She could
have been a gifted writer, and for a while she worked for
Mr. Hearst's deluxe quarterly *The Connoisseur,* but it was
only a courtesy job. Nobody took her seriously, she never
learned discipline, and drink and drugs got her in the end.
In 1935, she died by jumping out of a window in the psychiatric ward of a hospital in Los Angeles. She was twenty-five
years old. Not long ago, I came across her name in the index
of a book on Marion Davies, and it broke my heart. Then I
remembered a quotation from Goethe that I'd once typed
out. I've written it under the photo: 'For a person remains
of consequence not so far as he leaves something behind
him but so far as he acts and enjoys, and rouses others to
action and enjoyment.' That was Pepi."

Of all the names that spilled out of Brooks's memories
of America in the twenties, there was one for which she

reserved a special veneration: that of Chaplin. In an article for the magazine *Film Culture,* she had described his performances at private parties:

> He recalled his youth with comic pantomimes. He acted out countless scenes for countless films. And he did imitations of everybody. Isadora Duncan danced in a storm of toilet paper. John Barrymore picked his nose and brooded over Hamlet's soliloquy. A Follies girl swished across the room; and I began to cry while Charlie denied absolutely that he was imitating me. Nevertheless . . . I determined to abandon that silly walk forthwith.

For me, she filled out the picture. "I was eighteen in 1925, when Chaplin came to New York for the opening of *The Gold Rush.* He was just twice my age, and I had an affair with him for two happy summer months. Ever since he died, my mind has gone back fifty years, trying to define that lovely being from another world. He was not only the creator of the Little Fellow, though that was miracle enough. He was a self-made aristocrat. He taught himself to speak cultivated English, and he kept a dictionary in the bathroom at his hotel so that he could learn a new word every morning. While he dressed, he prepared his script for the day, which was intended to adorn his private portrait of himself as a perfect English gentleman. He was also a sophisticated lover, who had affairs with Peggy Hopkins Joyce and Marion Davies and Pola Negri, and he was a brilliant businessman, who owned his films and demanded fifty percent of the gross— which drove Nick Schenck wild, along with all the other people who were plotting to rob him. Do you know, I can't once remember him *still*? He was always standing up as he sat down, and going out as he came in. Except when he turned off the lights and went to sleep, without liquor or pills, like a child. Meaning to be bitchy, Herman Mankiewicz said, 'People never sat at his feet. He went to where people were sitting and stood in front of them.' But how we paid attention! We were hypnotized by the beauty and inexhaustible originality of this glistening creature. He's the only genius I ever knew who spread himself equally over his art and his life. He loved showing off in fine clothes and elegant phrases —even in the witness box. When Lita Grey divorced him, she put about vile rumors that he had a depraved passion for little girls. He didn't give a damn, even though people said his career would be wrecked. It still infuriates me that he never defended himself against any of those ugly lies, but the truth is that he existed on a plane above pride, jealousy, or hate. I never heard him say a snide thing about anyone. *He lived totally without fear.* He knew that Lita Grey and her family were living in his house in Beverly Hills, planning to ruin him, yet he was radiantly carefree—happy with the success of *The Gold Rush* and with the admirers who swarmed around him. Not that he *exacted* adoration. Even during our affair, he knew that I didn't adore him in the romantic sense, and he didn't mind at all. Which brings me to one of the dirtiest lies he allowed to be told about him—that he was mean with money. People forget that Chaplin was the only star ever to keep his ex-leading lady [Edna Purviance] on his payroll for life, and the only producer to pay his employees their full salaries even when he wasn't in production. When our joyful summer ended he didn't give me a fur from Jaeckel or a bangle from Cartier, so that I could flash them around, saying, 'Look what I got from Chaplin.' The day after he left town, I got a nice check in the mail signed Charlie. And then I didn't even write him a thank-you note. Damn me."

Brooks's souvenirs of Europe, later in the twenties, began with pictures of a burly, handsome, dark-haired man, usually alighting from a train: George Preston Marshall, the millionaire who was her frequent bedfellow and constant adviser between 1927 and 1933. "If you care about *Pandora's Box*, you should be grateful to George Marshall," she told me. "I'd never heard of Mr. Pabst when he offered me the part. It was George who insisted that I should accept it. He was passionately fond of the theatre and films, and he slept with every pretty show-business girl he could find, including all my best friends. George took me to Berlin with his English valet, who stepped off the train blind drunk and fell flat on his face at Mr. Pabst's feet."

The Brooks collection contains no keepsakes of the actress whom she pipped at the post in the race to play Lulu, and of whom, when I raised the subject, she spoke less than charitably. "Dietrich? That *contraption!* She was one of the beautiful-but-dumb girls, like me, but she belonged to the category of those who thought they were smart and fooled other people into believing it. But I guess I'm just being insanely jealous, because I know she's a friend of yours—isn't she?" By way of making amends, she praised Dietrich's performance as Lola in *The Blue Angel*, and then, struck by a sudden thought, interrupted herself: "Hey! Why don't I ask Marlene to come over from Paris? We could work on our memoirs together. Better still, she could write mine, and I hers—*Lulu* by Lola, and *Lola* by Lulu." To put it politely, however, Dietrich does not correspond to Brooks's ideal image of a movie goddess. But who does—apart from Margaret Sullavan, whose voice, as we know, she reveres? A few months after our Rochester encounter, she sent me a letter that disclosed another, unexpected object of her admiration. In it she said:

> I've just been listening to Toronto radio. There was a press conference with Ava Gardner, who is making a movie in Montreal. Her beauty has never excited me, and I have seen only one of her films, *The Night of the Iguana*, in which she played a passive role that revealed her power of stillness but little else. On radio, sitting in a hotel room, triggered by all the old stock questions, she said nothing new or stirring—just "Sinatra could be very nice or very rotten—get me another drink, baby —I made fifty-four pictures and the only part I understood was in *The Snows of Kilimanjaro.* . . ." In her conversation, there was nothing about great acting or beauty or sex, and no trace of philosophical or intellectual con-

cern. Yet for the first time in my life I was proud of being a movie actress, unmixed with theatre art. Ava is in essence what I think a movie star should be—a beautiful person with a unique, mysterious personality unpolluted by Hollywood. And she is so *strong*. She did not have to run away (like Garbo) to keep from being turned into a product of the machine. . . . What I should like to know is whether, as I sometimes fancy, I ever had a glimmer of that quality of integrity which makes Ava shine with her own light.

The next picture out of the manila files showed Brooks, inscrutable and somewhat forlorn in a sequinned evening gown, sitting at a table surrounded by men with pencil-thin mustaches who were wearing tuxedos, black ties, and wing collars. These men were all jabbering into telephones and laughing maniacally. None of them was looking at Brooks. Behind them I could make out oak-panelled walls and an out-of-focus waiter with a fish-eyed stare and a strong resemblance to Louis Jouvet. "You know where that was taken, of course," Brooks said.

I was sorry, but I didn't.

"That's Joe Zelli's!" she cried. "Zelli's was the most famous nightclub in Paris. I can't remember all the men's names, but the one on the extreme right used to drink ether. The one on my left was half Swedish and half English. I lived with him in several hotels. Although he was very young, he had snow-white hair, so we always called him the Eskimo. The fellow next to him, poor guy, was killed the very next day. He was cut to pieces by a speedboat propeller at Cannes."

Whenever I think of the twenties, I shall see that flash-lit hysterical tableau at Zelli's and the unsmiling seraph at the center of it.

From the fattest of all her folders, Brooks now pulled out a two-shot. Beaming in a cloche hat, she stands arm in arm with a stocky, self-possessed man in a homburg. He also wears steel-rimmed glasses, a bow tie, and a well-cut business suit;

you would guess he was in his early forties. "Mr. Pabst," she said simply. "That was 1928, in Berlin, while we were making *Pandora's Box*. As I told you, I arrived with George Marshall, and Mr. Pabst hated him, because he kept me up all night, going round the clubs. A few weeks later, George went back to the States, and after that Mr. Pabst locked me up in my hotel when the day's shooting was finished. Everyone thought he was in love with me. On the rare evenings when I went to his apartment for dinner, his wife, Trudi, would walk out and bang the door. Mr. Pabst was a highly respectable man, but he had the most extraordinary collection of obscene stills in the world. He even had one of Sarah Bernhardt nude with a black-lace fan. Did you know that in the twenties it was the custom for European actresses to send naked pictures of themselves to movie directors? He had all of them. Anyway, I didn't have an affair with him in Berlin. In 1929, though, when he was in Paris trying to set up *Prix de Beauté*, we went out to dinner at a restaurant and I behaved rather outrageously. For some reason, I slapped a close friend of mine across the face with a bouquet of roses. Mr. Pabst was horrified. He hustled me out of the place and took me back to my hotel, where—what do I do? I'm in a *terrific* mood, so I decide to banish his disgust by giving the best sexual performance of my career. I jump into the hay and deliver myself to him body and soul. [Her voice is jubilant.] He acted as if he'd never experienced such a thing in his life. You know how men want to pin medals on themselves when they excite you? They get positively radiant. Next morning, Mr. Pabst was so pleased he couldn't see straight. That was why he postponed *Prix de Beauté* and arranged to make *Diary of a Lost Girl* first. He wanted the affair to continue. But I didn't, and when I got to Berlin it was like *Pandora's Box* all over again, except that this time the man I brought with me was the Eskimo—my white-headed boy from Zelli's."

Brooks laughed softly, recalling the scene. "Mr. Pabst was there at the station to meet me. He was appalled when I got off the train with the Eskimo. On top of that, I had a

wart on my neck, and Esky had just slammed the compartment door on my finger. Mr. Pabst took one stark look at
me, told me I had to start work the next morning, and
dragged me away to a doctor, who burned off the wart. If you
study the early sequences of *Lost Girl*, you can see the sticking plaster on my neck. I hated to hurt Mr. Pabst's feelings
with' the Eskimo, but I simply could not bring myself to
repeat that one and only night. The irony, which Mr. Pabst
never knew, was that although Esky and I shared a hotel
suite in Berlin, we didn't sleep together until much later,
when *Lost Girl* was finished and we were spending a few
days in Paris. 'Eskimo,' I said to him the evening before we
parted, 'this is the night.' And it was—another first and last
for Brooks."

More fragments of Brooksiana:

I: Do you think there are countries that produce particularly good lovers?

BROOKS: Englishmen are the best. And priest-ridden Irish-
men are the worst.

I: What are your favorite films?

BROOKS: *An American in Paris, Pygmalion,* and *The
Wizard of Oz.* Please don't be disappointed.

I: They're all visions of wish fulfillment. An American at
large with a *gamine* young dancer in a fantasy playground
called Paris. A Cockney flower girl who becomes the toast of
upper-class London. And a child from your home state who
discovers, at the end of a trip to a magic world, that happiness
was where she started out.

BROOKS: You *are* disappointed.

I: Not a bit. They're first-rate movies, and they're all
aspects of you.

Postscript from a letter Brooks wrote to me before we met:
"Can you give me a reason for sitting here in this bed, going
crazy, with not one god-damned excuse for living?" I came
up with more than one reason; viz., (a) to receive the homage

of those who cherish the images she has left on celluloid, (b) to bestow the pleasure of her conversation on those who seek her company, (c) to appease her hunger for gleaning wisdom from books, and (d) to test the truth of a remark she had made to a friend: "The Spanish philosopher Ortega y Gasset once said, 'We are all lost creatures. It is only when we admit this that we have a chance of finding ourselves.'"

Despite the numerous men who have crossed the trajectory of her life, Brooks has pursued her own course. She has flown solo. The price to be paid for such individual autonomy is, inevitably, loneliness, and her loneliness is prefigured in one of the most penetrating comments she has ever committed to print: "The great art of films does not consist of descriptive movement of face and body, but in the movements of thought and soul, transmitted in a kind of intense isolation."

As I rose to leave her apartment, she gave me a present: a large and handsome volume entitled *Louise Brooks— Portrait d'une Anti-Star*. Published in Paris in 1977, it contained a full pictorial survey of her career, together with essays, critiques, and poems devoted to her beauty and talent. She inscribed it to me, and copied out, beneath her signature, the epitaph she has composed for herself: "I never gave away anything without wishing I had kept it; nor kept anything without wishing I had given it away." The book included an account by Brooks of her family background, which I paused to read. It ended with this paragraph, here reproduced from her original English text:

> Over the years I suffered poverty and rejection and came to believe that my mother had formed me for a freedom that was unattainable, a delusion. Then . . . I was confined to this small apartment in this alien city of Rochester. . . . Looking about, I saw millions of old people in my situation, wailing like lost puppies because they were alone and had no one to talk to. But they had become enslaved by habits which bound their lives to

warm bodies that talked. I was free! Although my mother had ceased to be a warm body in 1944, she had not forsaken me. She comforts me with every book I read. Once again I am five, leaning on her shoulder, learning the words as she reads aloud *Alice in Wonderland*.

She insisted on getting out of bed to escort me to the door. We had been talking earlier of Proust, and she had mentioned his maxim that the future could never be predicted from the past. Out of her past, I thought, in all its bizarre variety, who knows what future she may invent? "Another thing about Proust," she said, resting on her cane in the doorway. "No matter how he dresses his characters up in their social disguises, we always know how they look naked." As we know it (I reflected) in Brooks's performances.

I kissed her goodbye, buttoned up my social disguise—for it was a chilly evening—and joined the other dressed-up people on the streets of Rochester.

[1979]